The Well-Adjusted Dog

Books by Nicholas H. Dodman

The Dog Who Loved Too Much

The Cat Who Cried for Help

Dogs Behaving Badly

If Only They Could Speak

Puppy's First Steps (editor)

The Well-Adjusted Dog

The Well-Adjusted Dog

Dr. Dodman's Seven Steps to
Lifelong Health and Happiness
for Your Best Friend

Dr. Nicholas H. Dodman, BVMS

Houghton Mifflin Company   Boston / New York 2008

www.houghtonmifflinbooks.com

Library of Congress Cataloging-in-Publication Data
Dodman, Nicholas H.
  The well-adjusted dog : Dr. Dodman's seven steps to lifelong
health and happiness for your best friend / Nicholas H. Dodman.
      p. cm.
  Includes index.
  ISBN 978-0-618-83378-8
  1. Dogs. 2. Dogs — Health. I. Title.
  SF427.D544 2008
  636.7'0887— dc22 2007045894

All illustrations by Beth Mellor
Photo on page 150 is reprinted courtesy of Elite Pet-Havens
Book design by Joyce Weston
Printed in the United States of America

MP 10 9 8 7 6 5 4 3 2 1

AUTHOR'S NOTE: In an effort to protect the innocent, the names
of some of the dogs in this treatise have been changed. That said,
all the cases discussed, or employed as examples, are dogs I have
known or treated as clinical patients. They either did or still do
exist, and the tales about them are true.

To my family — my wife, Linda, and my children,
Stevie, Victoria, Keisha, and Daniel —
and to dogs everywhere

Contents

A Note to the Reader

Gender-conscious readers will note that throughout *The Well-Adjusted Dog*, I refer to our canine companions as "he." Please accept my use of the male pronoun in the spirit it is intended — as a nonspecific term and not an indication of any gender bias on my part. On the contrary, I have equal affection for both male and female dogs.

Introduction

There is no faith which has never yet been broken, except
that of a truly faithful dog.
— Konrad Z. Lorenz

While making small talk with a few friends at a cocktail party, a man mentions that his dog has started "having accidents" on the rug when the man is away from home. This behavior, he adds, is causing him a great deal of distress, not to mention wrecking his formerly close relationship with his dog. One of his friends, trying to be helpful, says, "I've heard the best thing to do in that situation is to push their nose in it to show them it's wrong." (*The dog would have no clue what was going on if the man did this and would probably consider his owner's behavior, well, strange.*) Another individual chimes in: "You should punish him for that. After all, he knows he's done something bad. I would rap him on the nose with a rolled-up newspaper when you get home." (*Punishment after the fact is a total waste of time and will make your dog mistrust you.*) A third person believes that he has the best solution to his friend's predicament. "Put him in a crate while you're away," he says with conviction. "That worked for our dog." (*What this person does not realize is that a dog that has accidents only in his owner's absence probably has separation anxiety; such a dog may seriously injure himself in attempts to break out of a crate when his owner is away.*) As part of the continuing barrage of advice, a fourth individual suggests that the man put ammonia on the spot where the dog has urinated, to obliterate the urine smell and thus prevent the dog from returning to that spot. (*This will only make matters worse; ammonia smells like urine and the dog will often mark over it.*)

It never ceases to amaze me how much misinformation exists on the care and management of pets. I find it remarkable that the same people who consider themselves experts in the field of animal behavior would never think of offering advice on a medical question, like what antibiotic to use for a dog with a bladder infection or what problems may result if a dog's cholesterol level is too high. If you're a nonspecialist, the proper answer to these and other such questions is usually, "I don't know" (the three words a wise person uses most often). A reasonable alternative is, "Why don't you check with your vet and see if she can help or refer you to a specialist?" Even veterinarians don't venture advice unless they know it to be sound. I am reminded of a quote that appears on the first page of each issue of one of the British medical journals: "I would have everie man write what he knowes and no more" (Montaigne). I've always adopted this as my personal maxim—whether writing or speaking.

The man at the cocktail party might also have turned to the Internet for advice about his dog's behavior. The problem is, much of what is found on the Internet is written by guys like the ones at the cocktail party. There is more information out there than you can shake a stick at, but it's hard to know what or whom to believe. With the World Wide Web, it is definitely a case of user beware. You may read about the efficacy of Bach flower essences and other "natural" antianxiety medications. You might find yourself musing about aromatherapy, touch therapy, and dog yoga, or you might even be taken in by an "animal communicator." Then again, you might wind up at the sites of hard-line dog trainers who will tell you that you have to be "alpha" and advocate such supposedly dominance-establishing techniques as rolling, pinning, and chain jerking.

So how do you know what's right and what's not among all

the information out there? First, assess the source. If the author-adviser is certified by the Animal Behavior Society or the American College of Veterinary Behaviorists, you can trust that you are receiving an educated opinion. If the author is a dog owner turned dog trainer/behaviorist, you should be more skeptical. Next, make sure you are comfortable with the advice being offered and fully understand what resolution of the problem entails. If what is being said makes sense from a logical and practical standpoint, then you are probably on the right track. Finally, avoid any training program that involves physical punishment as a means to an end. Know that "a correction" in trainer lingo is a euphemism for punishment or warning of imminent punishment. Also know that chain jerking and electric shock treatment are inhumane and outmoded training methods. In my opinion, the only time the word "jerk" should be used in dog training is when referring to those who employ this technique.

One of my goals in writing this book is to dispel some of the myths and misconceptions about how to look after dogs, how to manage them, and how to train them to be well-adjusted, good canine citizens. One of the most prominent falsehoods is that once a puppy is housetrained and has graduated from a puppy-training class, a dog owner's work is done. Nothing could be further from the truth. While it is true that the first few months of a pup's life—even the first year—are formative times, plenty of consideration must be given and actions taken throughout a dog's life if optimal welfare is to be sustained. Caring for an adult dog does not simply involve feeding him and taking him for short walks around the block for elimination purposes. A high quality of life for dogs, as for humans, requires more than basic sustenance. Providing a healthy lifestyle for a dog and attending to his physical and psychological needs are lifelong commitments. Training should be thought of as an ongoing process of continuing education extending long past puppy "kindergarten." Dogs can and do learn well into old age and should not be denied the opportunity to expand their communication skills and repertoire of responses throughout the course of their lives.

A dog's lifestyle, daily routine, and interactions will, to a large extent, determine how he feels and how he behaves. When behavior is out of kilter, it is important to address the bigger picture rather than try to suppress the symptoms of an underlying problem. The uninformed approach tends to be, "You tell me what your dog is doing wrong and I'll show you how to stop him from doing that." A behaviorist, however, asks why there is a problem, and has a broad, long-term approach to resolving it. I will share with you the latter approach: treatment of the whole dog within the context of his environment, not just the symptom or symptoms of the problem. Furthermore, the information I will provide is based on scientific studies and my thirty-seven years of clinical experience: it is not just my personal opinion (though I am not shy to offer one based on the facts). Objective assessment of outcomes is the best way to find out if treatments actually work in the short and long term, and studies of this sort are what scientists do. It is not sufficient follow-up to ask an owner how a dog is doing and if they say fine, chalk it up as a success. Most people, trying hard to please (and justifying their expenditure of money, time, and effort), will volunteer that their dog is doing better even when he's not. Or owners may be so pleased with minor improvement in one area of behavior modification that they report in superlatives, laying their praise on inordinately thick. Some owners fail to call back. That might mean the problem has been resolved, but it could mean exactly the opposite. Optimistic trainers think no news is good news, but it could be that the dog's behavior is unchanged or has deteriorated. Owners may have given up asking for further advice because nothing is working out, or they may have even had the dog "put to sleep." It's impossible to tell what's what without proper organized studies in which the behavior is rated as objectively as possible. Behaviorists take this approach, and share their findings with their colleagues in print. This book seeks to relay to dog owners all that has been learned from such empirical studies.

Since dogs' behavior problems should be addressed in the larger context of dogs' daily lives and interactions, lifestyle adjustment is imperative prior to implementing recommendations to deal with specific behavioral problems. It is probably true to say that many behavior problems exhibited by dogs originate because of unhealthful lifestyles—failure to accommodate the dog's needs—mismanagement, and poor training. The recommendations presented in this book are intended to help prevent behavior problems from developing in the first place and to assuage them if they have already surfaced. A dog that is exercised sufficiently, fed appropriately, communicated with clearly, led effectively, and has an interesting and purposeful lifestyle is not likely to be afflicted by the many behavioral problems that plague domestic dogs today. Your job as a dog owner is to try to understand your dog's life from his point of view, and to lead and protect, not to dominate, punish, and force a dog into submission, as popularized on too many of today's TV shows. Real leaders in the human world, as in the dog world, do not have to resort to physical measures to get their point across. Real leaders do not dominate; they listen, think, and often defer. Real leaders do not intimidate; they instill confidence. People follow real leaders not because they have to but because they want to. If you bear this in mind and provide for your dog in the ways I describe, you will enjoy your time with your dog and, equally important, your dog will enjoy his time with you. The human–companion animal bond is not forged through the metal of the choke chain or prong collar but rather through mutual trust and respect.

Consider the predicament that Buddy, an effervescent adolescent Border collie pup, found himself in. Each morning he woke up in a crate and stared longingly at the young married couple who were his owners, as they bustled around getting ready for work. Somewhere between coffee making, breakfasting, and showering, one owner would head his way, open the crate, clip on a lead, and take him outside for a breath of fresh air. But it was only a breath. In temporary exhilaration, Buddy would leap and pirouette like a spawning salmon heading upstream, but before he knew it, he was on his way back to the confines of his crate. Soon the house was quiet and all that was heard was a ticking clock. Things to do included chewing a toy, licking his paws, and staring at the wall. Pretty soon he'd be bored and fall asleep, awakening at midmorning or lunchtime. Time passed slowly. By midafternoon he'd be out of his mind with restlessness. He could have tried counting sheep—if he knew what they were and if he could count—but all that was left to do was circle and whine. His bladder ached. *When will they be back?* As the shadows fell, and after he had all but given up, there would be sounds that he recognized—a car engine, crackling gravel in the driveway, and finally the key in the door. They were home! The husband would arrive first, throw his raincoat over a chair, and then look Buddy's way. "Wanna go out, boy?" he would say. *Do I ever!* Buddy would think. The crate door would be opened and Buddy would exit like he was shot from a gun. Ricocheting around the room, he would pray for the back door to be opened, which it was, in due course. He would then careen out into the postage-stamp-size backyard and, after relieving himself, would practically do cartwheels as he barked himself hoarse, venting all that pent-up energy. "No!" he would hear from the back door as he noticed his owner heading toward him. Before he knew it, he was being hauled back inside. In protest, he would mouth his owner's arm, wriggle, and try to break free. Once inside, he would continue to charge around and blow off steam, but before five minutes were up he would often find himself back in the slammer. During the evening, there wasn't much to do in the crate except eat dinner and watch his owners eat and slump exhausted in front of the TV. Yes, there was a nighttime visit to the yard, but that was it until the next morning and then the cycle repeated itself. It was a dog's life.

From Buddy's owners' point of view, they had a dog that was totally berserk. Whenever they let him out of the crate he went wild, running around the living room, tearing up the couches and curtains, barking, and disturbing the neighbors whenever he was outside. Confining him to a crate—even when they were home—was, for these owners, a desperate means to deal with a desperate problem. But denying Buddy an outlet for his pent-up energies only made matters worse. It was a Catch-22 situation: the more they confined him, the worse he became. Contributing to the problem, they hadn't trained him properly, did not exercise him enough, and fed him a high-protein, high-energy ration formulated for active dogs. Their treatment of Buddy had created a rod for their own backs *and they thought he was at fault.* First-time dog owners, they didn't know how to be good leaders, let alone educate him. What a mess.

When owners bring their dogs to me at the Tufts Cummings School Animal Behavior Clinic, they are often, like Buddy's owners, at their wits' end. In fact, our clinic has been described as the "Last Resort Nation" by owners and referring veterinarians alike. It's true I do see the toughest cases, the hardest ones to treat. Each one is unique; no two owners are the same and no two dogs or behavior problems are precisely the same—though similar general principles can be applied when attempting to resolve the issues. Whether a dog is hyperactive, exhibiting aggression, or chasing his tail, we put him through a tailored-to-suit broad-spectrum rehabilitation program, and the dog emerges all the better for it. We know this for a fact because we conduct the requisite follow-up studies.

All in all, there are seven lifestyle factors—or steps—that I discuss with clients, ranging from providing sufficient exercise to environmental enrichment, though not all of these elements need adjustment in every case. The five or six factors that need attention in any one case constitute the behavior-modification program for that dog. The approach is holistic, in that it attempts to simultaneously address and optimize *all* aspects of dogs' daily lives and interactions. In order to know what recommendations to make in an individual case, I must first learn about the dog and his problems in detail. To this end, I inquire about all aspects of the dog's life, from birth to the present time—and do not simply quiz the owners about the problem itself, as behavior problems tend not to exist in splendid isolation of what is otherwise a healthy, well-adjusted life. I hear the owners' concerns and try to discern what is at the root of the problem (the behavior itself is usually the result of fundamental lifestyle issues). In addition, I carefully observe each dog to see if his temperament jibes with the problem reported and do whatever I deem necessary to reveal any underlying medical issues that might be contributing to the problem. The consultation provides me an opportunity to assess each dog individually and to tailor a program to suit that dog, rather than adopting a one-size-fits-all regimen that might have an adverse impact.

Treatment-wise, I usually start by addressing a dog's need for exercise. And most owners are bowled over by what it takes. Their response, when I tell them that their dog needs more than a mile walk around the block each day, is typically an astonished "I had no idea" (reminiscent of someone on *Antiques Road Show* who's just been told that something they pulled from the attic is valuable). Owners are just as much in the dark about the behavioral effects of some diets. "But the breeder told me to feed raw meat. She gives it to all her dogs" is the kind of response I hear. "Really. And where did you say the breeder went to study nutrition?" I might jive. That usually elicits a wry smile. To test whether the owner has a reasonable level of communication with her dog I might ask her to instruct her dog to sit. Then I watch. Often I witness this kind of scenario: "Sit, sit, *sit!* What did I tell you? Sally, sit! . . ." and so on. Finally the dog may actually sit—perhaps out of boredom—and the owner omits to praise him. We learn a lot about a dog's connection with his owner—or lack thereof—from this exercise. Then there's physical control. I stare in disbelief at some of the medieval-looking metal collars that owners have been told to use by spare-the-rod-and-spoil-the-dog hard-line trainers. "But the trainer says it doesn't hurt," owners declare. "As long as you don't get your fingers stuck in the collar when you jerk it," I retort. Physical control of dogs is another area for owner enlightenment. A fearful and aggressive dog on a loosely held ten-foot retractable leash is an accident waiting to happen. Then there's leadership. Dogs need strong leaders—but not abusive ones. Just because a dog stops complaining (growling) if you punish him doesn't make you his leader or him your follower. True leadership is something earned by fair and consistent actions. Inflicting pain might equate with domination, but it has nothing to do with leadership. Then there's fearfulness. Almost all dogs are frightened of something, even if it's only going to the vet's office (and can you blame them, considering that their first visit might have been for neutering). Sometimes trainers give reasonable advice to owners of fearful dogs, but sometimes they get it wrong. "My trainer says I should desensitize him to his fear of slippery surfaces by making him walk on them until his fear subsides." "That's not desensitization," I explain. "That is what is called 'flooding' and may have extremely detrimental effects." Desensitization is a gradual, layer-by-layer process of alleviating fear, not a Joan Rivers "Grow up" approach. Many owners are confused about what is the right thing to do. They are exposed to a lot of misinformation, conflicting information, and well-intended advice from friends and acquaintances who often simply get it wrong. Finally, far too many dogs are occupationally or environmentally challenged. It's as if owners have not thought of trying to look at the world through their dog's eyes. Dogs, like people, fare better when they are gainfully employed.

Though many dogs are faithful, perfectly behaved ones are not that easy to find. Almost half of the nation's 70 million dog owners report behavioral problems with their dogs, and some of these problems are severe enough to put a real damper on the owner-dog relationship. In fact, some 4 million dogs are surrendered to shelters annually, predominantly for behavioral reasons, and over half of them are subsequently euthanized. Most of the behaviors that lead to dogs' relinquishment arise through no fault of the dog's and are, in fact, normal canine behaviors that owners cannot properly control or direct. It is breeders' and owners' failure to understand what it takes to raise, care for, and communicate with dogs that underlies many potentially avoidable canine behavior problems. As the late Barbara Woodhouse used to say, "There is no such thing as a difficult dog, only an inexperienced owner" (*No Bad Dogs*). That's not far from the truth.

Back to Buddy. Buddy responded wonderfully to a combination of daily vigorous exercise, a sensible diet, training, and environmental enrichment. Long-term crating became a thing of the past and he finally got to lead a normal life with owners who had now learned how to care for him. Buddy responded exceptionally well to training, learning responses to various cues in record time. A better-behaved Buddy got much more freedom in the home and didn't even have to have the crate door shut when his owners were away. His owners felt much better about the new arrangements—and I know Buddy did, too. There are lots of dogs like Buddy who are misunderstood and mismanaged. The increasingly popular method for dealing with dogs' behavior problems is to punish them for unwanted behaviors, whereas a far more benign, logical, and effective approach is to reward desired behaviors, address basic needs, and lead dogs down the winding path to successful rehabilitation. It may take a little longer, but it is more humane, and the lessons and lifestyle changes produce lasting results. This is the approach that I describe in the pages that follow and the one I hope dog owners will adopt. Sit! Read! Learn!—and enjoy.

Part 1

Basic Needs

It should go without saying that a dog's physical and health needs must be taken care of as a priority to ensure his well-being and to provide a firm base for other, more sophisticated welfare measures. Ideally, every dog should receive an annual veterinary checkup, have any necessary blood work performed, and routine medications, like heartworm and flea and tick preventatives, prescribed. It is far better to take a preventative approach to dogs' physical well-being than to wait until things go wrong and then have to utilize a "fire engine approach" to deal with the conflagration.

What many dog owners don't realize is that routine veterinary care is not enough to ensure a dog's *optimal* health and happiness. Other factors essential for the dog's physical and mental health are sufficient exercise and a properly balanced diet appropriate to the dog's lifestyle, activity level, and temperament. Dogs also benefit from having a clear line of communication between themselves and their owners. They are at their best when they have confidence in their owners' ability to exercise leadership — including the use of humane forms of restraint when necessary. They also respond well to having a clear understanding of what's required of them and what their place is in the family unit. Many dogs, at one time or another, exhibit fear-based behaviors that erode their confidence and can lead to other problems. Owners must be able to manage fearful situations and use behavior-modification techniques when necessary to assuage specific fears. Finally, dogs thrive in user-friendly environments that support their canine agendas. All of these factors contribute to a dog's achieving optimal health and well-being, and to a relationship between dog and owner that is enjoyable and mutually fulfilling. In this section, I deal with the seven physical and mental needs that I see as fundamental to ensuring that dogs lead happy, healthy, well-adjusted lives.

1

A Tired Dog Is a Good Dog

Sufficient Exercise — A First and Necessary Step

If your dog is fat, you aren't getting enough exercise.
— Unknown

Sometimes canine behavior problems are so severe, they threaten the ability of people to successfully cohabit with their dogs. Other problems, though troublesome, simply fall into the nuisance category. In one such case, a couple came to the Animal Behavior Clinic at Tufts complaining about their two-year-old Dalmatian's constant whining, pacing, and circling. Seemingly neurotic, hyperactive behaviors such as these may be initiated by many complex causes, but they often stem from an imbalance of energy input and output. As a starting point in what would be a lengthy consultation with numerous recommendations, I addressed the dog's need for vigorous daily exercise—suspecting, as I did, that he may not be getting enough, because few dogs are.

"He gets walked around the block every day," the woman owner said when I asked how much exercise their dog, George, was getting. "Isn't that enough?"

"It's better than nothing," I replied, "but certainly not enough for a canine athlete like George. I used to take my eighty-year-old mother for a mile walk around the block each day when she visited from England, and neither of us was out of breath. Most dogs are born to run—and run hard. Dalmatians, in particular, were bred to run alongside stagecoaches and fire trucks for hours without tiring. Dogs' wild cousins covered huge distances in search of prey, so exercise is part of the natural and necessary canine agenda."

To illustrate the point, I told George's owners about my experience with a highly predatory and energetic Parson Russell terrier who used to accompany me and my father on long country walks when I was a teenager. While we were walking over hill and dale, the dog was running. When we had plodded several miles, the dog had covered many times that distance—and at full tilt. By late afternoon, when we returned home, the dog, who had been so jazzed up at the start of the day, was finally peaceful, relaxed, and happy.

"What George needs is a *minimum* of thirty minutes of aerobic exercise daily, and preferably more."

The couple then asked me to explain what constitutes aerobic exercise.

"Aerobic exercise increases oxygen consumption and makes the heart beat stronger and faster. It is exercise that causes dogs to pant and tires them out. It is usually only possible to achieve this level of exercise with a dog off leash—unless you use a treadmill. Gym people refer to this type of exercising as cardio (short for cardiovascular exercise). It leaves us with our hands on our hips, breathing heavily. This type of vigorous exercise is what most young, healthy dogs need."

"I see," the man commented. "The kind of exercise we get on a treadmill or Stairmaster or when we go for a jog."

"Precisely," I replied. "Exercise to the point of tiredness is what I am looking for. One of my favorite mantras is 'A tired dog is a good dog.' Do you think you'll be able to incorporate that level of activity into your routine with George?"

"He does get a fair bit of exercise on the weekend," the woman offered. "We like to hike and most weekends we take George with us. We walk several miles over hilly terrain. To our usual seven or so miles, he probably covers twenty-one. He's in perpetual motion—on the go all the time. That's enough exercise for him, isn't it?"

I had to admit that that level of exercise was more than any behaviorist could reasonably request for a dog. But, then again, it was only on weekends.

"And how is he on weekends after all that exercise?" I inquired.

Husband and wife looked at each other, smiled, then looked back at me. "Actually he's great, now that you mention it," the husband said. "We don't have any trouble with him at all on the weekends. It's during the week that we have most of the issues."

They had made the connection. I knew I had made my point about the importance of daily aerobic exercise. I also knew that these owners were going to take the message home and reorganize their schedules so that George could receive a suitable amount of exercise daily. This would entail a lifestyle change—perhaps involving a tag-team approach to the dog's management—but it would be well worth it. They later confirmed during a follow-up call that this change had made a positive impact on George's behavior problems.

Exercise is important for all dogs who are physically capable of it, but it has a greater behavioral impact on some than others. I have asked people, weeks or months after a behavioral appointment, to share their impression of the effects of exercise on their dog's behavior problem. Answers vary from "I think it makes a difference. He seems a bit calmer when he's been out for a run" to "Of all the things you mentioned, increasing his exercise has produced the most profound change in our dog's behavior." The latter is powerful testimony to the effect of exercise on behavior.

In general, dogs of the sporting breeds require a fair amount of exercise. Toy dogs and some very large breeds have low exercise

Different Strokes for Different Dogs

While it is generally true that all dogs need lots of aerobic exercise, breed requirements for exercise do differ. The amount of exercise a particular breed requires depends on the purpose for which that breed was developed. Dogs like Weimaraners, which were bred to run, will need much more exercise than lap dogs, such as Pekingese. "Runners" will require more than the statutory minimum of twenty to thirty minutes of aerobic exercise daily, though this minimum level may suffice for medium-energy dogs. "Couch potato" breeds may get all the exercise they need with a brisk walk around the block each day.

The Runners (high exercise requirements)

Working breeds (Siberian husky, Alaskan malamute, Portuguese water dog)

Sporting breeds (Weimaraner, pointers, setters, English springer spaniel, American and Irish water spaniel, Labrador retriever, golden retriever, Nova Scotia duck tolling retriever)

Nonsporting breeds (Dalmatian)

Herding breeds (Australian shepherd, Australian cattle dog, Border collie)

Terrier breeds (Parson Russell terrier, miniature schnauzer, bull terrier)

Hounds (foxhounds, saluki)

continued on next page

requirements. How much exercise a dog needs can be gleaned from his breed history. The American Kennel Club's *The Complete Dog Book* provides the best account of breed history and development for all AKC-recognized breeds of dog. Dogs that were bred to cover large distances at a fair clip will likely need more exercise than those bred for sedentary purposes, like lap dogs. Bear in mind that the energy level and thus exercise requirement of dogs also vary from individual to individual and are not solely determined by breed. I have met sluggish setters, couch potato pointers, and hyperactive hounds. Age (older dogs need

---

Different Strokes for Different Dogs, *continued*

The joggers (medium exercise requirements)

Working breeds (boxer, Rottweiler, mastiff, Doberman pinscher, Great
  Dane, Saint Bernard)
Sporting breeds (cocker spaniel)
Nonsporting breeds (chow chow)
Hounds (Afghan hound, beagle, greyhound)
Herding breeds (Old English sheepdog, briard, German shepherd)
Terrier breeds (Scottish terrier, soft-coated wheaten terrier)

The strollers (low exercise requirements)

Working breeds (Bernese mountain dog, Newfoundland, Great Pyre-
  nees, German pinscher)
Toy breeds (affenpinscher, Chihuahua, Pekingese, Shih Tzu, English toy
  spaniel)
Hounds (basset hound, Scottish deerhound, dachshund)
Nonsporting (bulldog, French bulldog, Lhasa apso, Shiba inu, bichon
  frisé)

---

less exercise) and physical limitations (e.g., hip dysplasia, arthritis) must also be considered when assessing how much exercise is
good for a dog.

Psychological Benefits of Exercise

While exercise is beneficial to dogs' physical well-being, my main
interest has always been in its psychological effects. Exercise has
both calming and mood-stabilizing effects, of that there is no
doubt. Anyone who has engaged in regular, sustained exercise, or
been actively involved in sports, already knows that exercise can
produce a night-and-day difference in a person's mood. During
my early days at Tufts, I sometimes finished work feeling stressed
out, with what seemed like all the troubles of the world on my

mind. Then, for health reasons, I would head for the gym. An hour and a half later, after a workout and a shower, I would emerge de-stressed, reinvigorated, and ready for anything the world might throw at me. This is the way exercise seems to work for dogs, too, and yet many owners and some veterinarians haven't made the connection. As basic a benefit as exercising a dog would appear to be, the science underlying the psychological benefits of exercise has not been appreciated until relatively recently. Even in the mid-'80s, medical reports stated that theories concerning the psychological benefits of exercise, though widely touted, had not been adequately tested. It was not until the mid- to late '90s and into the twenty-first century that the psychological benefits of exercise in humans saw sufficient study; and there is next to nothing on the subject with respect to dogs even now.

What is it about physical exercise that produces relaxation and well-being in us and in dogs? The answer is that it causes changes in brain chemistry. Most of us have heard of the expression "runner's high," which was once solely attributed to endorphin release in the brain (endorphins are nature's own morphine-like substances). According to the opioid theory, a good dose of exercise produces an opium-like high that dispels depression and makes the world seem a much rosier place. This concept has merit but may not be the whole story. Princeton University professor Barry Jacobs reports that exercise also releases serotonin, and that this brain chemical contributes to exercise-mediated well-being. Jacobs's take on serotonin is different from the one we usually hear. Serotonin's beneficial effects on mood are well known, but Jacobs notes serotonin's overwhelming importance in modulating the activity of large muscle groups that keep us ambulatory and upright. When we run or engage in fatiguing physical activity, our serotonin system kicks into overdrive. Enhanced mood stabilization is secondary to this process and may have evolved as part of nature's intrinsic reward system. Whereas physical activity increases activity in serotonin nerves, a sudden call for mental activity shuts them down, leading to decreased physical activity. A call for high mental activity, as occurs in stress, might contribute to the development of depression and languor by decreasing activity in serotonin nerves. In that case, augmenting exercise would seem a natural way out of the loop—and so it appears to be.

A year or two ago, I was talking to a friend of mine, Dr. John Ratey, a clinical psychiatrist and assistant professor at Harvard Medical School, about his book *A User's Guide to the Brain,* the bottom line of which, according to Ratey, is that "exercise increases serotonin so dramatically that its action on mood is even more powerful than the antidepressant Prozac." Who wouldn't rather exercise than take a pill to feel better, I thought, as I contemplated the beneficial effects of exercise in dogs and the way I feel when leaving the gym. It's interesting that depression in people is associated with decreased serotonin in the brain and (sometimes) compensatory overeating, while both exercise and Prozac increase serotonin, stabilizing mood and, at least in the short term, decreasing appetite.

To some, whether the beneficial effects of exercise are mediated by the release of endorphins or serotonin is moot. The net effect—mood stabilization, peace of mind, serenity—are the Holy Grail of behavioral medicine. Exercise is a natural way of helping us and our dogs deal with the pressures of modern life; in addition to making us happier, it also makes us smarter (by promoting the maturation of new brain cells) and helps us sleep more soundly.

Physical Benefits of Exercise

Aside from psychological benefits, exercise has important physical benefits for dogs, as it does for humans. The quality as well as the length of life is important for us and for our dogs. The Nutrition Center at Tufts University has coined the term "health span"—as opposed to "life span"—to describe the long, healthy existence for which we all strive and want also for our dogs. Exercise is an important component of a lifestyle offering the best chance of achieving a long and happy life.

Exercise builds muscle, burns fat, and strengthens the cardiopulmonary system. In addition, it staves off Alzheimer's disease in humans and, in all likelihood, has a similar brain-cell-sparing effect in offsetting the canine equivalent, canine cognitive dysfunction (see chapter 9).

It has been known since the turn of the twentieth century that the most important determinant of life span in animals is net caloric balance. If the caloric intake is in excess of output, fat will accumulate at a rate proportional to the imbalance. I'm reminded of Mr. Micawber's observation in Charles Dickens's *David Copperfield:* "If a man had twenty pounds a year for his income and spent nineteen pounds nineteen shillings and sixpence, he would be happy, but if he spent twenty pounds one he would be miserable." Paraphrasing: Intake seven calories an hour (for a small dog), expenditure six calories an hour, result, weight gain and eventual misery. Carrying extra weight shortens dogs' health span and leaves them prone to various medical problems ranging from heart disease to orthopedic problems to cancer.

Obesity in our canine companions has reached the same epidemic proportions that it has in humans—and for similar reasons. Indeed, one in three dogs in the United States is overweight. There are three factors that affect body mass index (body mass index is weight adjusted for a physical size). The factors are: food intake, metabolic rate, and activity level. There's not much you can do about a dog's metabolic rate, unless he is hypothyroid, in which case thyroid hormone levels can be adjusted by hormone replacement therapy. That leaves two components, intake (food) and output (exercise), as malleable variables. Of course, on the intake side of the equation, it makes perfect sense to ration a dog's diet properly, but it is equally important to control the output side,

Exercise and Aging

The psychiatrist John Ratey calls exercise Miracle-Gro for the brain. Wheel-running rats have been shown to have fewer damaged brain cells than their sedentary counterparts. Researchers have recently shown that aging people who exercise regularly have more brain cells in the frontal cortex—a brain region responsible for higher-order thinking, memory, and attention. The same people also had increased connections in a structure important for enabling the right side–left side communications in the brain. These results—which, no doubt, also apply to dogs that exercise regularly—are attributable to increased blood flow to the brain during strenuous physical activity. The take-home message: Run for your life.

which is exercise. All good weight-loss programs should address both sides of this equation. Dogs that are regularly exercised live up to 30 percent longer than their sedentary counterparts.

Practical Considerations

Okay, so let's say that at this point we agree that exercise is physically and mentally good for dogs. Should it therefore be a prescription for all dogs every day? The answer is yes, if at all possible. That said, some people have difficulty finding *time* to exercise their dogs, like the couple I mentioned earlier. In such cases a solution must be found, whether it is in the form of a paid dog walker (dog exerciser) or a few days a week at doggy daycare —which can really tucker dogs out.

Another problem can be finding a suitable place to exercise your dog. Dog parks are great but they aren't available in every town, and sometimes they come with strings attached—like no off-leash exercise. I have written several letters to local authorities explaining—on behalf of pro-dog action committees—that dogs really need an opportunity to run free, but I can't tell how much influence my opinion has had on canine-phobic committee members. Even if they have access to a place where they can exercise their dogs, some owners find it difficult to engage in this activity during the winter months, especially if they live in northern climes. It's true that sled dogs work in extreme weather, but most pet dogs (and many owners) aren't up for frolicking in the park when the temperature is twenty degrees below. In this situation, I sometimes recommend a treadmill, and there are some relatively inexpensive ones, retailing for about $150 and up, that are designed specifically for canines.

It is not difficult to train a dog to use a treadmill—it just involves getting on the treadmill with the dog on leash and starting to walk. Like us, most dogs, when given the opportunity to use a treadmill, seem to regard it as an enjoyable, rewarding experience. The speed of the treadmill can be gradually cranked up to trotting pace and an owner can then take off the dog's lead and slowly move away from the treadmill (so that she doesn't have to stand right next to the treadmill the whole time the dog is "work-

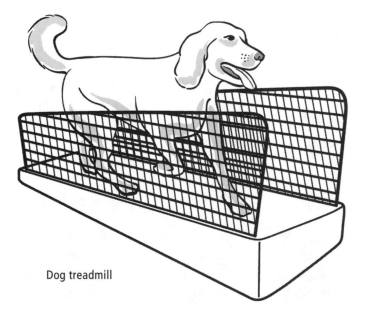

Dog treadmill

ing out"). Ultimately it may be possible for an owner to be sitting in a reclining chair reading a book and enjoying all the creature comforts of home while the dog gets twenty to thirty minutes of aerobic exercise on the opposite side of the room. Let's be clear about treadmills, though. For a dog that enjoys the experience, they can be used in the benign way described, but they should never be forced on a dog. No dog should be tied to the treadmill, left unsupervised, or run to the point of collapse. That constitutes abuse.

There are also "dog factors" that must be considered when implementing an aerobic exercise program. You can't take a dog that has been lying around on a rug accumulating weight for years and suddenly expect him to run the equivalent of a marathon. Dogs that are unfit, like people who are unfit, must be slowly acclimated to exercise via a program that increases distance and effort over time, as tolerated by the dog. Vigorous exercise may be contraindicated for some dogs for reasons of existing medical problems or plain old age. For such dogs, exercise may have to be conducted at more modest levels. Short walks around the block may be all that can be tolerated without producing deleterious effects. Here the philosophy must be: some exercise is better than none.

Limitations imposed by medical problems can sometimes be circumvented by utilizing a different form of exercise, for example, swimming, or freestyle low-impact aerobics in which the dog and owner engage in coordinated moves to music, and exercise can sometimes be facilitated by appropriate medical treatments. I know a German shepherd owner whose dog suffered from degenerative myelopathy (which causes German shepherds genetically predisposed to the disease to progressively lose control of their hind legs) to an extent that the dog was incapable of running. If this owner had resigned himself to the fact that his dog could not be exercised, its muscles would have atrophied and its physical function would have rapidly deteriorated. Instead, this dedicated owner drove his dog forty-five minutes each way three times a week to a special equine- and canine-only swimming pool where he put a lead on the dog and did laps with him for an hour each time. This enabled the dog to maintain strength and delayed the progression of this miserable disease.

Another dilemma that some owners face in trying to implement an exercise program for their dog is that the dog may be aggressive to other dogs or people and cannot be allowed off lead in public because of safety concerns. In such cases, I recommend that people find an unpopulated area to exercise their dogs. One such place is an empty tennis court, in which a dog can chase tennis balls to the point of exhaustion without risk to others' life and limb. Slightly more daring is an early morning outdoor excursion onto an enclosed running track or ball field. If that is out of the question, a dog can get a fair amount of exercise in an open area while affixed to a long lead, for example, a thirty-foot nylon washing line. With practice, an owner can run the dog on this long lead and "reel it in" rapidly at the first hint of danger. (One caveat is that the owner must be strong enough to reel in the dog when circumstances dictate.) Finally, for the hardcore canine, there is nothing that beats a properly fitted basket-style muzzle, like the ones police K9 handlers employ. Such muzzles allow a dog to pant, drink, take food treats, and do everything he would otherwise do — except bite. This measure gives owners reassurance that their potentially aggressive dog won't be a threat to people and other animals encountered during exercise.

But what happens if you meet up with an aggressive stray or dog whose owner did not take safety precautions like using a muzzle, and you or your dog is threatened? One of my clients fills a long-range, high-power water pistol with a combination of aversive (to a dog) substances like lemon juice, Tabasco, garlic, and pepper; she calls it "vamoose juice." She would level the spray at any marauding dogs in defense of her own dog, apparently with great success. Another client used a hand-operated, radio-

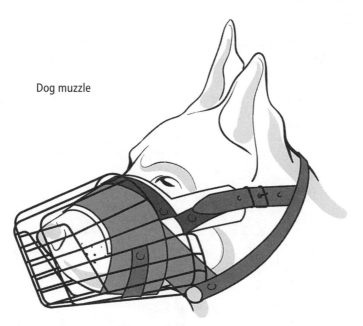

Dog muzzle

controlled citronella collar, activating it whenever her dog looked like it was heading for a fray. To her amazement, she discovered that when she activated the device, both would-be combatants took off in different directions. Such collars, as well as handheld citronella sprays to deter unwelcome canines, can be purchased at pet-supply stores. (For more on citronella and other types of collars, see chapter 4.)

The Bottom Line

The importance of accommodating a dog's need for exercise cannot be overstated. Exercise is a key part of a balanced approach to managing canine behavior and ensuring a dog's well-being. If there are logistical problems associated with exercising a dog, I work hard with owners to find ways around these obstacles. I encourage all dog owners to do what it takes to incorporate daily exercise into their dogs' routines. Pent-up energy has to be vented or it will manifest in destructive and unacceptable ways. Anyone whose children have ever suffered from cabin fever will immediately identify with the consequences of inactivity. Horse owners know that exercising horses by lungeing helps calm even the feistiest of equines. Informed cat owners know that aerobic play—encouraged by moving toys—helps neutralize antagonistic behaviors. Let's face it, exercise is behaviorally beneficial for all ambulatory species, and there's often trouble afoot when it is in short supply.

There is a long litany of dog behavior problems caused or compounded by lack of exercise. Aggression, barking, compulsive behavior . . . and that's only the ABC of it . . . the list goes right through to Z (as I describe in *Dogs Behaving Badly*). Underexercised dogs are likely to be more moody, aggressive, and fearful, and may develop any one of a number of compulsive behaviors, ranging from tail chasing to acral lick dermatitis (ALD). These are problems about which I am often consulted, and exercise—when feasible—is an important aspect of treatment.

Finally, exercise is a form of occupational therapy. When you take your dog for a breeze in the park, to doggy daycare, for a swim in the ocean, or for flyball or agility training, a number of social and lifestyle factors are simultaneously addressed. Environmental enrichment is a spin-off benefit of exercise. Think about it: dogs have been bred for a variety of physical activities and are social creatures. To exercise your dog is to address one of his most fundamental needs and is an undertaking that should be viewed as mandatory. If exercising involves the company of other dogs and people, so much the better. For owners having difficulty making a commitment to exercise with their dogs, ponder this: Studies have shown that people who walk and exercise with their dogs are generally happier and healthier and live longer. So, if you aren't motivated to take your dog out for his sake, do it for your own.

2

Food for Thought

A Proper Diet — Vital to Health and Well-Being

Life goes faster on protein.
— Martin H. Fischer

We all accept that a proper balanced diet is necessary for the maintenance of health and life, but the topic of whether different foods make a difference to dogs' behavior is controversial. It's another one of those subjects about which everyone has an opinion yet many disagree.

The first time I considered a possible connection between a dog's diet and behavior was when a visiting trainer asked the owner of an aggressive dog, "What do you feed him?" I wondered why this question was relevant to the problem at hand.

"Performance rations—only the best for my dog," the owner answered.

"That's rocket fuel," the trainer said. "It'll put your dog into orbit."

"So what *should* I be feeding him?" the stunned owner replied.

"A low-protein, all-natural ration—preferably lamb-based," the trainer said.

"How would that help the aggressive behavior?" I asked, genuinely puzzled by the advice.

"I'm not certain *how* it works, only that it does," the trainer answered. "Some people say it's the percentage of protein that makes the difference; others say it's the type of protein; others blame artificial preservatives. All I can tell you is that when you change all these things simultaneously, it can sometimes make a major difference."

"Have any studies been done to confirm that?" I asked.

"I don't know," the trainer answered, "but I can tell you from my own experience that feeding the right diet can really help. I've seen it over and over again. I don't know whether it's the protein source or the level of protein or the absence of preservatives— that's why I make the across-the-board change."

I had no reason to doubt this trainer's experience, since he had probably trained over twenty thousand dogs, but I was curious about the results he got and why. I pondered the subject of diet and behavior for several weeks. I had never given any thought to the possibility of this effect before and had certainly never heard anything about it at scientific meetings I had attended. If the trainer was right in his contention that diet affects behavior, that finding would be a useful contribution to canine behavior management.

In researching the subject, I found that numerous lay authors agreed with the trainer that diet can make a difference to dogs' behavior, and most attributed the effect to the protein content of the diet. Some of the proponents of the protein hypothesis were trainers or breeders, but others were veterinarians and one was a veterinary consultant for a pet food company. Most of them felt that lowering protein in the diet reduced aggression, though to complicate matters, one very well-known trainer, Bill Campbell, held the exact opposite view, that increasing protein content had a calming, antiaggressive effect. I decided to organize a study to investigate the effect of protein on dogs' behavior and began to look for a sponsor. I first contacted research scientists with Pedigree pet food company to see if they were interested in pursuing studies about the effect of dietary protein concentration on behavior. They asked me to draft the experimental protocol, which they approved, and soon funding for the study was in place.

The Effect of Protein on Behavior

Our study was designed to investigate the effect of protein on three different behaviors in adult dogs: owner-directed (dominance) aggression, territorial aggression, and hyperactivity. A "control" group of dogs that did not have behavior problems was also included. I farmed out the dominance-aggression and hyperactivity studies to two other veterinary schools; the "control" study of nonproblem (well-behaved) dogs was conducted by Pedigree scientists at their research center in England. I personally conducted the territorial-aggression component of the study here at Tufts. Pedigree supplied the food: custom dry food rations containing either 32 percent protein (the high-protein diet), 25 percent protein (the medium-protein diet), or 17 percent protein (the low-protein diet). The level of protein in the low-protein diet was the minimum necessary to meet a dog's maintenance requirements. The other two diets—one typical of many diets sold in stores (the 25 percent protein diet) and the other similar to high-performance rations (containing 32 percent protein)—supplied more protein than the necessary level for healthy adult dogs who are not pregnant, nursing, or being worked really hard. By the way, puppies (dogs less than 1 year old) need 28 percent protein to meet their needs; low-protein diets are not appropriate for them at all.

The diets for the dogs with behavior problems were coded A, B, and C. Investigators knew the protein content of each of the three foods, but participants in the study did not know which diet they were feeding their dog at any one time. The owners were asked to feed their dog each diet for two weeks and record the dog's behavior daily on a form. The order in which the diets were fed to the dogs over the three two-week intervals was randomized among participants. We spoke to owners every two weeks to make sure they were following the study protocol and filling in the forms correctly. Sometimes owners needed encouragement to keep them going. Sometimes they asked questions we were not allowed to answer. "Is the next diet likely to help him more?" they might ask. "I can't tell you that, I'm afraid" we would have to say. "You'll just have to keep going and all will be revealed at the end of the study."

After all of the study was completed, the results were charted and analyzed. They showed that territorial aggression was significantly reduced on the lower-protein diets. The decrease in aggression was almost linear when plotted against protein level—less protein equaled less aggression and the finding was statistically significant. A subset of territorially aggressive dogs motivated by fear or anxiety responded particularly well. One of these dogs was an Old English sheepdog, called Rosebud. Rosebud epitomized the behavioral change in the subset. After two weeks on the medium-protein diet (similar to the diet the owner had been feeding), Rosebud's behavior—lunging and barking at people entering the woman's photography studio—remained unchanged. On the low-protein diet, Rosebud was so much improved that her owner wanted to quit the study and feed her that diet for the rest of her life. On this diet, Rosebud only raised her head slowly from the pillow and woofed once or twice when someone came into the studio, before going back to sleep. I managed to persuade Rosebud's owner to complete the study; with only two more weeks to go, she agreed to comply. In the last two-week phase of the study, on the high-protein diet, Rosebud became so aggressive that her owner could no longer keep her in the studio. She had to be left at the woman's home and had lunged at and tried to bite someone in the street for the first time ever. You can guess what we recommended the owner to feed Rosebud after the study; that's right, a commercial low-protein diet—and things got better right away.

Many other stories we heard from owners of territorially aggressive dogs were similarly impressive. Since no concurrent behavior-modification therapy was included in the study, we felt we had categorically demonstrated an aggression-lowering effect of a low-protein diet—at least in territorially aggressive dogs.

As it turned out, neither of the other two behavioral conditions the study focused on—owner-directed aggression and hyperactivity—were affected by the protein content of the diet. It was my distinct feeling that these nonresults—particularly in the case of dominance aggression—were contaminated by poor owner compliance; I determined to repeat the dominance-aggression study at a later date. The control group of dogs, by the way, did not show any change in behavior on any of the diets. Though negative, that is an important finding and confirms, as we suspected, that high protein levels in the diet do not actually cause behavior problems, but they may exacerbate them—at least in the case of territorial aggression.

Around this time, I decided to recommend artificial-preservative-free, low-protein diets to owners of all aggressive dogs in the hopes of acquiring additional anecdotal data. Sometimes owners reported back stories of amazing success. One woman called me about her dominant-aggressive cockerpoo, Benji. I made an appointment to see her and advised her in the meantime to try changing Benji's diet to a lower-protein version. She did not show up for the appointment. A year later the woman called me again. When she reminded me about our previous con-

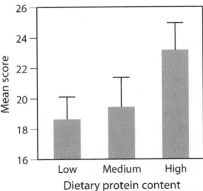

Territorial Aggression Scores for 12 Dogs

versation, I asked her why she hadn't kept the appointment. She said that the low-protein diet had worked so well for Benji that she didn't need to come in to see me. What had changed? I asked her.

"Benji developed skin allergies," she said, "and my veterinarian recommended a fifty-fifty chicken and rice diet for a while. A few days later, Benji's aggression returned and he bit me quite seriously."

Chicken is around 90–100 percent protein, depending on whether it's skinned or not, so she had just put Benji on a *high-protein* diet, and paid the price.

"Come in next week," I told her, "and we'll deal with Benji's problem in its entirety." This time she did show up.

Many of my clients find that their aggressive dogs improve following the implementation of multiple recommendations, including dietary change, but they are not sure which change is responsible for the beneficial effect. In some instances, owners who report feeding their dog its original high-protein ration—to see whether it makes a difference—state unequivocally that the dog's behavior suddenly deteriorates. Typically, they report that their dog becomes more tense and nervous following the switch back to high protein. On reverting to the low-protein diet, all is well again. Anecdotal information like this is hard to ignore, though it doesn't amount to scientific proof.

Brain Chemistry and Nutrition

My experiences with high- and low-protein rations led me to ponder the mechanism by which protein produces its effect. With this in mind, I paid a visit to the Friedman School of Nutrition Science and Policy at Tufts in Boston to listen to a talk by Professor John Fernstrom, a protein guru. I learned that carbohydrate (in the form of sugar), contrary to popular opinion, actually has a calming effect on behavior. The calming effect, which is evidenced in rodents within three hours of a carbohydrate meal, is blocked by dietary protein. The explanation is complicated but goes something like this: When sugar is absorbed into the body, insulin is released to transport it into cells. In the process, some amino acids are cleared from the bloodstream into cells. Only one amino acid, tryptophan (a precursor of serotonin), is resistant to this effect and remains at a relatively high concentration in the bloodstream: the ratio of tryptophan to the other amino acids is increased. Tryptophan is now able to cross relatively easily into the brain to be converted to serotonin, which has mood-stabilizing effects. Bingo! However, when enough protein is fed simultaneously, run-of-the-mill amino acids increase in concentration, and compete with and overwhelm tryptophan at a common entry point into the brain. Serotonin levels are negatively impacted and the mood-stabilizing effect of carbohydrate is thus lost. Imagine the common entry point for amino acid transport into the brain as a turnstile at a football game. Now imagine the run-of-the-mill amino acids represented by people wearing black T-shirts, while tryptophan is represented by people in white T-shirts. The more black shirts there are relative to white shirts, the more black-shirted people will color the crowd at the stadium. But if a lot of black shirts are diverted away from the turnstile, leaving white shirts in greater preponderance, the crowd will have a generally lighter, whiter appearance. This competition for the entry portal is only a theory but—like the theory of gravity—is supported by evidence.

Dr. Robin Kanarek, chair of the Psychology Department at Tufts, has written on the subject of the effect of diet on behavior. Her evidence bears out our observations and clinical data. Dr. Richard Wurtman of MIT has a similar view. Wurtman is often asked to appear on television at Halloween time to explain the effect of candy on children's behavior. The hyperactivity that candy produces, he says, has nothing to do with its sugar content, because sugar has a calming effect. The craziness that candy induces, Wurtman believes, is attributable to the coloring, preser-

The Effect of Dietary Protein on Brain Serotonin

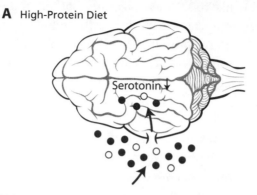

A High-Protein Diet

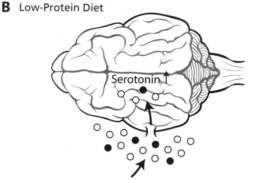

B Low-Protein Diet

vatives, and other components of candy. So, Wurtman not only confirms the calming effect of carbohydrate, but his theory lends some support to the notion that artificial preservatives in foods can cause behavioral changes.

Wanting to confirm and extend our own observations, as well as learn something more about the effect of various amino acids on behavior, I approached Hill's Pet Nutrition company for intellectual and financial support for this venture. The scientists at Hill's were enthusiastic, and a second dietary protein study was under way at our hospital before you could say Science Diet. This time, rather than simply looking at the effect of high-, medium-, and low-protein diets on behavior, we decided to look at two extremes, high protein and low protein, each diet supplemented or not supplemented with the "good guy" amino acid, tryptophan. The purpose of the study was to corroborate our earlier observations and try to confirm the purported role of amino acids in causing the behavioral effect. The study was overseen by my then resident, Dr. Jean DeNapoli. The behaviors studied were owner-directed (dominance) aggression, territorial aggression, fearfulness, and hyperactivity.

When the results were in they showed that the level of dominance aggression was essentially the same on the low-protein diets and the tryptophan-supplemented high-protein diet. The tryptophan-unsupplemented high-protein diet, however, was associated with nearly twice the level of aggression as the low-protein and tryptophan-supplemented high-protein diets. This is the result I expected to find—that high-protein diets can exacerbate dominance aggression. The study also showed that tryptophan supplementation of a high-protein diet cancels out the aggression-promoting effect of high protein (presumably because the number of "white shirts" at the entry point into the brain is increased). Another significant finding of the study was that tryptophan-supplemented low-protein diets were associated with reduced levels of territorial aggression. Neither frank fearfulness nor hyperactivity was affected by the manipulation of protein content or tryptophan supplementation.

The information we garnered from this study supports the notion that diet can affect behavior, not all behaviors all of the time, but some behaviors some of the time. It also sheds some light on the mechanism of the effect. To me, these findings, taken together, provide enough support for the protein theory of aggression to justify switching an aggressive dog's diet to a lower-protein one to see if the change helps. The effect, if it is going to happen, is quick—almost immediate, in fact. If the trial works, great; if it doesn't, it's no big deal to switch the dog back to his original diet. Keep in mind, though, that dietary changes should be made gradually, over a few days, to avoid gastrointestinal problems like vomiting and diarrhea.

Other Dietary Factors Affecting Behavior

And what about the effect of artificial preservatives on behavior? Pet food companies have no interest in exploring the link between artificial preservatives and dog behavior because omitting chemical preservatives would hamper their ability to store food for more than a few months, which would negatively impact the industry. Numerous trainers and veterinarians are convinced that artificial preservatives have a detrimental effect on behavior, at least in certain preservative-sensitive dogs. The prime culprit is deemed to be ethoxyquin, though there is no reason to discount the effect of other artificial preservatives, such as BHA and BHT. Some trainers have extremely strong views on the negative impact of ethoxyquin on behavior. Gail Fisher, a New Hampshire–based trainer, believes that ethoxyquin is the root of all evil in dogs. Gail's position is not entirely unfounded. Anecdotally, some dogs do seem to benefit behaviorally when artificial preservatives are excluded from their diet by feeding rations preserved with "natural" preservatives, such as vitamin C (aka ascorbic acid) or vitamin E (aka mixed tocopherols). Another downside to ethoxyquin is possible long-term toxicity. There is little information documenting ethoxyquin's safety when administered every day for years, perhaps the entire lifetime of a dog. Some people believe that ethoxyquin causes skin problems and others that it affects thyroid function. Nobody really knows for sure and it will take a long time to find out. Meanwhile, the FDA's Center for Veterinary Medicine requested, in 1997, that pet food manufacturers voluntarily reduce the maximum level of ethoxyquin by one-half, to 75 parts per million. Maybe they know something we don't? If 150 parts per million is not good, is half that amount okay? Maybe, maybe not. Anyway, even the possibility that artificial preservatives might exacerbate behavior problems is reason enough to try avoiding them when a dog is exhibiting problem behaviors, and that is usually my recommendation. If, after a two- to four-week trial, feeding rations preserved with vitamins C and E does not improve a dog's behavior, then it is reasonable to revert to the dog's original diet.

The last element of diet that has been postulated as shaping mood and behavior is the *type* of protein fed. One possibility as to how protein might alter behavior is if a dog is allergic to the protein source. I am not absolutely convinced that food allergy can alter behavior, but one anecdotal report I received does seem to support the hypothesis. The dog in question had the troubling problem of showing aggression to family members. Among other recommendations, I suggested switching the dog to a natural, low-protein, lamb-based diet. A few weeks later, the dog's owner reported back.

"Thank you so much for the recommendation you made about diet," she effused.

I was starting to feel pretty good about myself when she added, "It made him so much worse."

"And you're thanking me?" I asked.

"You helped me realize how much diet affects his behavior," she explained. "I had completely forgotten that he is allergic to carrots, and the ration you recommended contained carrots. When I started feeding the new diet, his allergies flared and his behavior deteriorated. So I went to the pet store and bought a different low-protein, lamb-based diet—one that didn't contain carrots. Now he's better than he's ever been . . . and it's all thanks to you."

I expressed gratitude to her for both her magnanimity and her report, as I learned that in this case, allergies, irritability, and aggression went hand in glove. As dietary allergies are relatively common, behavior problems caused by allergies may be common as well. Forty percent of all dietary allergies are to the protein source, and the most commonly fed protein sources are beef and poultry. This explains why switching to a lamb-based diet, or a diet with an alternative protein source, say, duck or venison, over time (at least eight weeks) could theoretically help resolve behavior problems related to dietary allergy. If lamb is a component of an allergic dog's normal rations, switching from lamb to another type of protein would be the logical switch.

One thing that's missing from the otherwise attractive hypothesis that allergy (dietary or otherwise) may affect behavior is a consistent link between allergies and behavior problems. This is not to say that no such link exists, just that it has yet to be definitively established. Veterinary dermatologists, who deal with allergies on a regular basis, often recommend a diet trial for allergic dogs, switching from one source of protein to another to test for and hopefully alleviate dietary allergies. In the process of making their recommendations, they may take a dog's full dietary history into consideration and advise the owners to feed a ration that avoids exposing the dog to any of the previous dietary constituents. For a dog to have an allergic reaction, he must have prior exposure to the food to which he is allergic (the allergen): no exposure, no allergy. Although the link between allergy and behavior is tenuous, some scientific articles are beginning to emerge associating skin disease and behavioral problems. To me, the connection is intuitive. How would pruritus (severe itching) not cause irritability, restlessness, sleep problems, and so on? But until the final verdict is in, it is a not unreasonable course to try changing the dietary protein source of an aggressive dog's diet on spec, as it were, to see if it helps—particularly if the dog is simultaneously displaying physical evidence of allergy (e.g., skin rash, pruritus, etc.). Be aware, though, that the hoped-for change may take a couple of months or more to become evident.

Other areas of dietary management that could possibly alter behavior include modification of dietary carbohydrate, fat, minerals, and vitamins. Dr. Fernstrom's studies, mentioned earlier, were rather unique as he was evaluating a pure carbohydrate diet. Such a ration cannot be sustained long term, as it omits other components of a life-sustaining ration. The question becomes, can varying the carbohydrate content of a diet within acceptable limits make any difference to a dog's behavior? This aspect of diet and behavior was studied by one of my colleagues. She investigated the effect of carbohydrate on the behavior of kenneled dogs and came to the conclusion that, at least in normally behaving dogs, changing the level of carbohydrate in their diet made no difference at all to the dogs' behavior. What she didn't study was the effect of changes in dietary carbohydrate in the management of clinical behavior problems. It can be surmised from Fernstrom's and Wurtman's work that high levels of carbohydrate might be beneficial. Presently, however, there is no information on the value of carbohydrate manipulation to treat behavior problems, and which, if any, problem behaviors might respond.

The situation regarding fat is even more obscure. Too little fat can create physical problems during pups' development because fat is required in the formation of nervous tissue (brain, spinal cord, nerves). Low-dietary-fat intake at a tender age can have far-reaching negative effects on an animal's learning ability and intelligence. What is not known is whether manipulating levels of fat in adulthood has much if any effect on behavior, though dietary fat is needed to transport fat-soluble vitamins into the body. On the other hand, too much (saturated) fat impairs learning and memory in adult rats, so, as applies to everything else in life, you can have too much of a good thing. Also, the ever popular omega-3 fatty acids have been shown to alleviate pain to some extent and have been recommended as a treatment for arthritis. Whether this treatment would improve the temperament of a cranky old dog is unknown.

As far as minerals and vitamins are concerned, not much is known about their effects on behavior, except in the extreme situation of absolute deficiency. Gail Fisher, the trainer, did have a theory about calcium that I found rather interesting. She heard that calcium supplementation can help alleviate mood swings in people. Knowing that meat is low in calcium and high in phosphorus, she extrapolated that high-protein diets might have a deleterious effect on dogs' mood—and thus behavior—by lowering a dog's blood calcium level. It's an interesting theory but there is nothing to substantiate it at this time. Regarding vitamin deficiency, behavioral effects, especially of vitamin B, may precede the classic physical consequences of deficiency (which are myriad). Vitamin B complex is taken by people to reduce nervousness and stress and some people give it to their dog for the same reason. Certainly several of the B vitamins are required for normal neurological function. Vitamins B_1, B_6, and B_{12} are most important in this respect, but deficiency of these vitamins is unlikely in a dog fed a balanced diet, so supplementation is rarely necessary.

Bon Appétit!

Finally, it is important to feed a dog what he needs in order to thrive. Unless you are an expert in nutrition, you shouldn't think about making your own dog food; it's far better for the dog to be fed a proprietary ration that has been tested in a feeding trial approved by the Association of American Feed Control Officials (AAFCO). This information is right on the bag or can but is not always easy to find. There is a question on the national veterinary board examination that goes something like this: If an owner asks you (the veterinarian) if it's okay to feed a dog table scraps, how should you answer? The only correct answer is that the owner should be informed never to feed her dog table scraps. This expert view may be rather an extreme, and you can argue that a little bit of what a dog fancies won't do him much harm, but the point is, you shouldn't feed great globs of human food to a dog, especially if you don't know what you're doing. And anyway, feeding a dog table scraps can lead to unwanted behaviors down the line—like hanging around the dinner table, begging, and pawing at people for food.

Dogs that eat nothing but dog food that has been tested in AAFCO-approved feeding trials have better diets than most children in this country. Complete dog foods are properly balanced in terms of all required nutrients. However, to choose just the right ration for your dog, it is best to read the label to make sure the food supplies everything your dog needs. Labels can be somewhat confusing, so don't hesitate to seek input from your veterinarian if there is anything you do not understand. If you plan to put your dog on a low-protein diet, you have to know how low you can go. Dogs need about 17 or 18 percent protein in their food to meet their nutritional needs, so going below this level, unless under the direction of your veterinarian and for some specific reason, could lead to protein deficiency. In time, too low protein will cause a dry, brittle coat, nails that are easily split, and eventually more serious problems. As mentioned earlier, growing pups, pregnant and nursing bitches, dogs with certain medical problems, and certain working dogs need more protein than healthy nonpregnant, nonnursing adult dogs. Pups should be fed puppy food; large breeds are best fed large-breed food; old-timers fare better on senior rations; and there are numerous approved custom rations designed for other special circumstances.

Summary: Nutrition and Behavior

Sugar has a calming effect (in people as well as dogs), protein blocks this effect (and may have some effects of its own), and rations to which dogs are allergic produce physical symptoms that can lead to irritability and possibly aggression. Fat doesn't seem to have much effect on behavior, though unsaturated fatty acids (components of certain fats) can help alleviate pain. Minerals and vitamins do not adversely affect behavior unless they are deficient in the diet or, in the case of certain of these nutrients, present in gross excess.

While it is a good idea to feed your dog a ration appropriate for his stage of life and energy requirement, it's also important to pay attention to his enjoyment of it. Even the most favorite food can become boring over time. None of us would like to eat the same food, day in and day out, for the whole of our lives and I doubt that dogs appreciate this kind of monotony either. So, within the limits that are acceptable for your dog, it's a good idea to switch food periodically. Variety is, after all, the spice of life — but don't forget to make any change in ration a gradual one.

3

Dog Speak

Communication — The Key to a Rewarding Relationship

The art of communication is the language of leadership.
— James Humes

I try to impress on dog owners the importance of communication. Clear communication between humans and dogs is a lifestyle enhancer for both parties. Our ability to communicate unambiguously with our canine companions reduces anxiety and stress, and helps ensure their good behavior. Elementary communication—training a dog to understand and act on words like "Sit," "Stay," and "Down"—is all very well, but dogs have the capacity for so much more. Training them to better understand what is required of them reduces the incidence of undesirable behaviors and the possibility that they will be placed in another home or surrendered to a shelter. The right type of training enhances mutual understanding between humans and dogs and increases the extent to which dogs are able to share in their owners' lives. Vocal communication on the part of dogs—by way of barking, whining, or howling—is not well understood by most owners. It is our job to listen to and learn from their auditory cues, just as we expect them to listen to and learn from ours.

Nonverbal communication is also important. Dogs need no

lessons in how to interpret our body language, but owners are often unclear in reading theirs. Dogs pretty much know—just by looking at us—what mood we are in as well as what our intentions are toward them. But the knowledge we glean from observing them is, at best, rudimentary. Being able to read your dog's body language so that you know how he is feeling or what he is attempting to convey is an important and (to my mind) necessary asset. Most owners need to improve on their interpretive skills in this respect because communication, even the nonvocal variety, is, or rather should be, a two-way street.

Communication and Training

In the bad old days, the standard way to realize communication between owner and dog was through obedience training. But the very term "obedience training" has a domineering ring to it; the implication being that you are master and the dog must obey— not a particularly flexible arrangement, and definitely not a two-way street. Obedience training—even today—often involves punitive measures that owners reluctantly accept as necessary. Many obedience trainers automatically reach for a choke chain or prong collar to begin the lesson and use "chain jerking" to force a dog to comply. They refer to the snapping of the leash and tightening effect on the collar as a "correction," though it is really physical punishment, akin to spanking, or rapping a child's knuckles with a ruler (considered an indispensable technique at my grade school some fifty years ago). The technique of chain jerking is intrinsically aggressive and is designed to force a dog to submit to an owner's authority. It is not intended to engender an affectionate relationship between dog and owner and it doesn't, even though some dogs—bless them—endure it with a wagging tail. (That's a testimony to the dog's spirit, not the aptness of the method.) Certainly, punishment can get a dog to do what you want—but at what price? Punishment can cause fear of the person doing the punishing, can be physically harmful, and can increase a dog's anxiety and aggressiveness. It is true that punishment may suppress an unwanted behavior for a while—as long as the threat of punishment exists—and it can be used to intimidate a dog to comply with a previously taught command (negative reinforcement)—but in the long term, the effects on the dog's behavior—not to mention the relationship between dog and owner—are deleterious.

The Nobel laureate and behaviorist Konrad Lorenz wrote about training in his 1948 book *Man Meets Dog*, "Even the best dog . . . will only collaborate as long as he is enjoying the work. Correspondingly, punishment is here not only incongruous but even harmful, since it is calculated to disgust the dog with this special activity, and to make him useless for it." Think about the unfortunate relationship that physical punishment creates. Who among us would want to be raised in a house of correction in which we were commanded to obey and punished for noncompliance? Fortunately, the spare-the-rod-and-spoil-the-child philosophy has all but disappeared from child-raising practices. It is now illegal to strike a child under four years of age in California (why only under four is my question, and why don't all states have such laws?). The writing *was* on the wall for dog trainers using punitive techniques until recently, when a few charismatic TV dog trainers stepped in to create an upsurge in punitive methodology. I happen to believe that harsh training is unnecessary as well as inappropriate and, in the long run, counterproductive. People train every other species under the sun using reward-based ("positive") training methods and achieve ingrained and sophisticated responses—so why is it that some owners and trainers feel the need to physically punish a dog during training? Try training a dolphin to do somersaults while he's restrained by a choke chain. You won't get too far. It's far better to train a dog (or a dolphin) to do something you want him to do than punish him for noncompliance. With positive training, you can train a dog to do almost anything your heart desires. Yanking on his collar is simply unnecessary. Dog owners should insist on positive training methods to achieve their training goals with their dogs and not rely on punitive methods that intimidate the dogs into submission. Punitive techniques may seemingly produce the results in short order but the effects are not sustained in the long term. Lorenz also said, "Punishment teaches a dog nothing except how to avoid punishment." He was referring to the application of a noxious or painful stimulus—like the sharp jerk of a choke collar.

The training methods I recommend, as part of a comprehensive behavior-modification plan, are based on positive reinforcement of a successfully completed task—with *negative punishment* utilized as a consequence of a dog's failure to respond. The opposite of reward is not punishment; it is the absence of reward (negative punishment). Negative punishment involves the withholding of a valued reward as a consequence of noncompliance. A human example might be, "Dad, can I have the car keys?" To which Dad responds, "Did you mow the lawn as you promised?" If the answer is no, then Dad's response should be, "Then no car for you today." The punishment is not one of violence, but of withholding—and that leads to deference and respect. Despite what hard-liners may think, this is not an approach for wimps. It requires more mental discipline and consistency than simply punishing a failed response with the jerk of a chain. The lesson it teaches is also more indelible. Using positive training and negative punishment in tandem as the situation dictates, owners can achieve anything they want with their dogs while maintaining a healthy, affectionate relationship: a relationship based on mutual respect and trust, not on fear and intimidation.

The principle of positive reinforcement is diametrically opposite to the physical-punishment-based methods employed by many dog trainers. Naysayers often smirk at the "positive only" approach, asserting that you need to engage in physical punishment of dogs to ensure a reliable response (though they might not say it quite that way). They criticize positive trainers for being "soft" and their techniques as ineffective—much the same objections as you might hear from traditionalists favoring the use of physical discipline for children. Trainers who employ physical punishment also tend to use the same faulty justifications for their methods, like "If you teach a dog to work for food, he will only obey you if you have food." What they fail to understand (though they may pay lip service to it) is the principle of intermittent positive reinforcement, which strengthens dogs' motivation to perform consistently. They also do not understand the power of negative punishment, which if used consistently as part of a leadership program is a very effective tool.

The Basics of Interspecies Communication

Let's remind ourselves, before delving into the mechanics of proper communication between dogs and humans, that dogs are sentient creatures who think, remember things, and act a certain way because of what they have learned from experience. They are not androids to be programmed for our convenience. We need to cut them some slack. A professor of veterinary cardiology once told me, as I was preparing for an interview on the subject of canine emotions, that he believed dogs are not self-aware and behave simply as Skinnerian automatons, a compilation of conditioned reflexes. I wondered if this professor had ever owned a dog and if so, what their relationship was like (probably not very fulfilling, for either party, I would think). Now, it's true that dogs will never deliver moving oratories (even if they were equipped with a bark interpreter), paint the ceiling of the Sistine Chapel (even if they had opposable thumbs), and they do not have powers of abstract thought (e.g., they do not consider where they came from or where they might be going at the end of life). Dogs can be thought of as having the same mental capacity as a three-year-old child—capable of simple communication, a good deal of affection, and an array of other emotions. They see the world as it is now, not the way it was a while back or how it will be in the future, and they want their rewards immediately. However, dogs are capable creatures in their own right. They are arguably more worldly, more independent, and more vibrantly in touch with life than most humans. They are especially talented in their own biological niche and would survive a lot better than us in the wild, even without a survival course.

Some people manage to communicate with their dogs in an almost subliminal way, both parties seeming closely in tune with each other's wants and needs. How do owners achieve such effective interspecies communication? The answer: clearly, simply, and directly. But interestingly, it's not a result of spoken language. Some owners erroneously think that dogs understand lengthy monologues and follow every word. Not so. Sure, a dog may look directly at you when you speak, cock his head to one side, and appear interested in what you are saying. He may even become excited if he hears the word "car" or "treat" buried in a sentence, but he certainly is not following the conversation. The RCA logo featuring a terrier supposedly listening to his master's voice broadcast from an old-fashioned gramophone is plausible, because the dog could recognize the voice as belonging to his owner. However, he would not be waxing emotional at the content of the recording. While dogs can understand the meaning of certain sounds we make—sounds we call words—they do not have language genes or language centers in their brains and are incapable of deciphering meaning from the various arrangements of words in sentences (syntax). Because of this limitation, words that are addressed to a dog should be short, enunciated clearly, and isolated from other verbiage. The late Barbara Woodhouse appreciated this notion as she popularized the use of certain monosyllabic, clipped words, like "Sit," "Out," and "Quit," in dog training. All of these words can be clearly articulated and all

One Smart Dog

An owner once told me that, at one time, she thought her dog was a mind reader. Every morning she would go either to a sitting area on an upstairs landing of her home to enjoy a cup of tea or to her sunroom for coffee. Whenever the owner was about to go to either area, the dog would race there first and sit and wait for her. How did the dog know whether she was going upstairs or to the sunroom? The owner decided to conduct an investigation to find out. After a few trials, she learned the dog's secret. It was the presence of a teaspoon on the saucer that cued the dog in to where she was going. The woman took sugar in her coffee but not in her tea, so when the dog saw a teaspoon in the saucer (or heard it clink against the saucer), he knew she was heading for the sunroom. When she prepared her beverage without using the teaspoon, and then went to the sunroom, the dog was completely fooled, already upstairs, waiting for her on the landing. It's amazing the little things dogs notice and remember. Without the "teaspoon signal," it's a good bet that this dog would have adapted his practice, perhaps learning to determine his owner's intended destination from the odor of the beverage instead.

end in a hard sound, a consonant. I encourage people to use such one-word voice cues and advise using them in isolation. Following the issuance of an action word the desired behavior can be shaped by rewarding successive approximations to it. A dog that is hungry for food or attention will soon figure out what he needs to do to win the ultimate jackpot.

If you want to see how not to communicate with your dog, just come to our front reception desk at the Cummings School of Veterinary Medicine at Tufts, or stand on any street corner as dog owners try to control their dogs. What you will hear (often at ever increasing volume) is something like "No, no, no! . . . Come here, Rover. Rover! Sit. Sit! What did I say? *Do it!* No. No, Rover! Sit. Sit!" Not a very effective exchange. As the old saying goes, most

B Is for Bozo

One client at Tufts told me that her dog, Bozo, knew the alphabet and could spell.

Her reasoning was as follows: Initially, every time she and her husband used the phrase "open the door," Bozo would get overly excited because he thought he was going to go out. To avoid these outbursts of hyper behavior, they decided to spell the word out: "D-O-O-R." This new lingo solved their problem, for a while. Pretty soon, the dog understood that collection of sounds, so they switched to calling the door simply "D." Soon Bozo knew that "D" meant door. Later he picked up "T" as standing for treat, "C" for car, and so on.

Smart dog—but no linguist.

dogs in this country think their first names are "No." Lesson number one: shouting gets you nowhere (it's the same when trying to communicate with people). Colonel Potter, of the TV series *Mash*, once said something to the effect of, "If they [the Koreans] don't understand when you speak to them in English, they won't understand any better if you shout." Multiple commands are pointless, too. Most dogs will either ignore commands reiterated countless times or they will perform the desired action only as a result of tedium or boredom. These dogs have been trained to expect multiple commands, so owners will have to say "Sit" seven times before they respond. Even when whispered, perhaps especially when whispered, one-word commands given by an effective leader one time are much more effective. If you consistently use one-word commands and enforce them—by taking time out of life and focusing on the job at hand—your dog is far more likely to sit when asked. He will learn that there is no escape from your softly spoken, fair-but-firm instructions. Don't worry that your dog might not have heard you (unless he is deaf) or that he has forgotten what you said. Dogs have a much better sense of hearing than we do and can remember a spoken word for a couple of minutes. If they don't respond, it's because they don't want to (more about this in chapter 5, "Leadership Program").

There are a number of ways to teach a dog to perform a simple exercise on cue—to understand what a spoken word, or sound, means—and none of them involves physical punishment. There is the capture method, in which you simply wait for the dog to do something you want, like sitting instead of jumping up, and then "mark" the desired behavior—when it occurs—with the appropriate word (in this case, "Sit"). As soon as the dog's butt hits the deck, he should be rewarded with praise, petting, or a food treat. In teaching a dog to sit, the lure method might also be employed. In this method, a food treat pinched between one's fingers is moved in an arc over the dog's head so that he must sit back on his haunches to access the treat. The word "Sit" can be appended to the exercise when the dog takes the desired position. Initially, you can "shape" the behavior by rewarding progressive approximations to it—in this case, rewarding first a slight crouching movement, then a more definitive crouch (so that the dog's butt almost touches the ground), then a fleeting touch of the butt on the ground, and finally a definite sit for a few seconds (or longer). The point is to advance in stages, rewarding the dog as he succeeds at any one level. Another method involves placement. Using this method, the dog is placed into a sit perhaps by giving him a little squeeze across his loins using your thumb and middle finger like pincers and at the same time applying very gentle downward and backward pressure. Success should always be rewarded immediately—within one half second of attaining the goal of the exercise. No matter what method you use, the dog will learn that the cue word—"Sit," in the examples given—means that if he subsequently sits, he will please you (which most dogs want to do) and will be rewarded in some way. If food treats are involved—though they don't have to be—the whole learning process works faster if the dog is hungry at the time, because he will be more motivated. After teaching a dog what various words mean, so that his response is reliable under optimal circumstances, the degree of difficulty can be gradually increased. He can be asked to respond when there are slight distractions around, say, another dog. He can be trained first inside and then outside in the yard or, eventually, the park. This is what I call the "taking the show on the road" part of the exercise; this is an important part of training, because you eventually want your dog to behave appropriately anywhere—even when there are distractions around. Many people I speak to tell me that their dogs are well behaved at home but impossible to manage when out and about and are preoccupied with goings-on around them. That's why it's important to expose the dog to a variety of environments and distractions during training.

Once a reliable response to a single-word cue has been well and truly established—for example, if your dog reliably sits when prompted to—it is time to put the reward on an intermittent schedule. Reward him two times out of three, then every other time, then every third or fourth time, and so on. Remember, if the reward schedule is fixed, say, rewarding every third time, the dog will learn this schedule and may slack off immediately after receiving his treat. So mix it up: go back to rewarding him for each proper response two or three times in a row and then skip the reward for a few repetitions. Finally, completely randomize the reward schedule so that he never knows when a serious reward is coming. *Intermittent, random reinforcement* is the most powerful reward schedule; this is what keeps gamblers riveted to their seats at slot machines or the blackjack table. In time, food treats can be supplied relatively infrequently or can even be phased out—but I see no point in going this far. I had occasion a few years back to watch a police handler put his adoring German shepherd through his paces. The dog was trained to heel and barely took his eyes off the handler as he was led through a maze of objects from traffic cones to half pipes and fences. The circuit was a cross between an obstacle course and an agility course and the dog navigated all of the objects flawlessly. At the conclusion of the circuit, as the dog sat like a statue beside the policeman, the officer leaned forward with a proud look on his face and petted his dog ever so briefly, muttering some glowing words of approbation almost under his breath. That was the reward that this dog anticipated and worked for—not food, but the warm appreciation of his grateful handler. Some dogs work for food, some for praise, others work for petting or toys. It is important to find out what motivates your dog while training him and to use it in training.

There are certain words all dogs should learn, preferably in puppyhood. "Sit," "Down," "Wait" (or "Stay"), "Leave it," and "Come." These are the ABCs of training that will help keep your dog out of trouble. If you see a pack of dogs that looks like trouble on the other side of the street, you can say "Sit" and "Stay" and, if properly trained, your dog will conform to your wishes until the danger passes. Alternatively, your dog may be dashing toward a busy main road and you can address the situation with three simple words: "Rover!"—using his name to get his attention—"Come!"—the appropriate command—and "Good boy!"—praise that tells him he is not in trouble and reinforces his good behavior. Your dog should turn on a dime in this case and run back to you immediately, averting a potential accident. Finally, your dog may be on the opposite side of a road when you see a car coming and you do not want him to run to you. In this situation you can use the words "Down" and "Stay" to make him "freeze," thereby ensuring his safety.

Beyond the Basics: Continuing Education

Unfortunately, most people who have taught their dogs the basics of communication do not continue to build on them. It's a cultural thing, I think. We are conditioned to expect a dog to respond to words like "Sit," "Down," and "Stay," and believe that if he knows these words, then his vocabulary is complete. This needn't be so and, optimally, shouldn't be so. The more words a dog under-stands, the better the bridge of communication between him and his owner and the more robust the bond between the two of them will be. We now know that dogs can learn hundreds of words.

- In a recently published study, a Border collie was reported to understand some two hundred different words.
- A client of mine told me that her dog knew approximately five hundred words (she stopped counting when she reached three hundred and fifty words).
- I once encountered a dog trainer who claimed that her dog knew over eight hundred words.
- A deaf Dalmatian patient of mine knows forty-three words of American Sign Language.

With children, we painstakingly point out certain objects to them, anticipating that they will remember the names. "Cup," we might say, demonstrating the object and repeating the word over and over again until the child knows what it means. But we don't do that with dogs. We quit before they've learned even ten words and are proud at that accomplishment, even though dogs are capable of so much more. I encourage dog owners to pursue the *continuing education* of their dogs to increase their dogs' vocabu-lary and thus to attenuate the verbal barriers that otherwise exist. To illustrate the point, I often ask my clients how they would feel if they found themselves in downtown Turin without being able to speak a word of Italian. "Stressed," "confused," "anxious," are the sort of replies I've received. But when even a few important words are at one's disposal, words like "food," "bathroom," "tele-phone," "hotel," anxiety can melt away. Life is a lot less stressful when we are armed with the ability to communicate. This is how it is for dogs too, I believe. They can be taught to understand when you want them to wait, or that they are going for a ride in the car, or that dinner is about to be served. They can be taught to fetch any number of different things ranging from your slippers to the morning paper. They can be taught to ring a bell to go out and to close cupboard doors. The list is endless.

Advanced training is probably best accomplished using a secondary reinforcer, most commonly a clicker. A clicker is a handheld, lightweight noisemaker, often in the form of a small plastic box containing a deformable strip of sprung steel that, when pressed, clicks back into position, making a metallic clicking sound. These devices are widely available now at pet supply stores, though a Snapple bottle lid does equally well. Using a clicker, some very sophisticated behaviors, like teaching a dog to close a door or get you a beer from the fridge, can be taught. Good luck training behaviors like this with a choke chain! In clicker training, the dog is first trained to understand that the click of the clicker signals reward (usually a food treat). This is called "charging" or "priming" the clicker. Second, desired behaviors, or even approximations of them, are "marked" with a click and the dog is rewarded. Third, a voice cue is added so that the behavior is clicked and rewarded only following a cue—for example, only when the dog is cued to sit (by hearing "Sit") and does so does he earn a click and then a reward. If the voice cue is not added, the dog can volunteer the behavior ad libitum and expect to be clicked and rewarded every time. This is not what we want, so each behavior is ultimately trained to its own voice cue.

So much has been written about clicker training that I do not intend to elaborate on it here, but, suffice to say, it can lead to a high level of training and responsiveness in dogs. It is, if you will, the ultimate way of teaching advanced communication. Once a dog has been clicker-trained to perform a certain behavior, the clicker itself, a learning tool, can be dispensed with, though a reward for the behavior, preferably on an intermittent, random schedule, should remain in place. I know trainers and some owners who prefer not to use clickers because they are mechanical devices that must be carried around (or worn dangling from a belt). They prefer to make a clicking sound with their tongue or use an enthusiastic "Yes!" to mark the successful accomplishment of a behavior. There are several variations on this theme, but it is the basic concept of using a secondary reinforcer (any secondary reinforcer) that is important to grasp.

The Language of Dogs

Thus far my focus has been on communication from owners to their dogs; that is, teaching dogs to understand what we say and to act upon it. But we have to understand what they are telling us, too. There are two methods by which dogs try to communicate with us in their own idiom. One is by vocalizing—whining, barking, growling—and the other is through body language, which they assume we understand though we often don't. Cartoonist Gary Larson published a now-famous cartoon in which somebody had invented a machine that translated dogs' barks into English. At long last, it would be possible to know what it was that dogs were actually trying to say to us. Unfortunately, yap, yap, yap, yap, yap merely translated as hey, hey, hey, hey, hey. Believe it or not, there is now a collar-mounted bark-translator device—the Bow-Lingual, which was invented in Japan. Supposedly, it turns barks into words. However, it's a gimmick rather than a serious tool and, scientifically, has been shown to produce an unreliable, inconsistent translation. One of the first people in Japan to purchase the bark-translator collar for the princely sum of about two thousand dollars eagerly fitted it to her dog, waiting to hear the first words that he would utter. Woof, woof, woof was translated by the collar as "I don't like you," a disappointing result for the doting and formerly optimistic owner. Studies conducted by Dr. Sophia Yin at the University of California at Davis have shown that the bark-translator collar emits different English phrases in otherwise identical situations, so the "translations" are, at best, equivocal and, at worst, confusing.

A few years back an article in *Smithsonian* magazine took a scientific look at barking to see if it really did mean something, rather than just being an effluence of energy. After meandering through subjects like alarm barking and long-distance communication, the article finally concluded that dogs bark simply because they can and the noise means nothing at all. I don't share this view and have known many owners who can tell what's going on from the nature and intensity of their dogs' bark. Owners describe, for example, a friendly bark when somebody they know is coming down the path versus a more offensive type of bark when a stranger approaches the door. I agree with these latter observations that different barks do mean different things and encourage owners to learn the significance of their dogs' barking so that they can respond appropriately. One common species misunderstanding occurs when territorial dogs bark to alert their owners that someone is approaching. The uninformed owner shouts, "Stop that noise, Rover! Be quiet!" The dog continues barking. If he could speak I'm sure he would say, "No, there really is someone coming, I promise you, they're out there. They're coming up the path right now." The continued barking elicits another tirade from the frustrated owner, propagating a noisy vicious cycle. Some dogs may think their owner is getting in on the act and may enjoy the vocal support. Now both parties are completely confused about what the other is trying to convey. I call this sad situation "interspecies dyslexia"—and unfortunately it is all too common. A better approach to deal with a dog that is barking out of territorial concerns is to praise him for bringing your attention to the stranger's approach. "Good dog, thank you." Sometimes this recognition alone is enough to stop a dog dead in his tracks. *By George, I think she's got it,* the dog might think. But if the barking continues beyond the glowing acknowledgment, an owner should communicate, "Enough," "Stop it," or "Quiet." But please remember not to punish a barking dog. Rewarding silence—when he comes, which he will—is a far better approach . . . and it works.

Growling is a warning: *Come one step closer and you'll get it.*

Rather than punishing a dog for this behavior, we should attempt to understand the dog's problem so that we can address it. Engaging in a confrontation with a growling dog is counterproductive and ignores the message the dog is transmitting. Figuring out why a dog is growling, what his gripe is, and addressing the issue at the root cause is the most logical approach. Dogs growl and bare their teeth to express frustration over something. Using our large human brains, we should be able to figure out the dog's concern pretty quickly. It is not smart to confront a dog on his own level and reduce ourselves to behaving like another dog. That really doesn't make sense and can be quite dangerous. One of my residents from a few years back used to make this point with clients by saying, "If you get into a confrontation with a dog, you must be prepared to fight to the death, because the dog certainly is." While this statement was a little extreme, it did get the point across. Here's a test. A dog growls when you put your hand in his food bowl. Do you (a) keep it there, because the dog must learn to tolerate the intervention; (b) respect his wishes and remove your hand; or (c) not put your hand in his food in the first place? (answers b and c are correct). If you engage strategies b and c, your dog will appreciate your deference and his anxiety around the food bowl will drop. Pick your battles. Needing to have your hand in the dog's food shouldn't be one of them.

I once attended a canine behavior symposium where four hundred people were in attendance. A colleague of mine, Dr. Ian Dunbar, asked any person who had *never* become angry at someone and said something they later regretted to please raise their hand.

No one did.

Next, Dunbar asked that anyone who had never pushed or struck another person in anger to raise a hand.

Only one person, a woman, put up her hand.

"Bless you, madam, you're a saint," Dunbar responded.

We humans are not perfect when it comes to controlling our own tempers and yet we expect our dogs to be perfect in this respect. That isn't reasonable. Dogs, like us, may become frustrated enough to display occasional aggressive responses, and this is acceptable as long as aggressive events are infrequent and, when you think about it, understandable.

To help avoid aggression, it is important for all dog owners to learn how to interpret canine body language. Basically, all parts of the dog's body, his posture and movements, can tell you what frame of mind he is in. For example, are his eyes looking directly at you or are they deflected to one side? Long looks—especially if the dog's pupils are enlarged and other aggressive signs, like hackles raised, are evident—indicate a threat. Dogs don't normally stare at one another unless they're issuing a challenge. In dog language, it is rude to stare. It's the same for humans, come to think of it. Check it out the next time you are driving around a rotary

---

No One Is Perfect

Occasional growling is acceptable but may progress to more severe forms of aggression if the communication is consistently ignored or punished.

Snapping is not biting; if a dog wants to bite you, he will.

Biting ranges from marginally acceptable to totally unacceptable, depending on the circumstance and the dog's commitment level. The various levels of bite are as follows:

- Level 1: Bark, lunge, no teeth on skin (i.e., more of a snap)
- Level 2: Teeth touch skin, no puncture
- Level 3: 1–4 shallow punctures from a single bite
- Level 4: Single crushing bite, deep puncture, much bruising
- Level 5: Multiple bite attacks plus multiple deep wounds
- Level 6: Biting that removes portions of flesh, leaving an open wound(s)

Level 1 and Level 2 bites may be acceptable, depending on the circumstances, and in any case can easily be trained out of a dog's behavioral repertoire.

Aggressive dog

Submissive smile

and accidentally cut someone off. That's bound to get a glare. It's okay for a dog to catch someone's eyes briefly during an encounter, but to hold a steady gaze usually indicates trouble and is a "come-on." What a dog is doing with his mouth is also revealing. Vertical retraction of the lips—the so-called lip lift—with teeth clenched and bared is a sign of potential offensive aggression. Horizontal retraction of the lips, however, into a "submissive smile" is not threatening at all and indicates deference. Know the difference! When a dog's mouth hangs slightly open, tongue lolling out to one side, he is relaxed. This is always a good end point in training.

Tense facial muscles and yawning are a sure sign of stress. If a dog licks another dog's or person's lips or mouth area in general, it signals deference. That's what pups do to their mom to get her to regurgitate food. Wanton face licking, or arm or leg licking, however, can be part of a dominant dog's willful agenda. If a dog licks his own lips and he hasn't just finished eating, it means he is nervous. Other anxious behaviors that a dog may display simultaneously include panting and salivating. Eye signs include blinking, which means that the dog is thinking hard and is a little confused and unsure. Darting eyes indicate nervousness, as the dog tries to look away from whatever is bothering him. Finally, if a dog is frightened, his eyelids will open wider so that the whites of his eyes (the sclera) show. This is sometimes called "whale eye."

Then there are several ear signs: For dogs with prick ears, ears up and forward is a sign that he is alert and attentive to whatever is in front of him. That's one reason for the heinous practice of ear cropping; if the ears are always up and forward facing, the dog looks more threatening. It's time ear cropping was banned in the United States. If a dog's ears are rotated sideways, it indicates that he is feeling somewhat insecure. Ears pinned back indicate submission. Lop-eared dogs, and dogs whose ears have been cropped, are harder but not impossible to read. The same changes occur— it's just that they are more subtle.

If a dog's head is held high it indicates confidence, dominance, and focus. Holding the head low (like Eeyore of *House at Pooh Corner* fame) signals deference or defeat. Turning the head to one side is another deferent move, with the dog simultaneously averting his eyes and exposing a vulnerable area of his neck. A headlong look and advance indicate confidence and interest or a challenge and threat. If a dog's hair is raised (piloerection: hackles raised), he is responding to a threat by enhancing his appearance. The response is automatic but the message is clear. Finally, the tail: If a dog's tail is bolt upright, it is a sign of dominance and confidence. If his tail is straight out and wagging slowly, it indicates mild interest. If his tail is wagging fast and furious, it means that his energy and excitement level are high. When a dog is playing, tail wagging means that he is energized and happy—having fun. When a dog is showing signs of aggression and wagging his tail simultaneously—watch out! An energized, aggressive dog is not one to mess around with. Recently, research has shown that when a dog is attracted to something or someone, his tail will wag predominantly to the right—not that it's that easy to appreciate in real time. Alternatively, when a dog is fearful or apprehensive, his tail wags predominantly toward the left side of his body. Interesting though this may be, you really need to film the dog and replay the tape in slow motion to be sure of what you are witnessing. By that time, it could be too late if the dog was not enamored of you. More concretely, if a dog's tail is down or tucked, this is a sign of fearfulness and defeat. Dogs with docked tails and dogs whose tails are naturally curly and positioned up and over their back are hard, if not impossible, to read.

Playfulness is indicated by the well-known play-bow position. In this posture, the head is held lower than the rump, almost at ground level, so the dog appears to be sloping downward from back to front. In a play bow, the paws are extended forward and the tail is held upright and is often wagging slowly. The playful dog's mouth is usually held a little open and he appears to be

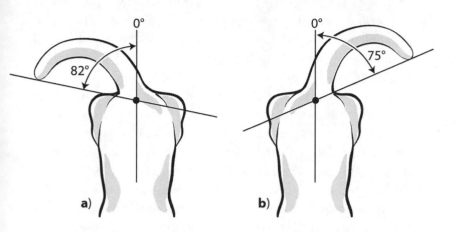

Seeing his owner, the dog wagged harder to his right (**a**). Shown an unfamiliar dog, the bias was to the left (**b**).

Play bow

smiling or laughing. Any behavior exhibited after a play bow is not serious, even if it involves growling or wrestling. Boxing—standing up on the hind legs and bopping another dog or person with the forepaws—is another playful behavior. Sometimes, in play or otherwise, dominance is signaled by a dog putting his paws on top of another dog's back or lying on top of a rival. Think about this the next time your dog puts his paws on you!

Submission is signaled by squatting and peeing or by rolling over to expose the vulnerable underbelly. Sometimes one rear leg is held up to give access to vulnerable, personal-scent-rich regions. This is a serious gesture of trust and submission when exhibited by a nonneutered adult male dog that has, almost literally, everything to lose. Not all dogs that roll over are showing submission. Some learn to roll over because their owners give them enjoyable belly rubs, equivalent to a back rub to humans. Owners complying with such dogs' requests are not demonstrating leadership but rather their compliance.

Communication Is a Two-Way Street

A dog's body language signs can be assembled in various patterns, but the patterns generally make sense to a person "in the know." With a dominant dog in full challenge mode, all the dominant signs—attentive, forward-oriented expression, tense musculature, tail up and rigid—are displayed simultaneously. An extremely fearful dog will exhibit the classic constellation of fearful or submissive signs: eyes averted, ears back, lips retracted, body hunkered, tail tucked, and so on. But sometimes dogs may exhibit mixed signals; so-called ambivalent body language. A mix of signs indicates a combination of dominance and fear and an unpredictable response from the dog. In the case of ambivalent body language, always assume the worst. For example, if you meet a friend when you are out walking your dog, and your dog barks, stands his ground, and raises his hackles while at the same time wagging his tail, do not assume he is delighted to see that person. Owners should understand such body language so that they can transmit requisite information to others about their dog's disposition for reasons of safety and convenience. This is what communication is all about: imbibing the obvious signs, both auditory and visual, and interpreting them in context. If we can understand what a dog is trying to tell us, we can react accordingly to meet some need or avoid some confrontation. Understand that dogs are good at reading our body language and in this respect need no lessons. A dog can practically see you sweat and will pick up even the subtlest signs of our changing moods and affect. There's no fooling a dog if you feel uncomfortable about him.

Of all the methods of communication that exist between people and dogs, their reading of our body language is the most innate and advanced. And it is not simply their superior senses that enable them to read us so well or the fact that body language plays such a major role in their interactions. Thousands of years of cohabitation of dogs with humans have honed dogs' inborn skills to the point where, even as pups, they can understand what we mean by certain gestures. That dogs can do this—and wolves cannot—was elegantly demonstrated by a Harvard researcher, Brian Hare, and his colleagues in a recent article in the journal *Science*. Hare reported, "During the process of domestication, dogs have been selected for a set of social-cognitive abilities that enable them to communicate with humans in unique ways." Of course, dog owners have known this for years, but it's nice to have it confirmed by a scientific study. The study also has implications about dogs' intellectual abilities—that they see themselves as unique entities and may have more complex emotions than scientists have previously ascribed to them. While this aspect of communication is well developed, all other areas need work. Dogs must be taught what verbal cues mean, and we have to learn what they are transmitting to us, actively or passively, through their vocalizations and body language. If we maximize the two-way communication that is possible with dogs, we will enhance our relationship with them, reduce their uncertainty surrounding certain events, and render them more socially compatible. It is extremely important to have sound communication in place in a crowded world where dogs and people often mix and mingle in extremely close proximity.

4

Command and Control

Physical Control — The Tie That Binds

> The number of problems reported by the owners
> correlated with the number of tasks for which their dog
> was trained using punishment, but not using rewards.
> — E. F. Hilby, N. J. Rooney, and
> J. W. S. Bradshaw (2004)

Many years ago I had a local dog trainer sit in on one of my consultations. He was doing a really good job at listening, refraining from intervening in my session with the client, though I could tell he was biting his lip. As I collected a detailed history from the owner, her dog, a German shepherd mix, was pacing anxiously around the room, whining and shooting us furtive sideways glances. The dog's restless behavior became quite distracting and was beginning to interfere with the consultation, as the owner repeatedly attempted to comfort the dog. Finally, the trainer leaned forward on his seat and, in a quiet and respectful voice, asked, "May I?" After receiving visual approval from my client, I said, "Be my guest." "Would you please attach his lead for me?" the trainer asked the owner. The owner reached down into a large bag she had brought with her to the appointment and produced a six-foot leather leash, which she then clipped onto the dog's collar. "Thank you," he said as he reached over and took the lead, then led the dog to where he was sitting. As he sat down, he stood on the dog's lead so that it had no slack; as a result, although standing, the dog was now hunched over in a semi-press-up position. The dog was clearly puzzled by his predicament and stopped whining, apparently absorbed in figuring out how to deal with the new situation. In the relative peace that ensued, the owner and I continued the consultation. Within about a minute, the dog had resigned himself to his fate, slumped down with a sigh, and lay quietly. He had clearly given up the struggle and, pinned by the lead, remained relaxed and recumbent for the rest of the appointment— calm, quiet, and under control.

"That's a neat trick," I said to the trainer, nodding to the owner upon conclusion of the consultation. The trainer responded with a statement that I will always remember. He said, "The only real control you have over a dog is with a collar and lead." That made sense to me. Here was a dog pacing anxiously one minute, and the next he was lying quietly on the floor, at peace. The difference was the lead, and the leadership. The formerly agitated dog was compelled to remain in one location by a person who had effectively established himself as the dog's leader. The dog no longer had to occupy himself with figuring out what the situation required—a troubling situation to dogs—because someone had taken charge, defining his role for the moment and dissipating his anxiety. Note that this control was not achieved using an aversive technique. The collar was a flat leather buckle collar and the lead was not jerked as a "correction." The lead had simply become an extension of the trainer—the leader—who had taken control in a decisive way.

The Need for a Lead

Certainly, some adult dogs can be trained to a fairly high level off lead, but these dogs are in the minority and even they are imperfect in their responses. I once witnessed some highly trained German shepherds performing in a Schutzhund trial. Schutzhund is a type of training that involves three components: tracking, obedience, and protection. One of the obedience exercises was for the dog to remain in a "down" position while his handler walked a distance away before turning and signaling the dog to come to him. The idea was that the dog should remain in the down position until called, but that didn't happen. In his eagerness and excitement, the dog sprang up prematurely and bounded toward the handler, losing points in the competition. If this was exhibition-level professional dog training, I thought, what hope did average dog owners have of controlling their dogs off lead? If that German shepherd had been on lead and secured by another individual, the error would not have occurred—but that was not the point of the exercise.

All dog owners need to think about and select an appropriate means of physical control for their dog, whether it is a buckle collar and lead or some more complicated device. The situations in which they will need to use the lead for control of their dogs are countless. A lead is necessary when walking down a busy street, vital when crossing a main road, helpful at social gatherings, at the vet's office, or in unfamiliar environments where various stimuli might cause the dog to startle and/or flee. It is useful when introducing your dog to people, ensuring good manners and making your guests feel more comfortable, and it is important for practically all basic training. On-lead training is to off-lead training like walking is to running—and you know which of these should come first. When you have a dog on lead, he is necessarily confined to a relatively small radius in close proximity to you, he is completely aware of your presence, and he is essentially under your control. No running away or remote investigation is possible for a dog on lead, and, with a modicum of skill, you can use a lead to become the center of your dog's universe.

Though very young puppies can learn some basics off lead, such as sitting or lying down when positioned by means of a food treat (the lure technique), it's not long before most trainers reach for a collar and lead to keep the pup in place. If you went to a training class full of energetic retriever pups careening around off lead, you wouldn't expect them to learn anything but how to wreak havoc. Adult dogs also need to be physically controlled in certain situations, and in certain public venues it's the law. Everyone's agreed on this, trainers, behaviorists, and pet psychologists—for once they're all on the same page. But here's the rub—everyone may be in agreement that a lead is necessary when it comes to basic training and control of dogs, but we don't all agree on what sort of collar the lead should be attached to. There are several choices, all with various pros and cons.

Choosing a Collar

The most basic type of collar is a flat or buckle collar, made of nylon or leather. This is the type of collar with which puppies are equipped as a first step toward their eventual physical control. If you attach a lead to this collar, you do indeed have your dog appended to you so that he cannot run away or get into trouble. With pups and some benign adult dogs, a flat collar may be all you need to hold their attention. But of all the training devices, a flat collar is the least likely to transmit a serious, authoritative message to your dog in situations where you need extra control. This type of collar permits a strong-minded adult dog to tow his owner down the street like a water-skier behind a powerboat. When you tug on a lead attached to a flat collar, the signal received by the dog can easily be ignored by the dog, as whatever pressure you apply is dissipated over a considerable area of the base of the dog's neck, especially if the collar is wide. For this reason, the so-called choke collar was devised.

A simple length of nylon cord or metal chain with a ring at each end, the choke collar is assembled by dropping one end of the cord or chain through the closest ring while holding the other, forming a letter P. The "P" is then put over the dog's head from the front so that his nose goes through the loop. Once the lead is attached to the limb of the P (the dangling piece of cord or chain), tension on it will cause the collar to tighten around the dog's neck, as the cord or chain slides through the ring. The choke collar is not just a neck collar that tightens; it also exerts greater pressure on the dog's neck than occurs with a flat collar, because there is less surface area in contact with the neck. This level of pressure will get the dog's attention more than that exerted using a flat collar, but even so, some dogs will try to ignore the signal and forge on regardless. This is where the choke collar trainer's skill comes into play, using a well-timed release followed by a sharp jerk to cause a momentary but unignorable (and, no doubt, unpleasant) sensation for the dog. Trainers sometimes introduce nylon choke collars to pups as young as four to five months of age, graduating to metal ones as the pup matures. While these collars can be used to produce immediate and spectacular results in some dogs, as you may have gathered by this point, I do not like them at all, especially for pups but also for adult dogs. The reason I object to them is that the principle by which they operate is punitive. That is, you achieve your goal by inflicting pain. It is pain or the threat of pain that makes the dog conform. So, if your dog is doing something you don't like and you physically punish him (with sufficient force and necessarily immaculate timing), he will decrease the frequency of what he is doing or even stop it entirely—for a while. That's how punishment works. Again, what dog trainers euphemistically refer to as "corrections" are physical punishments, and they can —often do—cause physical, structural damage to dogs' necks. Toy dogs, dogs with collapsing or narrow tracheas, and dogs with cervical (neck) vertebral instability should never be fitted with a choke collar, and it is highly questionable whether larger, physically sound dogs should be compelled to wear them either. At least, if they do wear them, the collar should never be jerked. A postmortem study of dogs trained using choke collars found that

92 percent of dogs had damage to either the soft tissues (skin, muscle, trachea, nerves, etc.) or hard tissue (bone) of their necks. This alone is enough to put me off. Some perseverant dogs mostly ignore mild to moderate jerking of the choke collar, take the hit, and keep on misbehaving. Reasons for their resilience include low skin sensitivity, a thick hair coat, and plain bloody-minded determination. Practitioners of the choke chain art then escalate to severe jerking, sometimes raising the dog off the ground with the collar ("hanging"), or jumping up and down in place with the collar taut, effectively stretching the dog's neck with each jump. Yes, that usually gets the dog's attention. And then there's the helicopter procedure . . . but let's not go there. Just because a technique appears to work and work quickly (good for TV) doesn't mean it is a valid technique, and certainly does not imply that it's a humane one. Long-term results and the maintenance of a good, mutually respectful relationship are far more important than short-term theatrics.

Extreme choke chain aficionados sometimes resort to using very fine-gauge neck collars for greater effect. These collars, which deliver more pounds per square inch of pressure than regular choke collars, force dogs to pay much more attention. In addition, they can be positioned high up on the dog's neck for additional leverage and greater pain-inflicting potential. Prong (or pinch) collars are also designed to deliver more pounds per square inch of pressure to dogs' necks. They operate on the stiletto heel principle that when the same force is transmitted through a very small surface area, more pounds per square inch of pressure are transmitted. In the days when stiletto heels were all the rage, women were sometimes banned from wearing them on wooden floors because the tremendous pressure delivered through the narrow heel left deep impressions in the wood. So it is with prong collars, though their impressions are left in the dog's skin—as well as in his memory. Sure, you have to tug less to achieve the same effect, but, even with a lighter pull, the pressure delivered is greater. Not satisfied with the simple prong collar, some trainers file the prongs of the collar into needle-sharp barbs. What dog wouldn't be forced into submission with a barbed wire equivalent wrapped around his neck? But is the technique appropriate or humane? I think not, on both counts. A further escalation over the sharpened-prong collar is the electric shock collar, which works on the same principle of inflicting pain. The fact that these collars can almost instantly get many dogs under control is hardly justification for their use. The end, to my mind, does not justify the means—but more on shock collars in a moment.

Most of what I have said thus far about neck collars has been pretty negative, and that's because I feel pretty negative about them. Flat neck collars can be used to good effect when leading and restraining dogs who acknowledge their handler as a leader, as was the case with the trainer in this chapter's opening anecdote, but they are not good for dogs who pull on lead or otherwise misbehave. The whole principle of controlling an unruly dog by the neck is an enigma to me. No other species is controlled by the neck. Not horses, not cows, not sheep, and not pigs. Every other species is controlled by the head. Horses are controlled with a bridle, cows and sheep with a head halter, and bulls and pigs with a ring in the nose or hog snare, respectively. Yet, for generations, dog trainers have focused their best and worst attentions on the dog's neck. When the flat collar doesn't work, some trainers escalate to the choke. When the choke collar doesn't work, they may escalate to the prong. When the prong doesn't work, some resort to electric shock collars, gradually upping the ante until the pain is severe enough that the dog has no option but to heed. The reason they must escalate, often to the point of using medieval-looking equipment, is that the base of the neck of a dog is poorly innervated with sensory nerve endings: it is not an area of the dog's skin well suited to receiving pressure signals. Suppose horse trainers insisted on trying to control unruly horses using a device that encircled the horse's neck. Even if they used barbed wire or a few electric dog collars strung together, do you think the horse would respond well to such a technique? Probably not, but he would likely become unmanageable and mistrusting once he figured out who the punisher was. That said, if I write off punitive neck collars for dogs (and horses) as unacceptable, I am obliged to make some other recommendation. I can't just leave *you* hanging.

My strong preference is for a head halter (aka head collar) for dogs and there are a number of different designs available. The design concept dates to the 1980s. Originally, there was the K9 Kumalong and the Alpha-M. The Alpha-M morphed into the Gentle Leader, and the K9 Kumalong evolved to become the Halti. The Snoot Loop, like the Halti, has side straps attaching the nose band to the high-riding neck collar to prevent it from slipping off the dog's snout. Whichever device you choose, controlling a dog by his head is the way to go to get your message across. Why is a head halter so effective for controlling and training dogs? To answer this question you need to know something about dogs' natural behavior. A bitch sends messages of disapproval when her pup is behaving badly by gently holding his snout with her mouth. Nature has programmed her to signal disapproval to the pup this way and has programmed the puppy to understand what it means. If you draw an imaginary circle around a dog's snout where his mom would have held it, this is the region gently pressured by the nose loop of a head halter when gentle tension is applied via the lead. This area is sometimes referred to as the "maternal point." It is densely innervated with sensory nerve endings that detect touch and pressure. If dogs had to read Braille, they would do so with their muzzles. The second loop of a dog's head halter rides high on the neck behind the ears. This is another well-innervated area that a pup's mother grasps as she transports him from one place to another. As the bitch's mouth clamps down on the pup's neck, the pup relaxes, knowing he is now in the hands (or rather the mouth) of his fearless leader. This area of the dog's head can be thought of as the "leader point" or "relax-

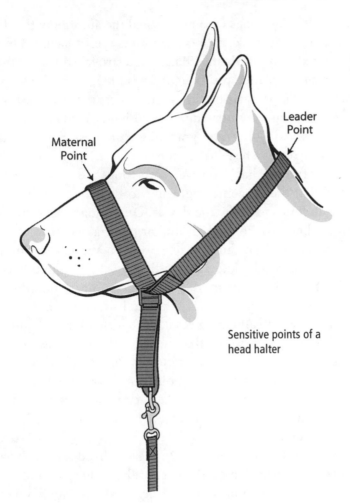

Maternal
Point

Leader
Point

Sensitive points of a
head halter

ation point." Pulling up on a lead attached to a head halter will
have the effect of pressurizing both the maternal point and the
leader point, thus enabling the dog to focus and relax. If all dogs
were fitted with these collars when they were puppies, they would
be quite used to them by the time they grew up, and wearing one
would seem natural.

The trouble is that a lot of people don't start dogs out with
head halters and try fitting them for the first time when their dog

is an adult. Older dogs who have tasted the autonomy that flat collars and basic choke collars permit may resist having a head halter fitted. Some of them will fight and struggle for more than a few minutes in attempts to get the head halter off. (It will not come off if it is properly fitted.) Many owners throw in the towel if their dog balks the first time a head halter is fitted, but it is worth persevering, however gradual the progress. Some say the more a dog resists a head halter, the more he needs it. There may be some truth to that. However, some dogs are so resistant to control that they become aggressive to their owner when the owner attempts to apply the device. Other dogs never give up rubbing their noses on the ground or pawing, trying to get the head halter off. That can be a real problem and may mean the dog is an unsuitable candidate for this type of restraint. Fortunately, these difficulties are relatively uncommon, and in many cases, adult dogs can be fitted with head halters with immediate and practically breathtaking results. Dogs that formerly pulled on walks stop pulling; dogs that lunged with malicious intent at strangers sit quietly next to their owners; dogs that barked incessantly may literally have their mouths shut. Because the way in which signals are sent and received is consistent with the dog's natural instincts, the results that are achieved using a head halter can be astounding.

Of course, the effectiveness of the head collar does not obviate the need for leadership on the part of the owner or handler. It helps, when applying pressure to a head halter, to look directly into the dog's eyes to transmit that you mean business—which you do. It also helps to use your voice properly (don't plead or shout, just say what you want to have happen, and say it once). And it helps to pet your dog firmly over the head with a gentle stroking motion from behind his eyes and over the top of his head to the nape of the neck, transmitting a powerful signal of your leadership. The control you get with a head halter can be immediate, and that control will facilitate the dog's learning.

After a few months of use, it may not even be necessary to apply tension to the head halter to get your point across, because the dog will have learned what is expected of him and will require merely a vocal cue.

Sometimes when I show clients how to use a head halter they say, "That's terrific, Doc, I'll take one. By the way, when can I stop using it?" To which I reply, "You haven't even started yet, and, if it works, why would you want to stop using it?" But if they insist, I explain how it is possible to wean some dogs off this training tool once a consistent response is obtained. I advise owners to start this weaning process only when they get the response they need without having to apply any tension to the lead at all; that is, when the dog has learned what is expected of him and is responding perfectly to voice cues alone. At this point, the head halter may be fitted without the nose band looped over the dog's nose. With the neck strap in place, the nose band simply pulls through the buckle underneath the dog's chin. If the dog continues to respond as if the nose band was in place, the next stage is to loosen the neck strap so that it rides lower on the dog's neck. If the dog continues to respond as desired, owners can take the plunge and switch to a regular flat collar.

I tell still-reticent clients about other people's success following the temporary use of a head halter. One of my favorite stories involves a client who called me up a few months after a consultation and said, "Dr. Dodman, that head halter that you recommended to us is the best thing since sliced bread. Ralph is now a perfectly well-behaved dog." "So, you use the head halter all the time?" I asked her. "No, we never use it. All we have to do is show it to him and he does what he's told." I've heard stories like that more than once, and they are powerful testimony to the efficacy of head halters. You could argue that the dogs responded to the sight of the head halter because they didn't like having it on. That's possible, but at least head halters do not inflict pain and they do help owners manage what would otherwise be untenable situations. It's the dog's choice whether he exercises self-control or has to have the head halter applied.

Head halters are difficult, if not impossible, to use on English bulldogs and some other brachycephalic breeds with short snouts. Neck collars are not suitable for these dogs, either; they have trouble enough breathing through their drinking-straw-caliber tracheas. When a dog's anatomy or temperament precludes the use of a head halter, harnesses are the next best option. A harness is a device that attaches around a dog's chest like a cradle and is secured by straps that pass in front of the brisket. I used to think that harnesses delivered no useful communication to dogs and were about as effective as a mud anchor on a boat. I learned otherwise when I met an expert harness trainer, Diane Arrington. Diane gave a talk at the Tufts Animal Expo one year on harness training in dogs. Later she sent me a video showing her in action, training a few behaviorally challenged dogs at her training center, PetPerfect Academy in Dallas, Texas. What she didn't know about reading a dog's body language wasn't worth knowing. She assimilated every blink, every look, every lick, every yawn, indeed every movement of the dogs in her charge. In teaching the "Sit" command, Diane would apply gentle upward pressure to the harness, simultaneously withdrawing attention from the dog until he responded. Once dogs were in the sit position, Diane would release tension on the lead and would shower them with attention and praise to let them know that they had done something that was truly appreciated. Her technique of training these dogs to sit took longer than most choke collar trainers would have patience for, but it made the dogs think and educated them to do what they were told to do, without inflicting pain. Whether wittingly or unwittingly, she was using the technique of so-called *negative reinforcement*, in which the frequency of performing a behavior increases in order to avoid some otherwise disconcerting circumstance—in this case, the cold shoulder. The reward, in negative reinforcement, is that the unpleasant situation or experience ends, though Diane also lavished praise to make the contrast between attention withdrawal and attention more pronounced. Diane used a similar technique for teaching "Down," which involved the laying on of hands (on the dog's back) with very light pressure, looking into the dog's eyes, and simply waiting for the desired response. When the dog lay down, which he invariably did in time, the pressure was released, Diane's intimidating gaze was averted, and attention and praise were liberally supplied, as before. Word cues were added later. At the end of these short learning sessions, Diane gave the dogs a brief shoulder massage to let them know that the session was over and that they had done well. All in all, it was a very impressive demonstration.

Choosing a Lead

Perhaps a slightly less charged issue than the type of collar you employ is what you attach to it. Here I am talking leads (also colloquially known as leashes). You can purchase leads made of different materials, different lengths, and ones with certain options. Nylon leads are inexpensive, but if a dog is prone to pulling, nylon can inflict the equivalent of paper cuts or rope burns on an owner's hands. I prefer leather leads and think of them as the gold standard. In time, the leather wears to become soft and pliable. But leads made of both nylon and leather can be problematic when it comes to leash chewers. While dogs can be trained not to chew their leads (using an "Out" command and snapping the lead from the dog's mouth), many owners never get around to teaching this lesson and go through scores of leads before they find a solution. Part leather, part chain leads were invented for just such dogs. The chain part that dogs can't chew through is nearest his mouth, while you, the owner, have the comfortable leather end in your hand.

For right-handed people, dogs are traditionally walked on the left side. The thumb of the right hand is put through the loop at the end of the lead—perhaps one or two turns of slack are taken around the wrist, as needs be—and the other end of the lead is loosely held in the left hand around midthigh. The right hand can be anchored in the region of the owner's midriff. It does little or no work in operating the lead. The left hand governs where and how the dog is led. For left-handed people, the opposite of this arrangement holds.

Leads vary in length but a decent length to start with is four feet. A four-foot lead gives your dog just enough freedom, and yet is short enough to ensure you have adequate control. Longer leads of five or more feet can be tricky to operate, especially for novices, who sometimes almost literally end up hoisted by their own petard. There is nothing worse than witnessing an unpracticed owner trying to control a dog on a long lead, shrugging apologetically as the dog cavorts around a twelve-foot radius, tying everyone within range in knots. This lack of control is also typical of retractable leads in the extended mode. While such

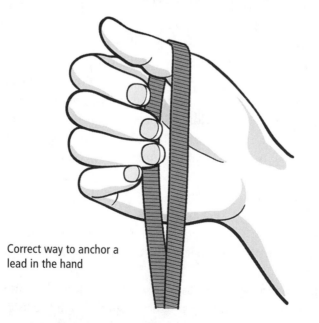

Correct way to anchor a lead in the hand

freedom may be acceptable in a park or open field, it is not help-ful in tight corners, on busy streets, or during training. Too much slack on a lead can cause a dog to start acting autonomously because, in effect, he is not under his owner's control. Long leads have their place, but it is not in the high street. Retractable leads are most effective when they are in the locked-in position—so you might stick to a regular lead unless you plan on going hiking.

Indoor training leads, as the name implies, are intended for indoor use only. They are long (up to ten feet long), lightweight, and loopless. Dogs can be obliged to wear them around the house when a certain unacceptable behavior needs to be addressed. Indoor training leads can be thought of as a penance for bad behavior. With training lead attached, a dog can be apprehended from some distance, should he become involved in any unaccept-able activity. The training lead provides a form of remote con-trol—and dogs know it. Just step on the end of the lead and you can stop a dog in his tracks, then reel him in like a fish. Having an indoor lead on a dog gives an owner better control and more authority. I find training leads helpful in the management of a variety of common canine behavior problems, such as raiding a garbage can, "counter surfing," and jumping up on people. They are also useful in helping the owners of dominant dogs to get their pets off furniture and off or out of other high places without getting bitten. This type of training lead is not designed for out-door use as it is too flimsy and can easily pull out of an owner's grip, since it has no loop. Sturdier and even longer training leads can be used to control dogs remotely in outdoor situations. A thirty- or forty-foot washing line, properly secured to a flat col-lar and with a handle attached, can give owners a lot more options when it comes to dealing with escape-artist dogs in a wide-open space. Along the same lines, long outdoor leads are also helpful for teaching dogs to come when called. Indoor and outdoor training leads, by virtue of the distance control they facilitate, add another dimension to training.

Controlling Dogs from a Distance

For controlling dogs at greater distances, so-called remote-training collars can be employed. These are collars that are activated by a handheld radio frequency transmitter to deliver a negative or positive signal to a dog off lead. The transmitter-collar combination almost literally allows you to "reach out and touch someone"—as the telephone company jingle goes. The most infamous remote-training collar is the electronic collar, which delivers a jolt or sustained burst of electric current to the dog's neck via a couple of prong-like electrodes on the inside of the collar. I must admit that the very concept of this collar makes me shudder, and I never recommend them to my clients. That said, a few of my veterinary behaviorist colleagues and any number of trainers do recommend electric shock collars under some circumstances and feel that they have a place in dog training. My former resident at the Animal Behavior Clinic at Tufts, Dr. Jean DeNapoli, is one behaviorist I know who uses electric shock to train her own dogs, and they seem none the worse for it. Jean is a high-level competition trainer of herding dogs, German shepherds, and when she worked with me, she possessed two fine specimens of this breed—as well as her own flock of sheep. In training her dogs to herd sheep in the manner of Border collies, she would first show them what to do on lead; then insist that they do whatever they had been taught using a choke collar; and finally graduate to off-lead control using mild electric shock as a remote correction device. Certainly her scheme worked well for her dogs, who were also her beloved pets. They were not frightened of her and seemed genuinely happy around her. I trusted that, as an expert, Jean knew precisely when to punish her dogs, knew the appropriate voltage to use (it was, in any case, very mild), and perhaps more importantly, knew when *not* to administer a shock. Bottom line: shock collars can work for some owners some of the time—but their effectiveness is dependent on the skill and knowledge of those operating them. One of our undergraduates informed me that she had trained her dog not to growl or snap at her using an electric shock collar and found that the briefest use of the collar produced a long-lasting effect. In addition, one client of mine, who owned a Bernese mountain dog that attacked pretty much every dog he saw, straightened out her dog's problem behavior using a shock collar (she later admitted to me sheepishly). Yet I continue to worry about this type of device; I've heard too many horror stories about inappropriate and even abusive use of shock collars, and as I have stated, I am not inclined toward any training techniques involving infliction of a painful stimulus. Random, intermittent electric shock has been shown to cause neurosis in dogs and to promote aggression. In addition, I have seen deep ulcerating wounds develop in the necks of dogs fitted with prong-type e-collars that are too tight or have been worn too long. For now, I pass on this type of punitive device and choose to promote alternative methods of restraint.

One remote-training collar I can live with is the citronella collar. When activated, these collars emit a puff of lemony citronella that the dog finds aversive. Though most people think of these collars as bark-activated antibark collars, there are ones that can be activated manually by a handheld remote controller. I don't have a lot of experience with remote-control citronella collars, but what little I have gleaned has been fairly positive. The one proviso with these remote-control collars is that they are punishers, however mild, and as such will merely discourage behaviors that you don't want. They aren't really much good at teaching behaviors you do want unless used as negative reinforcers (see earlier).

There are now remote collars that have a positive mode as opposed to exclusively delivering a punitive electric shock or a whiff of citronella. These collars vibrate or make some neutral sound that signals a job done well. They operate on the same principle as clicker training in that the vibration or sound serves as a secondary reinforcer, signaling success and good times to come. I had, years ago, come up with an idea like this myself: a new invention (I thought) to help owners recall their dogs from a distance. My idea was to fit a buzzer to the collar to train the dog to understand that whenever the collar buzzed, he would be given a very special treat. Then, when the dog was far away, the buzzer could be activated remotely, causing the dog to return for the treat. Unfortunately, I found I had been beaten to the punch when my patent attorney discovered that one shock collar on the market already had a positive mode, albeit not specifically for recalling dogs. As the most common cry of the dog owner is, "All I want them to do is come when I call," I thought I was onto a winner . . . but it was not to be. Later, I had the great pleasure to meet the owner of a deaf Dalmatian called Hogan, and this woman, Connie, had come up with something similar in attempting to recall her dog. "It's no good shouting upstairs to a deaf dog to tell him his dinner is ready," Connie said. "We use a cheap pager attached to Hogan's collar and activate it to vibrate by pressing a speed-dial number on a cell phone. It works well." These days, commercial recall collars are available for deaf dogs—and they work for hearing dogs, too.

Tie-Ups, Fences, and Pens

Various forms of restraint exist for controlling dogs in their owners' absence. One such method is the tie-up, by which the dog is attached to a runner or a stake in the ground. On the plus side, this allows the dog to get a breath of air while secured on the property; on the negative side, tie-ups seem to enhance aggression. Take the situation of junkyard dogs. Tethered by ropes or chains, junkyard dogs learn to charge at and intimidate strangers who approach within the radius of their confinement. Sensible people back off when the dog barks or lunges, so the dog's behavior is reinforced as he chalks up another victory. As the cycle is repeated, the dog gains confidence in his ability to repel intruders and becomes progressively more aggressive. The level of aggression seems to be inversely proportional to the length of the tie-up; the shorter the chain, the greater the aggression. This is a big disadvantage when it comes to tying up potentially aggressive dogs. Another major disadvantage is that people who inadvertently walk within the radius of the tie-up can be attacked. I was retained as an expert witness in two such cases in which the dog owner was found negligent. In the first instance, a young child let himself out of the back door while the grownups were engrossed in conversation and approached an aggressive pit bull secured to a stake. The dog savagely bit the child in the face, necessitating plastic surgery. In the second case, a Saint Bernard was tied to a tree, but the owners hadn't figured out that the rope by which the dog was tied allowed the dog to reach a nearby path. A visiting child running down the path was mauled by this dog as she came within the dog's reach. Because of stories like these, I do not recommend tie-ups.

More acceptable than a tie-up is a physical structure that will confine the dog. Many people opt for an invisible fence that activates a shock collar as being the least expensive way to confine a dog. When an invisible fence is first installed, the property is marked off with small flags delineating the boundary, and the dog is trained on lead not to cross the line marked by the flags. Typically, he is punished by means of a jerk applied to a choke chain for transgressing. Following the initial training, an electric shock collar is fitted, and the dog is led across the invisible fence line, whereupon he first hears an audible warning, a buzz or beep of some sort, and following which he gets zapped. Two shocks are usually all it takes to teach a dog that crossing the line is something to be avoided. Following that experience, most dogs stay within the delineated area, shying away from the flags whenever they hear the audible warning, knowing that the noise heralds a shock should they continue in that direction. After a few weeks, the flags can be removed as the dog understands his new limits. One brand of invisible fence (there are several) is approved by the Humane Society of the United States (HSUS) for the confinement of dogs. Its position must be that to condone the delivery of a mild punishing experience to a dog on a couple of occasions is in the dog's best interests when the alternative is the dog's running loose, getting hit by a car, getting lost, or becoming a public nuisance. Lost dogs may also wind up in shelters or pounds, and for some two-thirds of these dogs, this means euthanasia. I can go along with the rationale for using an invisible fence but prefer owners to invest in a solid fence—the gold standard of physical confinement, in my opinion. But when a solid fence is either beyond an owner's financial reach or is impractical for some reason, I have in the past advised an invisible fence. You might say this is counter to my position on electric shock training. It's true that I don't really much like electric shock training, but the difference with invisible fences is that the dog self-activates the collar, rather than the shock being administered by an individual. It is the dog's behavior that triggers the shock, and the shock does not come without warning. Also, following their initial exposure to the shocks, the majority of dogs will stay within the confines of the fence never to be shocked again. Occasionally, intrepid or just plain belligerent dogs (one invisible fence company calls them "hounds from hell") will bolt through the fence and take the shock, if the reward on the other side, say, an itinerant squirrel, is sufficiently motivating. On the other hand, there are some naturally timid dogs who, after receiving their first shock, will never leave the owner's porch to venture into the yard again. These so-called porch sitters are obviously too sensitive for an invisible fence. It would be best to identify these shrinking violets ahead of time, so that their owners might pursue a different course of action. Dogs not suited to an invisible fence, who may become these porch sitters, are those with a nervous disposition: the submissive urinaters, those with noise phobia, and those with anxiety-based conditions, such as acral lick dermatitis and separation anxiety.

Even assuming an invisible fence is deemed appropriate for a particular dog in a particular circumstance, and even if it does effectively confine the dog and prevent roaming, the downside is that people can still wander onto the property across the invisible fence lines without knowing it. This, coupled with the fact that a dog whose territory is so distinctly defined may become more protective of it, is a recipe for disaster in some cases. Fear-aggressive dogs, for example, can sit within the boundaries of the invisible fence like a spider in a web waiting for some hapless prey. Along comes the UPS man whistling on his way, only to be greeted by a lunging, snarling, Cujo of a dog that takes out the seat of his pants. Clearly, this is not an effective method of restraint for such dogs. Aggressive dogs should be confined by a real fence. A real fence provides much more reliable protection for the public and, though costly, is a lot less expensive than a lawsuit. Of course, it may be necessary to have a BEWARE OF THE DOG sign on the fence and a bell for tradesmen to ring. In addition, a real fence will protect your dog from the ravages of itinerant dog-aggressive dogs. All in all, a much more tenable situation.

One boundary safer than a fence is a dog pen. For owners with the need, the motivation, and the resources, a pen provides the ultimate physical control of a dog outside the house but on your property. It is what is insisted upon by courts of law for dogs who have attacked strangers in the past. Such dogs are effectively put under house arrest and are walked from the house to the pen or compound each day, where they are allowed to get their exercise. While somewhat austere, prison-like, and unpalatable to many owners, pens can be the only solution for some dogs, barring euthanasia. Personally, I think pens are okay if they are deemed necessary and are of an appropriate size. Clearly, the bigger the better, and it helps if the space is made more interesting, more user-friendly, by the incorporation of a dog house in which the dog can shelter during inclement weather and various structures to encourage exploration, play, and digging. In addition, the area should be enriched by including interesting toys and food puzzles (hollow, hard rubber or plastic toys in which food morsels can be hidden to provide the dog entertainment and reward).

The Mutual Benefits of Physical Restraint

With respect to the physical control of dogs outside the house, I should point out that most dog bites to people occur from dogs who are roaming unsupervised on their own property. Being unsupervised permits the dog to be a law unto himself, and being on his own property adds confidence and territorial motivation. Dogs that are properly supervised and controlled *off* their own property are responsible for the least number of bites. Remember, though, that "off the property" and "off the territory" (from the dog's perspective) may not be the same thing. Dogs often regard their territory as being not only the house and yard but also the immediate neighborhood and the streets they regularly patrol and mark with urine. Your dog will not have seen your legally defined plot plan and would not understand it if he did. He will make his own boundaries and for his own reasons.

Your consideration of the important issue of physical control of your dog on and off his home turf is of paramount importance to you, assuming you wish to avoid someone getting injured or litigation directed toward you—and is in your dog's best interest, too. Responsible dog owners immediately understand this point, but, unfortunately, some people need the threat of legal action to compel them to toe the line. Not everyone is a dog lover and there are people who are frankly anti-dog. There is even an anti-dog lobby. These folks' concerns center around dogs' fouling public places, creating a barking nuisance, and, perhaps most importantly, dog aggression. With the proper use of a collar and lead for dogs promenading in densely populated areas and proper supervision of dogs at home, whether on lead or by confinement, a lot of the problems that ignite the anti-dog lobby can and should be addressed. The last thing we want to do is give the anti-dog folk more cause for complaint. This is not to say that dogs need to be physically controlled at all times, but they certainly should be under close control when needs be. At home, it is usually safe to have your dog padding around off lead in the house or even in the yard as long as you are there to supervise. It is also safe to allow nonaggressive dogs to run free, off lead, in certain open areas, such as parks, woods, and beaches, especially if you have confidence in your recall abilities.

Since 42 percent of dog owners report that their dogs have a behavior problem, and the majority of problems fall into the category of aggression, and since some of these problems are so severe that they cause dog owners to give up on their pets, it is important to note the benefits afforded by using proper physical control. Think back to the words of the trainer at the opening of this chapter: "The only real control you have over a dog is with a collar and lead." Remember the benefits that we saw when the dog in the consulting room was properly restrained. Simple measures like this can go a long way toward controlling and preventing unwanted behaviors, not to mention inconvenience or injury to passersby. The message is clear: choose the appropriate tools for physical restraint, utilize them wisely, and don't feel badly for the dog because his freedom has been curtailed. Your dog won't hold it against you if you use physical control wisely; on the contrary, he will only benefit from being firmly under your direction.

5

Leadership Program

Good Leadership — A Prerequisite for Learning

> You do not lead by hitting people over the head — that's assault, not leadership.
> — Dwight D. Eisenhower

Many owners come to regard their dogs as family members — some even think of them as their children. It is from this sense of intimacy or closeness that many of the joys of dog ownership derive, but so do some of the problems, most notably owner-directed aggression if the dog has no confidence in his owner's ability to provide for and protect him. Most dog owners want a dog they can love and who loves them back, one they can have fun with and go for walks with, relax with and pet, and one that gets on well with all family members. That's fine, but you still have to be your dog's trusted leader and effectively run the show. A leaderless family is like a ship without a rudder and potentially disastrous when it comes to dealing with dogs, especially those who get wind in their sails. Whether starting out with a youngster or attempting to rein in an unruly adult dog, proper leadership goes a long way toward ensuring that you find yourself living with a relaxed and happy dog who respects as well as loves all family members.

Some dog owners, like some parents, try to win their charges over by spoiling them, thinking that that will generate love and loyalty. That's wishful thinking and often sends precisely the wrong message. Dogs of a certain persuasion interpret owners' unconditional kindness as amiable weakness and consequently do not trust them to make good decisions, both concerning everyday matters and when the going gets tough. For all dog owners, like all parents, there are times when you have to make your point and not fold if you want to maintain law and order as well as respect. Children may want to eat candy before dinner; they may not want to eat their vegetables, do their homework, or go to bed at a reasonable hour. Allowing them to decide what they will and will not do is not always good for them. It is a parent's responsibility to give clear and authoritative directions when necessary so as not to condone unhealthful or destructive behaviors. It's great to be your child's friend, but you must also be a parent — and that means not caving in to all requests. It's the same with dogs. What they want isn't always what's best for them, and dog owners have to become good "dog parents" — ones whose instructions must be heeded if the dog is to fit in with the family and, indeed, human society in general. You might think that children and dogs would be much happier if they were left to their own devices and desires — allowed to do whatever they want when they want — but actually they're not. Both children and dogs appreciate clear direction, knowing where they stand, and what's expected of them. They want to — need to — know the rules and live by them. Living within a consistent social structure alleviates a lot of anxiety and helps produce happy, self-assured dogs and children.

The Question of Dominance

A leadership program, formerly referred to as a dominance (control) program, can be implemented to bring pushy, nippy puppies in line and traditionally has been used to treat owner-directed aggression in adult dogs. One reason for the change in nomenclature is that the concept of "alpha dog" dominance with respect to canine pack dynamics has lately been subject to revision by animal behaviorists. Unfortunately, use of the term "dominance" in describing willful, disobedient, and aggressive behavior in dogs has led to the misconception that such behaviors must be addressed by humans through asserting physical dominance over dogs (i.e., by humans taking the "alpha" role). Most dogs with supposedly dominance-related behavior problems are not actually seeking dominance over their owners, however; rather, such dogs are typically anxious, confused, or even somewhat fearful of what might happen next. Waling on them to get your point across is thus hardly an appropriate solution. Owners can circumvent the most troubling aspects of this behavior through proper leadership and control without raising their voices, let alone their hands. Being your dog's leader doesn't — shouldn't — mean you have to be militaristic or unpleasant, it just means you have to *lead*. To do that, you must know what leadership is, how to be your dog's leader, and have some idea of the direction in which you want to go. Leaders set the pace, they initiate activities, they control resources, they are providers; they are not aggressive, but they are persuasive; they are fair, but they are also firm. Some people are natural dog leaders, while others need to work at it. What you should be striving to achieve is a relationship with your dog that is a happy and healthy one — but with you firmly at the helm. Think about it, it can't really be the other way around. Whether you like it or not, it's your responsibility to be the leader, and this arrangement is in the best interests of all concerned. When you feel like letting your hair down and cavorting and frolicking with your dog — go for it. But when it's time for the fun to stop, you should be able to peacefully draw the line and have your dog understand that the games are over and it's time to move on.

A dog's lack of respect for his owner — I call it the Rodney Dangerfield syndrome — leads to all sorts of behavior problems.

Lack of respect portends pushiness, lack of responsiveness, and general wayward behavior, including owner-directed aggression. An owner who is not his dog's strong leader will also find it hard to assuage his dog's fears because the dog will not consider him competent to manage the situation. Leadership is a fundamental prerequisite of most behavior-modification programs. If your dog is not following your lead, he will not be able to learn from you. Period. So important is a proper leadership program, some behaviorists require clients to engage in one — like the one I'm about to describe — for several weeks before embarking on a behavior-modification program to deal with specific problems. A leadership program can be described as Dog Ownership 101 — a basic requirement. While demonstrating clear leadership is important for all dog owners, it is especially important for owners of dogs displaying owner-directed aggression.

Currently, there is a great deal of debate about the cause of owner-directed aggression. Some of my veterinary behaviorist colleagues have determined that what was formerly called dominance aggression is frequently associated with fearful behaviors. They decry the "pack mentality-dominance" interpretation of owner-directed aggression and the hard-line corrective methods used to remedy it. While I applaud my colleagues for attempting to counter the outmoded and unacceptable practice of dominating dogs by force, I don't entirely discount the traditional theory of pack dynamics; wild canids do have societies that revolve around social status, and individuals within the pack do have different rights and responsibilities. Aggression within the pack, however subtle, exists to establish and maintain a stable hierarchy and serves a "cohesive" role that is both logical and functional. Even though humans have engaged in selective breeding of dogs for hundreds if not thousands of years, many of dogs' primordial instincts, including some remnant of the pack mentality, have remained relatively unchanged. Other deeply ingrained behaviors, such as predatory behavior (chasing varmints), circling before lying down (to flatten the grass), and howling (long-distance communication), have also survived relatively intact. I believe that while dogs displaying owner-directed aggression do not see themselves as pack leaders, neither does fear play a direct role in their response. They challenge their owners because they are lacking in direction, uncertain about their role in the family, and may be confused and anxious. It is underlying anxiety that causes them to be mistrusting and irritable when faced with perceived threats and challenges, but it is good old-fashioned dominance that causes them to lash out as opposed to deferring in these situations. Anxiety is merely the catalyst.

To complicate matters, anxiety and pack-style dominance coexist in different proportions in different dogs showing owner-directed aggression. In the clinic, I rate dogs' "dominance" on a 0–10 scale. A zero rating, which is rare, equates with no apparent pushiness or willfulness. A rating of 10, equally unusual, equates with ultimate confidence and independence. Most dominant-aggressive dogs score at the 5–10 end of the dominance scale. I also rate anxiety on a 0–10 scale and place dogs with anxiety-related problems somewhere on that scale. Certain dogs with owner-directed aggression seem to be reasonably confident, in-charge dogs who rate high on the dominance scale and low on the anxiety scale. These are dogs whose behavior equates more with the classical concept of dominance. Other dogs with owner-directed aggression score at the upper end of the range on both scales. These latter dogs are clearly confused and anxious about their owner's interactions with them. A spectrum of dominant-anxious personality types exists between the two extremes.

Most dogs displaying owner-directed aggression get on well with family members most of the time (typically, 95–98 percent of the time) and will often solicit — even demand — attention and petting from them. It's the 2–5 percent of the time that the dog becomes snippy, or even lunges or bites, that causes the owner concern. All dogs displaying owner-directed aggression will benefit from the institution of a leadership program. As an owner's leadership skills and confidence in dealing with the dogs grow, the frequency and intensity of the dog's aggression declines in parallel. It has long been thought — and we now have evidence to support — that tentative, nervous owners make their dogs nervous, too. If owners develop confidence and consistency in dealing with their dogs, the dogs will react positively, will be less anxious, and will be less prone to act aggressively.

Components of the Program

By definition, a leadership program puts owners in a leadership position with respect to their dogs, encouraging the dogs to look to them for direction, respect their wishes, and defer to them when the need arises. For owners whose dogs are out of control or showing aggression toward them, this is the only program that will really help — and we have demonstrated that it not only works in the short term but has lasting results.

The program has two basic components: (1) strategic avoidance of conflict and (2) controlling of resources. The former allays dogs' anxiety and prevents ongoing reinforcement of aggressive behavior. The latter demonstrates to the dog that the owner is in charge of all valued assets, like food, petting, and play, and therefore is in charge generally. Typically the two components are implemented concurrently.

The program can be adopted anytime from puppyhood to adulthood. The extent to which it is implemented is determined by owner concerns and the seriousness of the situation. Mildly challenging dogs may need only a modest level of implementation for the point to be made that the owner runs the show. Troublingly aggressive adult dogs displaying dangerous levels of aggression may need to have the book thrown at them (not literally, of course). Owners about to engage in a serious "tough love" leadership program often express the concern that the process will somehow adversely affect their relationship with their dogs or that the dogs might become sad or depressed. Quite the reverse is true. What actually happens is that when the owner steps into the leadership role, the dog responds positively. It's as if the dog thinks, *What a relief, for a moment there I thought I was in charge.*

The leadership program I employ is my customized version of a program variously described as "Nothing in Life Is Free" and "Working for a Living." I started using this program many years ago and have modified it continuously in the light of feedback from owners. My philosophy has always been that if something works, keep doing it. If it doesn't, change the plan right away. The definition of insanity is said to be "doing the same thing over and over again and expecting different results." That is not what I do. The program has evolved over some twenty years and is currently what I recommend to owners who come to our clinic. I have also shared the program with "remote" clients through our fax-consultation services and have monitored their progress. Interestingly, the program works as effectively for these distant clients as it does for owners whose dogs I have seen at the clinic. I suppose this result is to be expected, since the diagnosis in both cases is based on information the owner provides — not what we witness — and the advice given is identical. This is good news for readers of this book and anyone who lives too far away from a behaviorist to have an in-person consultation. One thing that is for sure, though: proper follow-up helps owners succeed. Ongoing advice and encouragement during implementation of the program makes a considerable difference to the short- and long-term success of the program. Make sure you have ongoing support.

1. Avoidance of Conflict

If the program is to be effective, it is imperative for owners to eliminate any ongoing stress or conflict between them and their dog. If a dog is growling, lifting his lip, snapping, or biting familiar people in any one of a number of different circumstances, owners should work to address issues that lead to these confrontations. If a dog growls at his owner for any reason, the dog's reaction indicates that he does not appreciate what is happening at that time. When confronted by a growling dog, owners should literally take a step back and carefully consider what is bothering the dog and whether the situation is potentially avoidable in future. In most cases, the solution is simply to refrain from doing whatever is upsetting the dog. That reduces stress all around. What more can a poor dog do than mutter his discontent about something he doesn't like? Well, he may escalate the warning to a snap or bite if his owner consistently ignores the communication, but why allow the situation to progress this far? I believe owners should listen to what their dogs are trying to tell them *before* the escalation occurs and take appropriate avoidance measures. All too often, owners are told to do exactly the opposite by well-meaning advisers, thus inadvertently exacerbating problems. I advise respect for dogs' reasonable requests for peace and independence. This strategy represents a considerable improvement over trying to coexist in an atmosphere of anxiety and confrontation. To this end, I have owners fill in a checklist of some thirty actions that are potential sources of conflict between owners and dogs, to help them identify the conflict-causing situations in their own relationship.

Ideally, as long as the owners understand and follow the recommendations, there will be no further aggression from that time forward, because there is no reason for it to occur. Avoidance of conflict allows the dog to relax in the owner's presence and is, in its own right, therapeutic. Aggression begets aggression, so it is important to immediately defuse all conflict situations if significant progress is to be made.

Specific actions in avoiding conflict

Some dogs growl — or worse — if you put your hand in their food bowl while they are eating. Dog trainers who use confrontational

Aggression Checklist Action by Owner	Growl	Lift lip	Snap	Bite	Not aggressive	Not tried
Touch food or add food while dog is eating						
Walk past while dog is eating						
Take away real bone, rawhide, or food						
Walk by dog when he has bone/rawhide						
Touch delicious food while dog is eating						
Take away a stolen object						
Physically wake dog up or disturb resting dog						
Restrain dog when he wants to go someplace						
Lift dog						
Pet dog						
Medicate dog						
Handle dog's face/mouth						
Handle dog's feet						
Trim dog's toenails						
Groom dog						
Bathe or towel off dog						
Take off or put on collar						
Pull dog back by collar or scruff						
Reach for or grab dog by collar						
Hold dog by muzzle						
Stare at dog						
Reprimand dog in loud voice						
Visually threaten dog: newspaper or hand						
Hit dog						
Walk by dog in crate						
Walk by/talk to dog on furniture						
Remove dog from furniture: physically or verbally						
Make dog respond to command						

Dog's Response

methods teach that you must be able to do this — that you have to make your dog tolerate this intervention to show him you're "alpha." This makes no sense to me at all. I know that I don't appreciate people sticking their hands in my food while I'm eating, and if a waiter did that to me in a restaurant, I would probably growl or snap at him. I can empathize with dogs in this situation and do not think they should have to tolerate such intrusion. My approach is to help owners appreciate that their dogs do not like their food touched while they are eating it, and I advise them not to do it. Insisting on your right to intervene will only confirm your dog's suspicions that you are a control freak and are not to be trusted. I saw a videotape once of an owner standing around a dog's food bowl at feeding time. The dog was hovering six inches above his food, head cocked, eyeing the owner shiftily, growling a menacing warning, and not even attempting to take a mouthful. Someone had told this woman that she had to be able to stand there while her dog was eating; that the dog just had to learn to accept that situation. Well, he didn't and the growling got worse, lasting for as long as she remained nearby. The scene was ludicrous and I felt sorry for the dog. Another avoidable confrontation sometimes occurs when owners walk too close to the food bowl while their dog is eating. The solution is to feed the dog in a place where he won't be disturbed. The reason why dogs growl when you walk too close to their food bowl is that they don't trust you to leave them alone . . . perhaps for good reason.

Another food-type issue involves dogs' protecting bones, rawhides, and other special food items. The answer to this problem is clear: Don't give your dog anything he may be so possessive of as to growl, or worse, when you or others perceived as threatening to take the object away come near. If you give a child a penknife and he insists on threatening you with it, you take it away. Ditto for dogs regarding butcher bones, rawhide, pig ears, Greenies, cow hooves, and so on. By the way, butcher bones are not approved by veterinarians for other reasons. Veterinary dentists say they break teeth and lead to root abscesses. Veterinary nutritionists and internists are concerned about the risk of infection from raw bones and intestinal obstruction or perforation from cooked bones. Some of these concerns are also valid for rawhide chews. Anyway, the general idea is to avoid conflict and not to adopt the confrontational approach of insisting that you *must* be able to take whatever it is away from your dog "because you have to be the pack leader." It simply goes against common sense to expect a tough-minded dog to give up a bone without a fight. It's better for all concerned to avoid any possibility of such a showdown. Simply deny dogs special food objects that provoke in them possessiveness and aggression. What the eye doesn't see, the heart doesn't grieve.

Favorite food, especially stolen food, may provoke aggression in dogs who may not guard their regular food. Once again, it is best to use our large frontal lobes to think our way out of this situation rather than taking a hard line and finding ourselves in open warfare with the dog. The first rule is a matter of preemption: Don't leave any food out that your dog might steal from you. When you finish your food, put the leftovers into a trash can with a dog-proof lid. Don't leave pizza, hot dogs, or meat lying out on the table unattended. Be smart, think ahead. But if despite your efforts your dog does grab something off the table or finds something on the floor, just accept that it's his. Your mistake, your loss, is his good fortune. I call this "the law of the floor."

Another common "dominance" issue involves the dog stealing and then protecting certain items, like socks, shoes, and even underwear. Dogs that steal such things and guard them do so because they get a rise out of their owners. If your dog steals a shoe, or anything else for that matter, and you stop what you're doing and become animated, this can provide rewarding excitement for the dog in the midst of an otherwise humdrum day. The solution is simple: Keep socks in drawers, keep shoes in cupboards, keep dirty laundry in bins with lids, and generally clean up after yourself. In other words, deny your dog the opportunity to take things you wouldn't want him to have, but, at the same time, ensure he has acceptable things around to amuse himself with. Of course, no owner will be perfect in the keep-away endeavors. If a dog does manage to steal something, the best course of action, if at all possible, is to ignore him and let him tire of it. Then pick it up and put it away.

A favorite item for dogs to steal is bathroom tissue. Some dogs steal unused tissues out of the box or used tissues from the trash can. Once you get the tissue from the dog, he knows the game is up so, hardly surprisingly, he wants to hang on to it for as long as possible and will growl to keep you at bay. The way to avoid this problem is to outsmart the dog by keeping new tissues in a place that he can't reach, say, in a cabinet or behind locked doors. Get a trash can with a pedal-operated lid or keep the trash can behind closed doors. Once again, owners will likely not be perfect in denying their dog access to tissues, so if your dog outsmarts you and succeeds in grabbing a tissue, let him have it. There is nothing intrinsically appealing to a dog about bathroom tissue — stealing it is simply an attention-getting behavior. This is a case that calls for conscientious attention withdrawal: ignore him. Let him chew away to his heart's content. It won't taste good, and, if it doesn't result in the desired hoopla, he'll conclude that eating tissue is not worth the time or trouble.

The same philosophy applies to dealing with most stolen objects, but there are exceptions to the "let the dog have it" rule. If the stolen object is your favorite pair of shoes and your dog starts chewing on them, some remedial action is mandated. Also, if the stolen object is unsafe for the dog, intervention is necessary. Typical examples of unsafe objects that you would need to retrieve from a dog might include your glasses, your remote control, and your wallet, which contains your credit cards (if he chews them up and swallows them, you won't be able to pay the vet bills for the surgery that he may need later). In such instances, diversion, not coercion, is the name of the game. Several different strategies can be implemented. One, for more territorial dogs, is to go to the front door and ring the doorbell to greet an imaginary visitor. Another is to get the dog's leash and ask him if he wants to go for a walk. A third possibility is to go to a location where the dog knows very special food treats are kept and fiddle around there for a while, making your dog fully aware of what you're doing. One thing you *should not* do is offer your dog a treat in exchange for the stolen object, as this bribery will only encourage more stealing. Once you have diverted your dog away from the object he is guarding, you can attach his lead, give him an instruction, like "Sit," and reward him with a food treat, petting, or praise if he obeys. If you have chosen to distract him by showing him his lead, you should take him for a brief walk; otherwise he'll see that he was duped; you might be able to trick him once, but don't expect him to fall for the leash ploy in the future. Once things are under control, however you have managed it, you can retrieve the stolen object. You may have to rotate diversions or even invent new ones if your dog wises up to your ruses. A client of mine used the doorbell-ringing technique very successfully to get her dog, Gipper, out of her bedroom. If allowed to take up residence on her bed, her dog would lie there and growl at her — space guarding, if you like. On my advice, she would go downstairs and ring the doorbell, whereupon Gipper would immediately leap up, barking, and run down the stairs to the door to see who had arrived. Meanwhile, the owner would sneak upstairs and shut the bedroom door. All worked well for a couple of weeks, until one day, she heard Gipper barking frantically at the door. She ran downstairs from the bedroom to see who'd arrived, and Gipper shot back upstairs to commandeer his favorite spot. There was no one at the door.

Postural interventions, such as petting a dog on the head or hugging, should also be avoided if they are annoying or aggravating to a dog. Remember when we were little how we didn't like it when Grandma came along and pinched our cheeks and ruffled our hair? That's how dogs must feel when people walk up to them uninvited and start patting them on top of the head or hugging them. Sure, they appreciate being petted by the right person at the right time and in the right way, but, if these conditions aren't met, dogs either have to tolerate unwanted petting or object in the only way they know how. If your dog growls when you pet him on top of his head, it's best not to do it. He is trying to tell you something. At the very least, you should modify the way that you're petting him so that he enjoys the interaction. You could, for example, switch from petting him on the head to stroking him along the side of his face in the same direction that his hair grows. Alternatively, you could scratch his chest. A lot of dogs prefer to be scratched on the chest than petted on top of the head. Petting a dog on the head, or any other intervention from above, may be perceived as a threat or challenge — not exactly what you intend. Learn from your mistakes and modify *your* behavior to keep things copacetic.

Personal space is a very personal thing. You can think about it as an invisible bubble around the dog's head and neck — like an imaginary space helmet. Some dogs have other sensitive zones, too. If you invade a dog's personal space by an up-close stare, grabbing his collar or scruff, or handling his feet, he may let you know he's unhappy about what you are doing. We all know how uncomfortable we feel when people come within our personal space. "Close talkers" stand three inches away and keep encroaching as you try to back away. We don't appreciate these personal-zone infractions and neither do dogs. The long and short of it — we shouldn't be subjecting our dogs to things they don't appreciate for our pleasure. One client of mine was bitten in the face by her German shepherd, Thor, three times while petting and kissing him. I told her she would have to curtail this particular interaction, but she said she could not help herself. I was dumbstruck. Petting, kissing, and hugging are not always appreciated by dogs, and owners should respect that wish. It doesn't make sense to pet a dog that doesn't want to be petted, kiss a dog that doesn't want to be kissed, or hug a dog that doesn't want to be hugged. Some of these gestures are interpreted by the dog as affronts and may cause him to recoil or rebel. If you want to test the water before imposing yourself on a dog, ask him to do something first (see next section). Then he can choose to obey, which is like saying *okay*, or not, which might mean *not right now*.

Another rude intervention that we can inflict on our dogs is to physically wake them up or disturb them when they're resting. While some long-suffering dogs may not object to being bothered, others certainly do. Just imagine if *you* were fast asleep and someone came up and poked you in the ribs. "Cut it out," you might say. "I'm trying to get some rest." Well, dogs can't speak for themselves, but what they can do is growl their objections, and, if you persist in your incursions, their warnings may become more severe. But you may have been instructed by an ill-informed trainer to force your dog to tolerate your waking him up, so you continue with your unwelcome advances. Your dog, believing you to be a slow learner, becomes progressively more anxious, even hesitant about resting when you're around, because he knows you're not to be trusted. Shakespeare penned the line "Let sleeping dogs lie" back in the sixteenth century. The Bard was right. A few centuries earlier Geoffrey Chaucer wrote, "It is naught good a sleeping hound to wake." Well, it's about time we heeded these ancient warnings. This is not to say you have to pussyfoot around your dog when he's sleeping. You don't. Just don't go up to your dog and shake him to wake him. No more shake and wake. If you're leaving for a car trip and your dog's asleep on his bed, you can say, from across the room, "Do you want to come for a ride?" He might open one bleary eye, decide whether he wants to come or not, and either join you or go back to sleep. Now you're communicating... and without conflict. In the event that you *have* to disturb a crotchety, recumbent dog, make sure he's fully alert before approaching him. Coax him toward you with some special favor before attaching his lead; and let him know that something good is about to happen. Act cheerfully as you attach the lead. Now, with him on lead and fully under control, you can lead him away from his resting area with relative impunity.

Another potential area of conflict, admonishments or physical punishment, should be appreciated from the dog's point of view. If *you've* just made a mistake by petting your dog on the top of his head while he's eating, holding his paw while he's trying to walk around, or prodding him awake while he's trying to sleep, and he growls, you should not start pointing, yelling, or hitting him with a newspaper or your hand. I do not believe in entering into verbal or physical confrontations with dogs; the chances are you will lose the battle anyway. Aggressive reactions on your part will only escalate conflict and propagate mistrust. Instead, you should learn from the dog's response and alter the circumstances so as to avoid the confrontation in the future. That's using your noggin.

Most of the conflict situations referred to above will be exacerbated if the dog is in an elevated position, such as on a couch or bed, or if the owner is on the floor with the dog. As a rule, it is a good idea to keep all dogs that display owner-directed aggression off high places. That means off chairs, couches, and beds. It is okay to let a dog have one particular piece of dog furniture that he can lie on as long as all family members know that when the dog is in that particular place, they should leave him alone. There are two basic ways of keeping dogs off beds and furniture without inducing conflict. One is through training and the other involves booby-trapping (the use of a remote punisher). Of the two techniques, I prefer the former. As described in chapter 4, I have owners attach a long, lightweight, loopless training lead that the dog wears around the house. I instruct them that when they see their dog on off-limits furniture, they should pick up the end of the training lead and say the word "Off"— once only. If the dog obeys by getting off the furniture, he should be praised immediately and perhaps even given a food treat. If he doesn't obey, owners should exert steady, increasing tension on the lead until the dog topples off the furniture and winds up with four feet on the floor. "Good dog, thank you," should be the owner's immediate reaction, even though the event was assisted. If this approach is logistically difficult or ineffective, booby-traps can be contrived. One fairly well-known technique is to put upside-down mousetraps underneath some stiff wrapping paper on the piece of furniture in question, so that when the dog jumps onto it, he experiences something like landmines exploding under his feet. Another way is to string a piece of thread from one side of the couch to the other to create a tripwire effect and attach the thread to a towering pile of shake cans (empty soda cans with pennies inside) or to something else that makes a loud sound when it falls down. As the dog jumps onto the couch, he trips the wire, the cans come crashing to the floor, and, hopefully, the negative experience deters him from that location in the future. There are other ways to scare a dog off, too, some involving air horns and water balloons, but the important thing is that if you use any such aversive techniques, you should not be seen as the punisher. Rather, these deterrents should come out of left field and be attributed by the dog to the couch. That involves planning and stealth — but if such a scheme is well executed, it can be very effective.

If all these measures are adopted and a dog no longer has to worry about his owner's invasiveness — the hand in his food, being petted on top of the head, having his collar or scruff grabbed, or being disturbed while resting — there is no need for him to be "on guard" or aggressive. He can be confident that his environment is safe, and a self-assured dog is a candidate for positive learning.

2. Controlling Resources

Prerequisites and mindset

Your dog must be made to understand that all good things in life come only and obviously from you. Some dogs just don't grasp this inescapable fact because their owners don't send them the correct signals. Even a dog that is skulking around and showing aggression to all family members is actually dependent on them — he just doesn't know it. It is we humans who provide the roof that keeps the rain off a dog's head and protect him from the elements. It is we who go to work to earn the money to pay for heat in the winter, air conditioning in the summer, and provide food and entertainment. It is humans who give a dog access to the outside by opening doors and taking him for walks or rides in the car. It's humans who give him treats (that he may try to protect from us) and a bed or crate (that later he may guard with his life). The fact is, any dog, however irascible, however unheeding, and however badly behaved, would not survive long in a domestic setting if it wasn't for us. There would be no food for a start. As unpalatable as it may seem to some owners, it is sometimes necessary to communicate with dogs that all the good and necessary things in their environment do not arrive like manna from heaven but rather are supplied by us, their true leaders. This philosophy can go a long way toward increasing a dog's respect and trust, as well as ensuring that owners are able to control their dogs' behavior when the chips are down. To have it any other way would be like having the tail wag the dog. We have to be in charge — it is our responsibility.

In chapter 3 we discussed communication and how important it is for dogs to understand cues like "Sit," "Down," and "Come." Once a dog understands what these basic words mean, the leadership program can begin. In my experience, most dog owners believe that they have the basics of communication down, even when they don't.

"Oh, yes, he knows how to sit, he learned that very quickly in puppy-training classes," is most owners' response to a question about whether the dog understands the basic word cues.

My next question is, "How often does he sit when you prompt him to?"

"He obeys about 70 percent of the time," is a typical response. "He's better when I have a treat."

"He obeys when he wants to," I translate.

If you say a word like "Sit" to a dog, and you know he understands but fails to respond, it's an indication of lack of respect. Failure to respond should lead to some negative consequence; again, I don't mean yelling, hitting, or any other form of physical punishment. But you do need to follow through by, say, withdrawing your attention or withholding a resource. Ignoring a failed "Sit" command by continuing to interact with the dog or inadvertently rewarding him in some way informs him that sitting when asked is an option, something to be acted on only when he's in the right mood or if a valued reward is in the offing. The pop group the Fixx had a lyric that went, "Say what you mean, mean what you say, one thing leads to another." That's a good mantra for dog owners. Paraphrasing, if you don't say what you mean and mean what you say to a dog, one thing will lead to another — his not listening to you. Some wives complain that their husbands hear them but do not listen. As if to make the wives' point, one husband was heard to say, "My wife always says I listen but I don't hear." Busted. Well, we don't want dogs to be like that, especially at times when you really need them to comply quickly in the interests of safety or simply for your pleasure. You can't have a dog that sits only some of the time when you cue him to do so in a quiet environment and then expect him to follow your directions as he is bounding out of control around your visitors. There are no ifs, ands, or buts when it comes to this simple fact; dogs who don't listen simply don't respect their owners' authority.

Specific actions in controlling resources

How we demonstrate our control over a dog's resources is per-haps best illustrated by the way in which we provide his food. Food is like money to a dog and, as such, should be earned. Dom-inant-aggressive dogs especially need to learn that we control this valued resource. My grandmother used to say that whoever con-trols the purse strings (in a marriage) controls the house. Well, it's the same with dogs, except the resource is kibble. Once an owner has demonstrated control over this vital resource, the dog will better appreciate his position in the hierarchy. The trick is to make your dog work for all of his food, for every meal. He must realize that he must listen to you and follow directions, if he expects you to produce the goods. It is especially necessary to make this point with dogs who respond slowly to voice cues, who fail to follow directions, or who exhibit owner-directed aggres-sion. It is helpful for some other dogs, too, to let them know from the get-go that there are house rules. For owners of dogs who need a dose of this medicine, there are two things to bear in mind: First, don't feel sorry for your dog because he has to earn his food because, after all, you have to earn your living. There is no free lunch for any of us. If you stop going to work, your paycheck will stop arriving. What's good enough for you is good enough for your dog. Second, in terms of implementing the program, it's the details that count. Many people might think they are engaging in a "no free lunch" approach, when, in fact, they're giving it away.

One example of how not to do it is to have your dog sit and wait as you prepare his food, and then, when it's ready, you say *okay* and he comes over and starts to eat. People who engage this approach think that because their dog is sitting and they have issued a release word, they have instructed him in an authoritar-ian manner, but the dog may beg to differ. A dog sitting while you prepare the food is like a person sitting in a restaurant while a waiter goes back to the kitchen for the food. When the waiter puts the food down in front of you and says *Bon appétit!* (i.e., go for it), you chow down. The waiter is not exerting any control over you in this situation. But just imagine if the waiter approached your table with the food and said, "Get down on your knees or you don't eat," and you couldn't leave because the doors were locked. You might try to resist the waiter's demand, but as you got hungrier, your resolve would weaken and you would do what you've been told. Now who's in charge? The waiter, of course. I tell people I don't want them to be the first type of waiter, the one who simply serves up the food and tells you to go for it. I want them to be the second kind of waiter — one who must be obeyed. Remember the "Soup Nazi" from *Seinfeld*? That's what I'm talking about. To do this, first put the food in a bowl, go to wherever you feel like feeding your dog, and give a one-word command, either "Sit" or "Down." The dog must respond to your instruction, so if he is already sitting, tell him "Down." If he's already down, tell him "Sit." He must obey the one-word command, whatever it is, within, say, three seconds initially, in order to receive his food. After you've given the word, count *one Mississippi, two Mississippi, three Mississippi*. No response in that time means no food until the next mealtime twelve hours later. *Next!*

A lot of dogs in need of this correction for their disdainful attitude may take their own sweet time in responding. This is what I call dumb insolence. It is behavioral apathy, inertia, a resistance to follow directions. That's why we impose the three-second rule. But fair's fair; once the instruction is obeyed, the food goes down quickly and the dog is left undisturbed to eat. For dogs who fail the test, the whole procedure is repeated *by the same person* at the next mealtime. Dogs who know the cues "Sit" and "Down" but do not obey are simply refusing to do what you say — they're refusing to give in. I've had some tough dogs go three to five days without eating before doing what they were told, even though they knew precisely what their owner was instructing them to do. But they all succumb in the end. After that battle has been won, we stick to the three-second rule for about one week and then up the ante. The dog must now respond within two seconds, and it's his duty to find that out, not yours to make it work for him. And yes, you guessed it, by the third week we will be requiring one-second or immediate response. You say "Sit" and your dog's rear end should hit the deck and stay there. Your job is to put the food down immediately when that happens. Now, with an immediate response in place and the option of one of two commands, you have a dog who must listen and who must obey. Now that's attention . . . and respect. It's a good idea to extend this concept to food treats as well, so when you have anything that's tasty, a meal or a treat, your dog should have to work for it. If this method of providing victuals is enacted unwaveringly, formerly disrespectful dogs will grasp the concept that you are in charge of the vital resource of food and that you must therefore be in charge generally. It's a tough lesson but an important one. If you teach a young puppy to sit for all food and treats, you will never be disrespected in the first place, and the phrase "owner-directed aggression" or "dominance aggression" may never be a concern for you.

Physical affection is another resource subject to an owner's control. Petting can be an extremely powerful reward, and as such it can and should be earned. Petting is often an automatic response on the part of dog owners, thus some dogs take the action for granted. Owners often sit in my consulting room petting their dogs continuously. When I ask them, "Why are you doing that?" they shoot me a puzzled look. "What?" they ask. "Why are you petting him?" I say. "What did he do to deserve it?" "Nothing, I suppose," is the usual reply, and then, "Oh, I see what you mean," as the penny drops.

Instead of giving it away, petting, like food, should be meted out as deserved, as a result of a dog's actions. I don't mean that all dogs should have to earn petting all the time, but many need to learn that petting is something that can be provided or withheld at an owner's pleasure. Owners should not be like automatic vending machines, always there to supply the goods when their buttons are pressed. In giving bossy dogs everything they want, whenever they want, and not asking for anything in return, compliant owners create a situation where the dog is in charge; not a good behavioral strategy. So what should they do? How can they ration petting? Consider an owner, placidly sitting in a chair reading the newspaper, suddenly disrupted in this activity when his intrusive mutt nudges him with his wet nose, demanding to be petted. The owner, a good-natured person, interrupts his reading to pet his dog. Most times this is the incorrect response. It is better to ignore a pushy dog's initiative and create one of your own. If you need to, stand up and walk away and wait until the dog has given up on any efforts to solicit petting. This is the time to turn to the dog, say, "Come" or "Sit," and when the dog comes or sits, that is the time to pet him. Now we have clear communication going on between the two parties. The dog learns quickly that if he obeys a directive, something good will happen, in this case, petting.

When an owner initiates the activity, it's good for the dog as well. Sometimes an owner will seek to pet a dog who, for whatever reason, simply doesn't want the attention. In this case, the dog can simply refuse the advance. That's okay, if the owner respects the dog's wishes to be left alone. The dog has avoided an unwanted postural invasion (petting) and a potential conflict has been averted.

Toys are yet another valued resource, and many dogs have so many around so much of the time that they get bored with them. Some dogs practically have to pick their way across a room strewn with toys they may show little interest in. The best plan is to put the toys into a dog-proof box, drawer, or cupboard, and to rotate them so that each remains novel and interesting. But a novel and interesting toy, if sought by a dog, must be earned. Dogs learn very quickly where the toy drawer is located, and when you approach it, they will either ignore you — which means they're not interested at that time — or they will eagerly join you.

If a dog stands by the toy drawer, his eyes shining, tongue lolling, and tail wagging, you can be assured of his interest. In this case, open the door, produce what you perceive to be an interesting toy, and issue an instruction, like "Sit" or "Down." A marginally delayed or immediate response (according to the level of training) should be rewarded by immediately tendering the object, which the dog can play with for as long as he wants. He has earned that privilege. When he has finished playing with the toy, pick it up and put it back in the receptacle. When he wants the toy again, the whole procedure is repeated.

As far as playing with the dog is concerned, there are two things to remember. One is that rough games are never indicated for aggressive, willful, or unruly dogs. By rough games I mean tug of war, wrestling, slap boxing, or tickling. Competitive games encourage dogs to challenge your leadership, thereby potentially achieving a higher "rank" in the family; this could lead to trouble down the road. Again, I'm not saying that tug of war is inappropriate for all dogs at all times; there are some who might benefit from the increased confidence it instills. Appropriate games are fetch and hide-and-seek. In playing such games with your dog, you should be the one to both initiate and terminate the activity, to indicate that you are in control. If your dog finds a tennis ball lying around and you immediately fling it for him when he expectantly drops it at your feet, the dog has initiated the game. If he walks off after a few tosses of the ball and leaves you standing there, he has also terminated the game. This scenario will encourage the dog to see himself as *your* leader. Dominant dogs in a pack initiate all activities. *Woof, woof, woof* might mean to other dogs, "Let's all go down to the bottom of the hill." Pack members show their consent by following. *Woof, woof, woof* might next mean "Let's all go back to the den". . . and the other dogs, again, consent and follow. In the dogs' world, there are leaders and there are followers. And when it comes to your dog, as far as being the leader is concerned, you're it.

Regarding the rewarding game of fetch, the tennis ball, Frisbee, or whatever the fetched object may be should be in a place in your domain, a drawer or cabinet in the garage, for example, along with the dog's other toys. Playtime is determined by you as a reward for good behavior. To play, your dog must follow you outside and, when you throw the ball, must retrieve it and bring it back to you, allowing you to take the object gently from his mouth or dropping it at your feet. Any modification of your benign rules, like not returning the ball to you or not letting go when you try to take it out of his mouth, and the game is over — following an "Enough" command. Even if the dog is playing nicely and by your rules, as you see him tiring of the activity, exhort one last good repetition and then issue the "Enough" command. Then, with a smile on your face, return to the house and deposit the toy back in the cache of toys. You have now initiated and terminated the game at your discretion, as the dog's leader.

Bottom line: dogs must work for valued resources, whatever they may be. I sometimes advise owners to make a list of the six things their dog likes most and have the dog earn them instead of receiving them for free. Food should always be on the list. Some people include access to the yard as one such resource. This access is permitted by means of the owner opening the door — a concession for which the dog must now work. Other people include on the list car rides, back rubs, belly rubs, whatever the dog finds most pleasurable. On the list it goes. Implementing this program is not as tough as it may seem. It's more a mindset than anything else, a way of ensuring your dog's respect. In a manner of speaking, you are simply insisting that your dog says please before he gets what he wants.

Reaping the Rewards

If you have an unruly dog desperately in need of proper leadership and you implement the program outlined above, you have a

70–90 percent chance that your dog will be very much improved a couple of months after adopting the new approach. The improvement is maintained as long as some aspects of the program are kept in place, enough to remind the dog that you are in control. Dogs who previously growled or snapped over food or postural interventions may no longer show this aggressive behavior. First, you no longer give them any cause for aggression, and even if you do unwittingly trespass, you now have some indemnity — some behavioral cash in the bank. Second, dogs have more respect and will regard you in a different light. Dogs that previously wouldn't listen now pay attention and follow directions. And far from being miserable about the new order, they respond well to — and are grateful for — the structure and the leadership. Dogs, despite trying it on at times, don't *need* to be number one in their pack but do need to know where they stand. It is our job to make this fact clear to them. We *must* be our dogs' leaders because without our taking a leadership position, they become anxious and confused and make some really bad decisions. When we lead, they are happier, more self-assured, and considerably better behaved.

The end product of the leadership program is a confident, trusting, *well-adjusted* dog that can now engage in a mutually respectful relationship with his owners. Dogs trained by aversive methods may behave well when challenged because they fear the consequences, whereas dogs trained using the leadership approach are not intimidated by their owners or fearful of them. They will follow their owners' directions — not because they have to, but because they want to. One important point: those engaging in the leadership program will be able to signal their leadership to the family dog. This state of affairs decreases their likelihood of their being subjected to dismissive or aggressive behavior on the part of the dog. Anyone who has not established a leadership position over the dog — including neighborhood children, visiting relatives, and family friends — will not necessarily have this immunity

Dolly the Black Lab

Dolly was around two years old when her owner, a photographer for a local newspaper, spoke to me about her evolving bad behavior of growling at him when he was anywhere near her food bowl. This man could not understand why his dog regarded him as a threat to or rival for his food — which, after all, he supplied. The reason, of course, was that Dolly did not understand her owner's role in the provision of her food. My client was going to have to help Dolly understand that he was in charge of the food resource. First, I advised him to feed her in a place where she would not be disturbed, so that she could eat in peace, secure in the fact that her food supply was not threatened. Next, Dolly was going to have to earn every single meal by promptly responding to a command, like "Sit" or "Down." After a short hunger strike, Dolly began to comply, obeying a command as a precursor to receiving her food bowl. This became her new routine, and gradually she got the connection: her owner provided the food. Two months after the initiation of this highly focused mini-leadership program, Dolly's owner inadvertently walked by her more than once when she was eating. The growling did not occur. There was no further aggression toward him over the food bowl . . . ever. Naturally, I told him not to push it — to continue to give Dolly her space during feeding — but it was nice to know that if he got a little too close for any reason, he wouldn't be on the receiving end of a growl (or worse). The "fix" was achieved with no yelling, no hitting, and no chain jerking — and had lasting effects.

when in contact with the dog. So be ever mindful that your dog's good behavior stems from his relationship with you, his leader or leaders. Exercise supervision when necessary.

Ideally, the leadership program should be implemented by the whole family, at least all those who are capable of participating in it. Exceptions include children under six years old, who are unlikely to be able to convince a dog of their authority, elderly people who simply don't want to be bothered with Fido's training, and anyone with a physical or mental impairment preventing them from participating. The good news is that very young and very old people do not usually present a challenge for dominant dogs and are thus to some extent immune to their aggressive advances. Children between, say, one and six years old, if not properly supervised around dogs, can unwittingly press a dog's buttons (pull on his tail, for example), provoking an aggressive response. Proper supervision of children around dogs is mandatory. Children of six years of age or older are capable of being taught how to participate in the leadership program and are often thrilled at the results. Finally, they find there's someone below them on the totem pole . . . and that's how it should be. After all, despite what a dog may think he wants, his proper position in the family unit is at the bottom of the pack.

6

The Fearful Dog

Managing Fear — A Functional and Humane Necessity

> The psychological condition of fear is divorced from
> any concrete and true immediate danger.
> — Eckhart Tolle

Fearfulness is the most common cause underlying behavior problems in dogs. Whether a dog is aggressive toward
strangers, shy around visitors, panics when alone, or is terrified of
thunderstorms, fear is at the root of the problem. An owner's
masterly control can go a long way toward assuaging a dog's fear
of strangers, other dogs, sounds, and certain situations. But strong
leadership alone may be insufficient to deal with extreme irra-
tional fears. These must be carefully thought through before any
behavioral or medical management program is embarked on.
Fears may arise because of a dog's nature — genetic influences
make some dogs prone to excessive fearfulness. More commonly,
fears arise from adverse experiences in early life — failure of proper
socialization and/or exposure to terrifying events or circumstances during a crucial period of early development. Inadequate
and improper socialization as occurs, for example, in puppy mills
is the crime of the century in the dog world. It is important for
owners to understand that fear of real danger is normal and has

a protective function, though one can have too much of a good thing. Functional, protective fear is not only helpful but necessary. Having no fear — like experiencing no pain — allows the subject, unless closely supervised, to get into serious trouble. But when canine fears become excessive to the point that they cause a disruption in normal daily life, some remedial action is warranted.

The most fundamental treatment for fear — which I will describe in more detail later — is desensitization. Basically, desensitization is a process by which a feared person, animal, thing, or circumstance is presented incrementally so that a fearful response is not triggered. During the process the dog is fully aware that the feared stimulus is present, but the level of exposure is insufficient to generate full-blown fear. It's the behavioral equivalent of getting into a cold swimming pool very gradually; the body adjusts to the temperature so that full immersion becomes less uncomfortable. For owners to be able to desensitize their dog to a previously fearful stimulus, the stimulus must be controllable so that it can be presented incrementally and in a nonthreatening way. Also, during the whole desensitization process, the dog must be controlled closely and protected from being exposed to the full brunt of the feared stimulus. Sometimes the distance between the dog and the feared stimulus is used to reduce the level of threat. A feared person might be presented to the dog at a distance of, say, fifty yards, then, if all is well, at forty yards, and so on until the two parties are in close proximity without the dog's evidencing fear. In the case of noise phobia, it is volume that is manipulated. You make a recording of the feared sound so that it can be played to the

Example of Counterconditioning

Fear response: DOORBELL = STRANGER ENTERS = NEGATIVE ASSOCIATION (FEAR).

Counterconditioning: DOORBELL = HOTDOG FROM STRANGER = POSITIVE ASSOCIATION (APPETITIVE RESPONSE).

dog first at low and then gradually increasing volumes. Desensitization is usually used along with counterconditioning. Counterconditioning (literally, opposite conditioning) involves converting a previously fearful situation into one that is associated with pleasure — in other words, the complete opposite. Delicious food is often used to achieve the turnaround.

Dogs without a genetic tendency to fear who are raised properly, kept out of harm's way as youngsters, and are properly cared for have no cause to become overly fearful — and they generally don't. Conversely, dogs prone to fearfulness who are improperly socialized and exposed to early psychological trauma become the most fearful. These dogs are destined to drift into what I refer to as the Bermuda Triangle of fear — a hypothetical fear zone from which there is little chance of complete escape. Hybrid situations also exist: potentially fearful dogs raised optimally, genetically

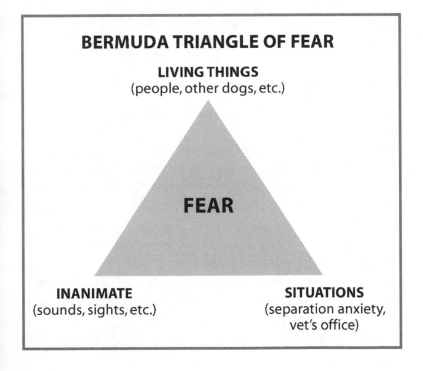

BERMUDA TRIANGLE OF FEAR

LIVING THINGS
(people, other dogs, etc.)

FEAR

INANIMATE
(sounds, sights, etc.)

SITUATIONS
(separation anxiety,
vet's office)

normal dogs exposed to suboptimal or oppressive early life experiences, and various shades of gray in between. The Bermuda Triangle is aptly named because it has three points of reference:

1. Fear of animate cues (creatures of the same or different species, including humans)
2. Fear of inanimate cues, most commonly sounds but also sights, smells, or even touch
3. Situational fears, like being left alone (separation anxiety), fear of the vet's office, or fear of riding in the car

The underlying factor in the development of any and all of these apparently diverse fear-based conditions is — for whatever reason — a fearful disposition. Many fearful dogs have more than one fear — two is almost the rule. Certain fears tend to occur together; for example, 40 percent of dogs with storm phobia also have separation anxiety. Some dogs have a "full house" of fears, having all three types of fear simultaneously. I refer to these dogs as having generalized or "global" fear.

Genetic Factors

There is a line of inbred pointers, formerly kept at the National Institute of Mental Health but now being studied at the University of Pennsylvania, that exhibit extreme, abnormal fearfulness with respect to certain stimuli. Note that pointers were originally bred to freeze in position and "point" toward game. Also note that freezing — along with "fight," "flight," and hugging walls — is one of the possible reactions of animals to a fear-inducing stimulus. This may explain why it is a line of pointers and not some other breed manifesting this extreme form of genetically induced fearfulness. Some of the affected dogs — but not all — can be retrained to some extent using behavior-modification techniques, but none ever becomes truly confident.

Another breed that seems genetically predisposed to anxiety

or fearfulness is the German shepherd. This trait may have arisen as a result of genetic manipulation of the evolving breed to produce dogs exhibiting "failure to commit"— to biting sheep, that is. Everyone knows what happens to sheepdogs who maul or kill sheep; they are "put down" for their crime, thus artificially selecting for hesitation, apprehension, and balking. Almost every German shepherd I have ever seen in our behavior clinic has a condition related to anxiety or fearfulness. They present with fear aggression, fear-based territorial behavior, thunderstorm phobia, noise phobia, separation anxiety, and compulsive licking — all of which are fear- or anxiety-based behaviors. In one study we conducted, 50 percent of all dogs with storm phobia were either herding breeds or herding breed crosses. That seems to say something about the genetic makeup of many of the breeds in this breed group.

But it's not just pointers and a few herding breeds in which a genetic basis of fearful behavior is apparent. Any breed — perhaps some more than others — may have genetically based fearfulness *in certain breed lines.* So when selecting the "best fit" dog for you and your family, make sure you ask the breeder about any family predisposition toward skittishness in the line before you commit to buying a pup — unless you're up for a challenge. Also note that it's possible to obtain an educated assessment of a dog's confidence level; pups and adult dogs can be tested for fearfulness before you acquire them — but you need to find an experienced trainer or behaviorist to conduct the testing.

Nature vs. Nurture in the Generation of Fearfulness

For owners of adult dogs, trying to understand why their pet became anxious or fearful in the first place may seem like a futile exercise. But for reasons that I will explain, I always try to find out whether nature or nurture (especially early life experiences) is the most influential factor promoting a dog's skittishness. If nature is the driving force, then neutering should be performed to prevent transmission of this genetic trait to scores of offspring down the line. A strong genetic predisposition to fearfulness also makes the problem harder to treat because genetic makeup is difficult to override and, even after retraining, dogs tend to gravitate back to their old ways. However, most anxious and fearful behaviors are homegrown; the result of suboptimal rearing practices as epitomized by the puppy mill/pet store scenario. Raise a pup like a battery hen, with only his mom and littermates for company during the first few formative weeks, and important windows of learning opportunity are missed. The critical (aka "sensitive") period of learning occurs during the first twelve weeks of a pup's life. Poor treatment at this stage causes Bermuda Triangle–style damage that is hard to reverse. If a pup is not exposed to a variety of benign strangers during this period, he will never be comfortable around strangers; and if not exposed to various real-life events and circumstances during the sensitive period, may develop other fears and phobias that owners will later have to address.

"But she has papers and comes from a long line of champions," frustrated owners of fearful dogs sometimes say to me.

"So does royalty," I typically retort.

It is the breeder's responsibility to socialize his or her pups, but too often socialization goes by the wayside. Some are too busy or simply unwilling to engage in this time-consuming activity, whereas others just plain do not understand its significance or what it involves.

"But we do socialize our pups," one breeder told me. "My husband and I spend ten minutes each day with the pups for that very purpose."

"That's handling, not socialization," I replied.

Finally, there's the so-called breeder who is simply out to make money and is running a puppy mill. Say no more . . .

Again, it's very unlikely that a dog with no family history of

The Socialization of Puppies

Early socialization is best accomplished by ongoing benign exposure to as many people and other dogs as humanly possible during the critical period of learning (three–twelve weeks of age). If the environment does not naturally avail the pup a variety of possibilities for interaction, you will have to create opportunities for such exposure by other means. Introducing the pup to as many people as possible in this case must become an active process rather than a passive one. One of the ways that this can be accomplished is by means of "puppy parties" in which people are invited around to your home in small groups for the express purpose of socializing your pup. Puppies as young as three weeks of age should be passed around your circle of happy friends until they are quite comfortable. Each person in the circle should hold the pup for a while, cooing to him softly and gently petting him. The whole experience should be engineered to be as rewarding as possible for the pup. Hopefully the people have fun, too. Puppy parties should be ongoing, preferably being conducted two or three times weekly until the pup is twelve weeks old. Hats, umbrellas, uniforms, loud talking, and so on can be introduced to pups gradually over the course of the sessions so that they are not perceived as unusual and will be readily tolerated by the dog later in life.

fearfulness, raised in a home with a loving family, and frequently exposed to kindly visitors subsequently turns out to be fearful. There's always some reason why dogs develop fear — fear doesn't just happen. In trying to circumvent fearfulness it is always best to remember that perfection is hard to achieve. A tad of maladaptive fear— through an omission of some aspect of early exposure — is perhaps unavoidable. That's where understanding of the situation leading to that fear and proper management become so important to ensure that any fear a dog shows lessens rather than intensifies over time.

Fear of Living Things

Some dogs are skittish or frankly fearful to the point of displaying "fear aggression" toward other dogs or people. Others are fearful of horses or flying insects. Species-specific fear arises from lack of socialization or from specific, unfortunate fear-inducing events, especially ones that occur at a tender age. Fear of other dogs often manifests as aggression to all unfamiliar dogs but may also take the form of a generalized fear of dogs of a particular size or body type. Ditto fear of people, which is often targeted at particular types of strangers, frequently men and children. Sometimes fearfulness is directed toward strangers with certain characteristics — beards, work boots, or distinguishing headgear. But clearly dogs are not born fearful of men with beards, big boots, or baseball caps. They become fearful because of lack of exposure or some negative experience when young. Children often bear the brunt of the dog's suspicion, and, when they do, boy children are the ones most frequently mistrusted. One explanation for this is that males, whether men or their younger counterparts, tend to be more aggressive than females. Horses kick and some insects sting, so it's not hard to figure out why either might strike terror into the heart of a previously sensitized dog. It's a terror that stems from negative experience — a déjà vu kind of thing. If fearfulness is in a dog's nature, the manifestations of that fear are personalized according to his experience.

The response of a fearful dog ranges from simply avoiding what he is frightened of (running away, hiding) to aggressively repelling borders (fear aggression). There's also the middle ground of appeasement, particularly in young puppies. Dogs are wired to display deferent gestures when the need arises. These gestures include squatting, rolling over, and urinating (as well as an assortment of facial expressions, including the submissive grin). "I bow to you, oh great one — please don't hurt me," is the message sent. Sometimes discretion is the better part of valor — and dogs know it. Submissive urination by a pup — sometimes lit-

Beware of Brandy

One dog, called Brandy, that my former resident, Dr. Jean DeNapoli, saw a few years back was, atypically, frightened of and aggressive toward women, according to Brandy's owner. Now Jean is a pretty straight-shooting, no-nonsense type of person who is really good with dogs. Brandy sat calmly throughout the whole consultation until right at the end. Jean had to leave the room to take some papers to the pharmacy, leaving my Japanese postdoc, Dr. Yoshiko Uchida, the only woman stranger in the room. Brandy took advantage of her slight trepidation and seized the moment. He leapt toward her face with his mouth wide open. Dr. Uchida defended herself with her forearm and was severely bitten in the hand, requiring medical treatment. We had all learned a vital lesson: Believe what people tell you and take no chances.

erally peeing on your shoes — signifies the dog's fearful nature. For submissive urination to occur, you have to have an underconfident dog on your hands. In this situation, a plethora of other fearful behaviors, including fear aggression, may develop at a later time unless proper steps are taken.

Prevention is better than cure when it comes to fear of living things, though sometimes that knowledge comes after the fact when adopting from less than ideal circumstances. But what can a poor owner do to accommodate their disturbed dog's fear and dread? Should the fear be indulged or punished? Should an owner sympathize or chastise? Neither of the above, is the correct answer. First, concerned owners should engage the lessons of earlier chapters: ensure that the dog has plenty of exercise ("a tired dog is a good dog"), a suitable diet (not a high-performance ration), and that the channels of communication are wide open. Think about investing in a head halter to facilitate proper control of the dog in difficult situations (see chapter 4). Finally, there's desensitization.

What Not to Do

1. Do not take a dog that is frightened of other dogs to a training center to meet a whole slew of other dogs all at once. Whatever anyone might try to tell you, that will make matters worse.
2. Do not take a dog that is fearful of children to a Little League game to "desensitize" him to children.
3. Do not take a dog that is frightened of strangers to the parking lot of a shopping mall to be exposed to hundreds of people in one afternoon. Bad idea.
4. Do not coddle or overly sympathize with a dog when he exhibits inappropriate fear; this reinforces that his response is okay when it's not.

Desensitization

The first rule of desensitization is not to expose the dog to whatever he fears, except as part of a carefully planned and structured desensitization program. In other words, keep the dog away from what he fears, whether other dogs or strangers. Of course, this is rarely entirely practical, but it is something to strive toward. If you see a fear-inducing situation on the horizon, do not go into consolation or sympathy mode. That will only assure the dog that there's trouble afoot or he will scan for it. It's also a bad idea to tense up on the lead — unless it is attached to a head halter — as this will telegraph your apprehension to your dog. Instead, act cool, calm, and collected. "Let's go," you might exhort your dog, as you stride off in a direction away from the offending dog or person. Then praise the response you have just insisted upon. Your dog will come to view you as his protector and will relax in the confidence of knowing that you will take charge. If you don't take charge of the situation, your dog may feel that he needs to look out for himself, and that's bad news.

The second rule of desensitization is that both ends of the

equation — for example, your dog and the other dog — are under control and are nonthreatening. To set up dog-to-dog desensitization exercises, speak to another dog owner about lending his well-behaved dog and his time to your cause. Arrange to meet in a park (or some other neutral territory) and have one of the two dogs positioned in a sit-stay or down-stay under the masterly control of his leader (that would be you or your acquaintance). The other dog is then promenaded around in wide but ever decreasing circles with a radius large enough to avoid a meltdown. Both dogs should be paying attention to their handler, not the other dog. Praise and reward each dog for remaining calm and following directions. Then try switching the dogs' roles. The dog in the middle can become the one who is led around in a circle. If things are going well, the radius of the circles can be decreased so that the dogs get progressively closer to each other. It may be that you can get within only six feet the first day, but there's always tomorrow. Never force the issue. If your dog balks at any point, go back to a "safe" distance and finish the session on a good note.

You may be lucky. The two dogs may learn to tolerate each other side by side in the park on the very first day — or acceptance may take longer. Be satisfied with any progress, and be prepared to repeat the exercise as many times as necessary to achieve harmony between the pair. Then engage the services of several other dog owners — one at a time — in hopes that your dog eventually generalizes his learning and eventually accepts most of his fellow kind. Once again, perfection is an unrealistic goal, but in time you can make huge strides toward your dog's improved tolerance of other dogs.

Training moves along more quickly and effectively if you offer some pleasurable reward to mark increments of progress. The reward could be in the form of a favorite food, a tennis ball, or a Frisbee. Whatever your dog's heart desires works best. Switching a dog's normal response — from fearful behavior at any level of exposure to the feared entity to excitement about or anticipation of fun or food — is counterconditioning. Having the dog sit and stay instead of lunging and barking is also a form of counterconditioning. Counterconditioning and desensitization (CCD) are techniques that are usually performed simultaneously.

Desensitization is conducted in a similar manner when fear of strangers is the issue. Again, the correct approach is *one person at a time*, not group therapy. Keep your fearful dog far from the madding crowd. Do not seek out crowded places to "desensitize" your dog. But it is unrealistic to think that you should keep all visitors away from your home, so you will have to use your discretion. If the number of visitors is small (say, one or two) and they are relatively nonthreatening and compliant, you could take advantage of the situation by making a training exercise for your dog. Alternatively, you can orchestrate such sessions with selected individuals (see below). If several people are coming over at one time, the experience could be overwhelming for your dog, as well as difficult to control. In this situation it may be necessary to protect your dog from what I call "visitor overload." This is especially important during large get-togethers, like Super Bowl parties or Fourth of July gatherings. Create a secured area at such times, with food, water, a bed, and toys, or leave him at a friend's house for the day. He will not learn anything positive from this avoidance approach, but at least people will be safe and his fear of people will not increase. With your dog's challenges minimized, you are now in a position to begin the reeducation process.

When conducting planned desensitizing exercises, ask a relatively nonthreatening (from your dog's perspective) person who is comfortable around dogs to assist you in the retraining program. Do not start out with someone who is scared of dogs or pushes the dog's buttons (the UPS man, for example). With your dog secured on lead (preferably using a head halter rather than a flat collar for fear-aggressive dogs), fully orchestrate and control the meeting and greeting of the "stranger" at the door. Have the stranger ring the doorbell. Control your dog. Bring him to the door on leash, have him sit and calm down. Open the door. Once again, if necessary, control your dog. Ask the visitor to step inside the house. Control your dog. Say something to the visitor like, "I would like you to meet my dog," as you hand the visitor a delicious food treat to drop on the floor for your dog. Make sure the person does not come on too strong. A fearful dog will not like a person who stares at him, reaches toward him (trespasses into his "personal space"), offers a clenched fist (to sniff), tries to pet him, addresses him directly, or walks straight at him. All these actions can be perceived by the dog as threatening — assaults on personal space. Instead, the visitor should simply toss the food treat onto the floor in front of the dog and then stand quietly. If the dog shows interest in the treat, that is good. (An interest in food and fearfulness are incompatible states.) If not, simply ask the stranger to come in, walk your dog around in a curved path, ignoring him, and then sit down on a chair (a much less scary posture for the dog). The visitor should never look directly at your dog and should refrain from any attempts to befriend him. Your job is to confidently take your dog to where you will be sitting and have him sit or lie down next to you on a blanket (an ordinary blanket that you reserve for this particular training that will come to be viewed by the dog as a safe haven). If your dog warms up to the stranger, you might allow him to approach the visitor — who can then shell out more delicious food treats, sliding them across the floor in the dog's general direction. You may need a long (ten-foot) loopless training lead to allow your dog to approach the stranger yet remain under your control. Always hang on to your end of the lead. There is usually no danger to a person if the dog is not showing aggression and approaches the visitor at his own speed. Trying to rush things is a recipe for disaster and can set your dog back in his training. Be patient, be calm, and maintain control. Be extra wary when your visitor has to stand up and move around. Be prepared to step in authoritatively, though not punitively. In time, maybe after several visits, your dog will learn that the visitor is not a threat because nothing bad happens: in fact, quite the reverse — good things happen. It can take a while and several visits for the full realization to set in, but it will eventually happen and the result is a new friend for the dog — one new friend. This exercise should be repeated with other strangers to build your dog a cohort of new friends. In time, with patience and luck, the learning about people will generalize. The dog will start to see that not all people are threats; in fact, some are quite fun.

The limitation is that the learning curve is asymptotic (never reaches the 100 percent acceptance mark), and backsliding can occur if pleasurable encounters are not arranged on an ongoing basis. Sure, you can back off somewhat in the frequency of the supervised encounters, but you must organize some schedule of such visits if you want to maintain progress. Such an arduous program is not for everyone. Not many people wanted to be a dog trainer when they grew up. But CCD is the most humane and effective way of rehabilitating a fearful dog — whatever the fear. A similar approach can be taken to desensitizing a dog to his fear of horses or flying insects, though finding cooperative subjects can be a challenge.

For the shrinking violets and submissive urinators, as opposed to proactive, fear-aggressive dogs, a kid-gloves approach to rehabilitation is required. These dogs have very little or no confidence and should not be tethered and forced to endure a potentially unsettling experience. Rather, their rehabilitation begins behind the scenes with what I call a reverse-dominance program. Supersubmissive dogs should not have to work for food, should be *encouraged* to play tug of war, and should get free access to toys, petting, and other privileges. That's the only way to convince them that they don't have a big "L" — for loser — on their forehead. They can be and should be winners, if you play your cards right.

Fear of the Inanimate

The most common fear in the inanimate category is fear of sounds, often thunder or fireworks but also gunshots, sonic booms, blasting, wood stove pellets exploding, and so on. The origin of noise fear is often obscure, but sometimes a psychologically traumatic event involving noise is known to have initiated the problem. The dog's initial jarring experience can be thought to induce a kind of post-traumatic stress syndrome, in which the particular noise — or anything reminding the dog of it — causes panic and an avoidance reaction. Sometimes fear is triggered visually, such as by the sight of flashing lights, darkening skies, plastic bags, or rope. In most cases the explanation is that the visual fear is generated by association with some traumatic event. Fear of flashing lights and darkening skies is usually (but not always) secondary to thunderstorm phobia. Fear of rope arises when a dog has been tied or beaten with rope. Fear of microblinds developed in one dog I know of who was shot with a BB gun from a window after the blind was raised. (How's that for an unforgettable experience?) Some fears do not involve things heard or seen but things smelled. Cigarette smoke or alcohol on a person's breath can be the trigger. The underlying scenario is not hard to fathom. I had three dogs who were frightened of the smell of lamb cooking. My guess is that they burned their nose on the stove while investigating the delicious smell and never forgot the experience. Slippery floors can lead to splayed legs — and especially if you are a big dog with hip problems — that can be a really painful experience. The lesson learned is stay off shiny floors: they bite.

So how do you, the owner, cope with a dog who has developed fear of an inanimate source? Take a page out of the animate fear book, that's what. Desensitization is the name of the game in most of these scenarios. Remember the golden rules?

1. Eliminate or at least attenuate exposure to the fear-inducing stimulus.

2. Arrange to control the feared thing.

3. Expose the dog to the feared stimulus during structured sessions in which the level of exposure is gradually increased as tolerated

4. Optional but highly recommended, undertake simultaneous counterconditioning.

If sound phobia is primary and uncomplicated — for example, a dog is scared of the noise made by the garbage truck — desensitization can be highly successful. Using the latter example, the dog should be prevented from being exposed to the full brunt of the sound during retraining. This may be the trickiest aspect of the program as it involves coaxing the driver to participate in your scheme. Next, make a high-quality tape recording of the sound of the garbage truck in action. Now training can begin. Play the tape to the dog at very low volume — setting number one on the control — and have your dog under control nearby and doing fun things (e.g., positive training — eating food treats, playing with a tennis ball). If your dog appears fearful, try again at a lower volume or greater distance from the sound source. Once your dog can tolerate the sound of the garbage truck at volume setting one, increase to volume two, and so on. Eventually, he should be able to tolerate the sound at a level equal to what the real truck produces. Then, and only then, is it time to have the truck come by again — as you continue to work with the dog to keep his attention and instill him with confidence. The program, like other desensitization programs, is time-consuming but does work for anyone determined enough to see it through.

Not all sound fears are easily desensitized. Take thunderstorm phobia, for example, which is particularly refractory to desensitization for some reason. That intractability could be because storm phobia is a composite fear that develops to include other storm-associated signs. Think about it. During a storm there is thunder, lightning, darkening skies, wind noise, rain; and there are other invisible changes such as with respect to barometric pressure, static electric fields, and even ozone content of the atmosphere. Which one of these is the primary fear inducer? The likely culprit is the sound of thunder. There is no doubt that the sound of thunder is unsettling for many dogs and is probably the primary cause of storm phobia for many. But all the other components of the storm that can be appreciated by storm-sensitive dogs are, to a greater or lesser extent, also involved in this complex phobia. That's why storm phobia is so hard to desensitize. There is nothing quite like a real storm, and the multifaceted challenge it presents is difficult to reproduce and control for desensitization purposes. Veterinary scientists have tried to desensitize dogs to storms in experimental settings designed to simulate real storms. They have equipped desensitization rooms with quad sound, strobe lights, and played lawn sprinklers on the windows (to simulate rain). Dogs can be desensitized with this experimental setting but quickly become distraught once more if exposed to the sound of thunder in a different room. That is, the learning does not transfer to a different situation. If that's the best the experts can do, what hope do regular mortals have of desensitizing their dogs to storms using tape-recorded sounds? Not much, I expect.

A new but equivocal development in the treatment of storm phobia has been the Storm Defender cape. This garment is supposedly like a Harry Potter invisibility cloak, rendering the dog "invisible" to static electricity. A conductive lining inside the cape makes it like a portable Faraday cage. I wrote about the static electricity theory of storm phobia in my first book, *The Dog Who Loved Too Much*. The theory was that some dogs became statically charged during storms (which I know to be true) and that they may get painful static shocks delivered to them (perhaps delivered to the tip of their sensitive nose) as they explore their environment — not an unreasonable hypothesis. This scenario would certainly explain why the onset of extreme thunderstorm phobia is often precipitous and why some storm-phobic dogs seek contact with electrically grounded locations, such as baths, sinks, Jacuzzis, and toilet tanks, during storms. It also explains how some dogs are able to sense storms before they are appreciable by us (though there may be other explanations for this apparent clairvoyance). Also, in support of this theory, the Storm Defender cape has produced some fairly impressive results for us when used as directed in storm-phobic dogs. More than half of the dogs become much less distraught during storms, with some owners reporting that their dog has been cured. The cape is simply fitted at the first sign of storm phobia — pacing, whining, attention-seeking, et cetera — and the owner is then instructed to pay the dog no attention (comforting, as I said earlier in the context of animate fears, can make matters worse). One dog in our study ran to where the cape was hanging and stared at it longingly when a storm was brewing until his owner got the message. Whether the jacket is working because it shields the dog from static or whether it acts as a secondary reinforcer of newfound confidence by taking owner input out of the equation (owners are instructed to apply the cape and then ignore the dog) was a mystery we set out to fathom. Early work seems to confirm the latter hypothesis as a dummy nonlined cape has produced almost identical results. The bottom line: however it works, it works!

Situational Fears

Epitomized by separation anxiety — a fear of being left alone — situational fears are fears that are precipitated by a particular set of circumstances. In the case of separation anxiety, the situation is either of being separated from an attachment figure or, in some cases, simply being left alone. Other situations that can engender fear in susceptible dogs include going to the vet's office, car travel, and going to dog shows. It's the whole experience that gives rise to the fear, not necessarily specific components of it alone. As with other fears and phobias, though genetic underpinning may be involved, there's usually a pretty good reason for the dog's trepidation. Separation anxiety arises in dogs whose early bonding has been interrupted and whose self-confidence has correspondingly been lost. Fear of going to the vet's stems from memories of the pain of injections or discomfort caused by other unwelcome interventions. Fear of riding in the car may be linked to motion sickness or some other a dysphoric (bad feeling) experience during a car ride. Fear of going to dog shows is a response to prior overwhelming circumstances or negative interactions at a show. Prevention being better than cure: Do not allow pups to become separated from attachment figures until they are old enough to cope; make car rides fun from the outset, and observe pups closely for signs of distress during car rides so that you can take action (like stopping the car and getting out for a fun break); make vet visits fun — employ special food treats; insist that your vet takes extra time, uses gentle restraint, and the smallest possible needles inserted by the least painful routes. Ease dogs gently into any performance roles — never force the issue. Go with the flow. Not all dogs are cut out for all things.

The best short-term solution to situational fears — and the first step on the road to recovery — is avoidance of circumstances that trigger them. For example, be cognizant of the early signs of separation anxiety (see box next page) and do whatever it takes to prevent reinforcement of the fear. If that means not leaving the dog alone for a while, so be it. Meanwhile, don't coddle your dog, because too much attention can make separation anxiety worse. Instead take positive action to build your dog's confidence and independence. When you are with your needy, anxious dog, try to teach him to be more independent — to be able to "stand on his own four feet" without your constant support. Discourage clingy behavior; don't be a human vending machine; engage a work-for-food program; schedule "apart time" when you are at home; gradually arrange for your dog to sleep at night where he will be during the day when you are away. If you are prone to lavish affection on your dog, restrain yourself in his best interests. His rehabilitation is not about your well-being — it's about his. You have to be firm to be kind.

If you must leave your dog with separation anxiety at home alone for a short while, try to make the experience a positive one for him. Feed him as you leave (and pick up any remaining food when you return). *Never* sympathize with him at the door — instead, act happy. Also, make sure he has several food puzzles around to occupy him when you have to leave (food-stuffed Kongs, Boomer balls, Buster Cubes do just fine). Chew toys are helpful, too, especially if made more enticing with the addition of a favorite odor, such as vanilla or anise. Enrich the environment in ways that suit your dog when you are away. Play tapes of household sounds; provide him a room with a view (that's like dog TV); have a comfortable crate available to him — with its door wide open; hide food treats around the place.

Signs of Separation Anxiety

- Dysfunctional history (mistreatment, broken bonds of early attachment, multiple owners, shelter history, etc.)
- Hyperattachment (shadowing/"Velcro" behavior)
- Predeparture anxiety
- Vocalization (whining, howling, barking) starting as the owner leaves
- Destructive behavior in an owner's absence
- Urination/defecation in the home when home alone
- Inappetance (lack of appetite) when alone
- Salivation (drooling) when alone
- Exuberant greeting on owner's return

(Answering yes to three or four of the above confirms the diagnosis.)

When you return, be low-key. Say hello by all means, and then head for the nearest chair; don't pay him any more attention until he is calm. The goal is to even out the emotional roller-coaster ride your dog takes upon your every departure and return.

If a dog shows signs of fearfulness or anxiety at the vet's office, implementation of a desensitization program is once again the best approach. Enlist your vet's support and cooperation, and put this plan into action at the first sign of your dog balking during a vet visit. Don't wait for the situation to deteriorate. Your vet should thank you for your perspicacity, energy, and proactive involvement because it will certainly make his job easier in the future. The first rule of desensitization: No vet visits except as part of the rehabilitation program. If your dog needs veterinary attention in the meantime, see if you can arrange a house call instead or have him sedated with a veterinary cocktail that includes a drug — like Valium — that renders the dog unmindful of the experience. The second rule is that you must be able to control both ends of the equation — you and your dog at one end and the staff at the vet's office at the other end. The veterinary office personnel must buy into what you are doing or it won't work. First, make sure your dog is trained to respond to voice cues while on lead. The "Sit," "Down," "Stay," "Relax" portfolio will do just fine. Then take your dog for a car ride to a neutral place — say, a park — and put him through his paces. Repeat this exercise as often as necessary until it becomes rote. After your dog has learned this routine, take him to the parking lot at your vet's office and go through the routine again. Start as far away from the office building as necessary for you to maintain control, making sure that you praise your dog warmly and give him food treats or some other reward (counterconditioning) for responding to your cues and remaining calm. If all goes well, repeat exercises progressively closer to the office building. That may be enough for the first day — and even the second, third, and fourth days. Once the car park routine is working well close to the vet's office, it's time for the next step. Bring your dog into the waiting room, where you have arranged for the office staff to meet and greet him, showering him with attention and food treats. Then go home. Repeat this exercise on a regular basis until your dog looks forward to his occasional vet office visits. Next, arrange for Dr. Scary to come into the picture — still in the waiting room, but without her white coat — and have her sit on a low seat (or on the floor) and bounce a tennis ball or slide food treats toward your dog until he accepts her as a nonthreatening, fun person. The two must become friends. Repeat this exercise as often as necessary until your dog remains upbeat and happy during these benign office visits. If your dog has a meltdown, you may have to go back a step or two in the program, but look at it as a temporary detour, not the end of the road. Finally, when your dog is perfectly happy sitting on your vet's examination table in her presence, some nonpainful veterinary manipulation can be performed, amid much praise and the frequent and timely presentation of delicious food treats.

Of course, at some point the "bad" things do have to happen, but they can be attenuated with your vet's cooperation. Ask her to take as much time as is needed to allow your dog to relax before proceeding with any uncomfortable interventions; have her use narrow-gauge needles for injection and use the least painful injection sites (injections given under the skin of the neck are usually least painful, those given intramuscularly — into the muscle of the thigh — are usually the most distressing). Gently rubbing or pinching the area of the intended injection site helps, too, by fatiguing neural pathways and acclimating the dog to pressure and pain sensation at the site. In addition, have the vet distract your dog at critical moments, causing him to look away from the proceedings, as his apprehension about what is about to happen only makes matters worse.

I have seen this desensitization approach work in dramatic fashion. Initially, the dog in question, Fletch, could not stand her vet — even though she made house calls — and had to be muzzled and manhandled for even the simplest procedure. Fletch went berserk when the vet's truck appeared at the end of the long driveway to the house. Luckily for Fletch, that vet left town and my wife, who is also a vet, took over. She took time to get to know Fletch before revealing her true identity. Sitting cross-legged in the drive, she engaged Fletch in her passion — chasing tennis balls — and became the dog's best friend before touching her with a needle. After that, Fletch was always overjoyed when she saw my wife's Toyota coming down the drive, knowing that it meant a game of fetch. It was only a matter of time before Fletch willingly accepted vaccinations for the first time in her life.

Desensitizing a dog to vet visits is a time-consuming process, and not everyone is up for it. The alternative is to use medications to facilitate veterinary interventions. Ask your vet to employ sedatives or anesthetics for procedures that are unavoidably painful — like irrigating a badly inflamed ear canal. Why cause your dog to suffer and build up even more negative associations with the vet's office? When my dentist asks me whether I would like local anesthetic for a short-lived but painful procedure, like tooth drilling, I always say, "Give me everything you've got." He obliges and I relax. The same concept can be employed for dogs.

The final fear I want to mention is that of car travel. Pay attention to your dog's behavior in the car. If he trembles, pants, or drools, he is not enjoying the ride. It's time to stop right there. No more car travel until you've figured out what is going on. Insisting that a dog just get used to it (again, the Joan Rivers "Grow up" approach) doesn't make much sense. Neither does flooding, which some trainers recommend; this involves exposing the dog to the feared stimulus continuously until the fear abates. I once heard of an owner whose trainer recommended she take her car-phobic dog for a car ride and just keep going until the dog settled down. She drove from Boston to northern Maine and back — many hours of travel. The dog never settled and was bug-eyed at the end of the seemingly never-ending rocky horror show. As you might imagine, his fear of car travel became considerably worse. That was a mistake. A much better and more humane approach is to think things through, go slowly and in stages, and address all possible concerns that your panicky pooch may have. First figure out when the problem first started. Was your dog always nervous in the car and did he always drool? If so, perhaps he has motion sickness. If this is the case, no amount of training will convince him he doesn't feel unwell. This problem can be addressed with veterinary help. Some vets give carsick dogs the sedative drug ace-promazine or an antihistamine, like Benadryl. Both have sedative and antiemetic properties and may work. I prefer Buspar — an antianxiety medication with anti–motion sickness and antiemetic properties. Recently a new drug, Cerenia, has been approved to treat motion sickness in dogs. That may be the best of all. What-ever works best is the way to go — but something must be done to alleviate a dog's distress before attempting desensitization. Per-haps your dog was okay in the car until one day when something bad happened — a car accident, maybe, or a sudden stop. One sound-phobic dog I treated developed a dread of car travel one day when the car wheel went over a cobbled strip at the side of the road and made a loud drumming noise. When fear of car travel has arisen suddenly as a result of some psychologically traumatic event, the gradual rehabilitation approach of desensitization is the best strategy. The stages are: no car rides for a while; feed the dog near the car for as many days as it takes to have him relaxed and comfortable in that location; feed the dog in the car until the same endpoint is reached; spend quality time with your dog in the car after he has eaten; start the car engine; rock the car back and forth in the driveway; roll the car out of the drive and back in; take the car for a short trip around the block; then try a slightly longer ride; progress from there. Each stage may take sev-eral days. As in the game of chutes and ladders, you may make good progress for a while and suffer a setback and have to go back a stage or two before resuming. But don't give up. As long as you are making overall progress, however slowly, you will achieve what you want — a dog that is more relaxed and not so scared in the car.

A Final Word about Fear

In psychiatry, fearful conditions are classified as anxiety disorders. Anxiety disorders include panic attacks (some dogs have something similar), agoraphobia (dogs develop that condition, too), specific phobias and social phobia (a dog may have either or both), obsessive-compulsive disorder (see chapter 7), post-traumatic stress disorder, acute stress disorder, generalized anxiety disorder, and anxiety resulting from a medical condition (chapter 9). So dogs and humans experience the same gamut of anxiety-related disorders. The treatments are similar, too. Whether you favor my Bermuda Triangle of fear classification or the psychiatric nomenclature is up to you. However you classify fears, you need to understand how to prevent them from developing in the first place and what treatments should be employed if they emerge. Don't follow hard-line trainers' supposedly no-nonsense, Joan Rivers–style advice or you will make your fearful dog's condition worse. To treat separation anxiety, hardliners recommend such techniques as confining the dog to an escape-proof, military, working dog crate or rushing back into the house and punishing him for exhibiting such "bratty" behavior. Such strong-arm tactics are inhumane and clearly not helpful to any dogs, let alone fearful ones. Fearful dogs should be retrained using the passive methods I have outlined above—with or without antianxiety medication for refractory cases (see chapter 10). With the correct knowledge and a modicum of patience, you can help your dog regain his confidence, and life can become much less stressful for both of you.

7

Environmental Enrichment

A Full and Meaningful Life — Supporting the Canine Agenda

The purpose of life is a life of purpose.
— Robert Byrne

There's no place like home. That's the way it should be for a dog, too, but sadly, it's not always the case. Take Billy the beagle, for example. Billy's natural instinct was to hunt with a master and other pack members and track down quarry, like wild hares, communicating his position en route by vocalizing to his master and the pack around him. But his actual life was quite different. He lived in a small house in Connecticut with a loving, hardworking family. Excursions outside the home were rare for him but included a short visit to the yard three or four times daily to "do his business" and a few car trips. In effect, he was a house pet and had to make the best of what he had there — rugs, furniture, TV, and a fleeting glance through the window at squirrels in the yard. To pass the time and exercise a few of his talents, he licked the rug and wooden furniture, lunged and barked at any animal he saw on TV, and barked at passersby and squirrels. These activities became his "job," but the results for his human family — general irritation and annoyance — brought them to me for help. How do we stop him from doing these things was the question of the day. First, we had to come up with alternative things for Billy to do along the lines of his genetic predisposition, to trump his invented "virtual" jobs. Trying to stop him from doing what he was doing without providing suitable alternatives would have been like attempting to bottle a genie. Part of the prescription was to take him for longer walks, give him more freedom, and let him see actual rabbits (rather than just the ones on *Animal Planet*). At home, another canine companion would have helped immensely, but this was not a solution to which these caring owners could commit. That left innovation, food puzzles, chew toys, and interactive games as the best alternatives for enrichment of his otherwise paltry indoor environment. Keep Billy's plight in mind as you read on.

When we plan our homes and lifestyles, most people naturally have their own agendas in mind, not their dogs'. When asked what makes our home an appealing place to be, people immediately think of (their) creature comforts. Some picture a comfortable recliner in front of a widescreen TV. Other peoples' thoughts drift to plush carpets, elegant decor, or electronic accoutrements, such as a personal computer, stereo system, and DVD player. None of these things, however, holds any intrinsic appeal for a dog. Even the four walls and closed doors of the house can be viewed by dogs as an unwelcome constraint. To understand what dogs want and need, you have to first know something about their biological needs and then imagine yourself in their shoes (or, rather, paws). With this empathic approach, you can strive to make your home and lifestyle as user-friendly as possible for your dog.

Think about it. You have removed your pet's need to hunt by supplying food. You have removed his romantic interests by neutering him. You have removed his social needs by depriving him of pack interests and competition. He can't even wander and explore his outside territory, let alone try to resolve his own problems — because there aren't any. You saw to that. So what's a poor dog to do? Channel his energies in unacceptable ways, that's what.

When a dog needs something to chase and the only things around are joggers, cyclists, and automobiles, what do you think the dog's going to do? Movement is trigger for predatory behavior, real or contrived, and all of those things move. Dogs with a high prey drive need predatory outlets. Owners must ensure that their dog's predatory instincts are discharged in ways other than chasing skateboarders or the neighbor's cat.

Dogs' social needs must also be provided for. As social animals, dogs need companionship — maybe more than some owners can provide if they have to spend long hours at work. Even if there are two or more dogs in the home, what are they to do all day while their owners are away? Read? I think not. The bottom line: you must keep a dog mentally occupied so that he does not find inappropriate ways of occupying himself. In chapter 8 I discuss some of the consequences of boredom and confinement in dogs. In this chapter I will discuss how to provide maximum entertainment for a dog within the constraints of a modern life, so that behavior problems stemming from inadequate behavioral outlets can be circumvented.

Predatory Outlets

Predatory behavior comprises two phases or components. First there is the so-called appetitive phase, which involves tracking, locating, stalking, and finally, pursuit of prey animals to the bitter end. Then comes the consummatory phase: actual eating of the prey. All phases of this instinctive behavior may be acted out as behavior problems if appropriate outlets are not provided. Some dogs wander off at the slightest opportunity in search of green pastures — so-called roaming. They may follow a trail or another dog to a place where good things happen — perhaps a slimy pond full of frogs or a landfill teeming with seagulls. For these dogs, the great outdoors holds more appeal than anything their uninitiated owners might have contrived for their pleasure indoors. Once outside, dogs with high prey drive may home in on humans and other animals, often chasing them and intimidating them or worse. Some nip or bite these ambulatory prey facsimiles in a manner nature intended for real prey, sometimes with serious consequences all around. Consummatory aspects of predatory behavior may also be expressed in such unacceptable (to owners) behavior as garbage eating, coprophagy (eating excrement), eating socks or undergarments, rock chewing, or pica — to the consternation of their owners. A dog's gotta chew what a dog's gotta chew.

As most pet dogs do not have a natural outlet for their predatory tendencies, how should their owners proceed? How can they best accommodate their dog's needs? First, let's consider the appetitive phase. Most dogs need to hunt something. If you don't like the idea of their hunting wild animals and perhaps catching them and killing them, you must find some other biologically appropriate outlet. For example, many dogs enjoy activities like tracking, lure coursing, flyball, earthdog trials, and herding. All these activities, which engage a dog's prey instinct in a controlled environment, are available throughout the United States; consult the yellow pages or the World Wide Web to find activities available in your area. A dog that is allowed to hunt a prey facsimile will be much less likely to chase bicycles or skateboarders, as he will be mentally and physically satiated. Sigmund Freud's and Konrad Lorenz's hydraulic model of behavioral drives makes sense to me. Simply put, the fluid level or pressure in the system builds up until it is either discharged naturally or overflows out of context. The concept of "vacuum behaviors"—those performed without apparent triggers — derives from this notion. Dogs with high prey drive and no outlet for this behavior sometimes chase shadows and lights or search for nonexistent prey beneath the floorboards. If prey outlets are not available, dogs invent them. It is far better for prey-driven dogs to vent their natural inclinations in a controlled and appropriate manner than to transfer what are irresistible urges to inappropriate prey facsimiles.

If organized activities to engage your dog's predatory tendencies are not for you, seek to arrange some predatory-type outlets at home. Throwing a tennis ball or Frisbee is a good way of discharging these types of energies in dogs so inclined. Some of my clients have set up agility courses in their backyards. While these may not specifically satisfy all aspects of predatory behavior, they do address some of the running, thinking, and navigating components of appetitive behavior and can provide a backyard version of the thrill of the chase.

Social Matters

Dogs are pack animals. They need companionship and meaningful social exchange. The worst-case scenario for a dog is to be raised alone and live alone. In this situation all kinds of bad things happen. One veterinary textbook describes the syndrome of "kennelitis," which affects dogs raised in complete isolation in kennels. The impact of such experience on dogs depends on the breed in question but can include slow learning, aggression, and hyperactivity. Monkeys raised in social isolation are unable to engage in necessary social play, leading some to enter into pseudo battles with their own limbs — the so-called floating limb syndrome, in which the monkey's hind foot, poised over his shoulder, is attacked as if it were an approaching adversary. I have seen a video of a dog doing much the same thing, attacking his own slowly advancing foot — which gave me a good idea of how that dog was raised. Dogs need the company of their own kind right from the get-go, for reasons of socialization and to learn proper dog etiquette. Dogs that are hand-raised (bottle-fed by humans) never learn how to signal defeat to other dogs or understand another dog's signals of surrender. Consequently, in a battle with another dog, dogs raised without a mother or littermates will keep attacking the other dog relentlessly, even if the other dog is submitting, since they will not have learned the signals for sub-

Breed-Specific Predatory Activities

Terriers: These dogs were originally bred for chasing and killing small varmints. They have a very high prey drive that must somehow be accommodated. The terrier's prey drive can be hard to satiate, short of an owner's releasing a few rats in the house each day. Earthdog trials are a good way to accomplish this. Dogs are released in the vicinity of an underground maze leading to a rat-scented rag (the "quarry"). They track the quarry by scent, and emerge victorious.

Hounds: Scent hounds are olfactorily driven. These dogs were bred to track by scent and are very good at it. They are happiest when they are allowed to do what comes naturally. Dogs can be trained to track anything by sense of smell. Typically they are put on a long line with the owner-handler walking behind as the dog searches. We trained a dog to track an endangered species of turtle so that the turtles could be relocated prior to a construction project that would have obliterated their habitat. Sight hounds were bred to track by sight. Lure coursing — chasing a mechanical lure along a track — à la greyhound racing — is just what these dogs need.

Herding: The activity of herding is derived from appetitive aspects of predatory behavior. A herding dog is never as happy as when he is herding a group of animals. Herding classes are available for dogs bred to control the movement of livestock. My former resident, Dr. Jean DeNapoli, has German shepherds and her own (small) herd of sheep. That may be a bit much for everyday owners. If herding classes are not up your alley, think about enrolling your dog in fly-ball. Even just having him retrieve tennis balls in your own backyard is a respectable outlet for predatory behavior.

continued on next page

mission; neither will they know how to deter a potential aggressor. Separation anxiety, depression, overeating, and destructive behaviors are other consequences of social deprivation. There's no escaping the fact that dogs need company throughout their lives and it's our job to provide it.

Breed-Specific Predatory Activities, *continued*

Sporting: All dogs of the sporting group have been selected for bird-dog tendencies that are directly related to predatory behavior (usually modified in some way). The ideal outlet for such a dog is hunting, by a hunter's side, out in the fields (or by the water in the case of the Irish water spaniels or Chesapeake Bay retrievers). Field trials, involving the hunting, flushing (or pointing), and retrieving of game, are available for dogs trained to do this type of work.

Nonsporting: This is a diverse group of dogs, but most will benefit from having some predatory outlet. A daily run around in a fenced-in yard, chasing anything that moves, may be all it takes for some of these guys.

Working: This breed is somewhat eclectic and not all members have a high prey drive, but some do. For example, Akitas were bred to hunt bears and Rottweilers to herd cattle. This means that their ancestors' prey drive was capitalized on and modified in the breeds' inception. Akitas can be trained to track. Rottweilers are sometimes used in Schutzhund, which has a tracking component.

Toys: Another mixed bag of characters. Toy terriers are still, well, terriers, and will benefit from any exercises that involve chasing or tracking. Italian greyhounds, small though they are, are sight hounds at heart, and appreciate organized chasing activity. For other members of this group, simply look to the activity they were bred for and try to approximate it in some way.

Almost all dogs enjoy human company; that's the basis of the human-animal bond. But we can't always be there for our dogs. Two parents both away at work all day with children at school for a good part of the day is a fairly common scenario these days. The dog is left alone. While some independent dogs may simply resign themselves to the situation and benignly while or sleep the hours away, many are not so self-sufficient and become bored, maybe even panicked, and unacceptable and destructive behaviors result. Seventeen percent of the nation's 70 million dogs suffer from separation anxiety (see chapter 6) — that's a whole lot of dogs! A good many more are unhappy about being left alone but do not "act out"; their owners may never know there's a problem. A video camera or "nanny cam" can be an invaluable aid in assessing your dog's ability to cope in your absence.

Being there all the time for your dog is impossible for most dog owners, and some must be away for extended periods of time. Does this mean that the latter people shouldn't have dogs? Not necessarily, because there are several ways to circumvent this problem. One solution is to have more than one dog. Another dog in the house is often not the answer to ongoing separation anxiety, but it could help prevent separation anxiety from developing in the first place. Be aware, though, that dogs can become so attached to their canine companions that they develop separation anxiety when separated from their buddies. When death of a close dog-friend causes the remaining dog to grieve, a new dog, a puppy perhaps, can sometimes help heal the wound. Another way around the loneliness problem is to drop your dog off at a place where he will have company in your absence. Some owners are fortunate enough to have a relative living nearby or a dog-loving friend willing to dog sit. If not, doggy daycare is often a good option, though it can be quite costly. Dogs who go to daycare come home tired and happy, only to sleep and dream of all the fun they've had during the day. Of course, the daycare operation must be a good one, one that caters to individual dogs' needs. Finding appropriate daycare for a dog may take as much research as choosing appropriate care for a child. No one size fits all.

Physical Provisions

Inside the house, dogs need a place to get away from it all — a retreat. They need their own sanctuary as surely as teenagers need a room of their own. Dogs, den dwellers at heart, do not need scads of space for their "home-within-a-home." A traditional crate *with the door left open* does just fine. Most dog owners think that crates are only good for housetraining puppies, and they dispense with them as soon as their pup is housetrained. Don't do that! Most dogs love their crates — at least, ones that have not had a punishing experience in one. It has been suggested — by dog psychologist Dr. Dennis Fetko — that if you want to be your dog's best friend you need to (1) take care of his health; (2) have him (or her) neutered (or spayed); (3) train him; and (4) provide him with a crate. That's not bad advice; and it's interesting that a crate is right up there in the big four. So why does a dog need a crate other than the fact that it approximates a den-like space? Here's why. You have the neighbor's children over, they are noisy and they all want to pet your dog. He is not obliging at the moment; for whatever reason, he wants to lie down in a place where he won't be disturbed. Guess where that place might be? Also, many dogs like to retire to their crates at night or when their owners are absent during the day. For a dog, there's something comforting about that snug space.

When supplying a crate for a dog, you should make sure that it provides the ultimate den-like experience. Size-wise, the Goldilocks rule applies: it should be just right, not too big, not too small. The rule of thumb is that a crate should be tall enough for the dog to stand up in without his head touching the top and long enough that his nose and rump do not touch either end, and it should be wide enough for him to turn around in easily. Preferably, the crate should be solid-sided; if it is made of wire, it should be draped with a blanket — for the dog's privacy and comfort. I always imagine a plain wire crate to be like a glass shower — too revealing for some tastes. Remember, in the wild, dens are not transparent. The floor of the crate should be lined with something comfortable, removable, and washable. Vinyl-covered foam rubber does just fine. Cushioned bumpers are a great idea, too; these permit a dog to loll up against the side in comfort without getting hatch-mark impressions in his coat.

It is best not to force a dog to use a crate if he is not used to one. Instead, try coaxing him by feeding him near and then just inside the crate. Also, make sure there are food treats hidden inside the crate, and perhaps a novel toy or two. Always praise a crate-shy dog when he goes in or near the crate, and never use a crate for punishment. Once a dog is comfortable in his crate, it should be possible to shut the door for short periods without causing him to panic. The period of time in which the door is closed can be incrementally increased, as long as the dog remains calm. This way, the crate becomes a tool for you as well as a retreat for him. When noisy children come around or there is some other environmental perturbation, he can be safely enclosed in his crate for his own comfort and protection.

When you can't be there for your dog, whether he is crated or not, make sure he has plenty to occupy him. If he can see out of a window, that's good. I think of window gazing as dog TV. You can make the program more interesting by feeding the squirrels or birds, unless your dog is so prey driven that the presence of small creatures outside causes him to bark or go berserk. The view of a busy street might entertain some dogs, but you may have to limit this experience if it provokes unacceptable behaviors such as excessive barking. If you can't arrange a view of the great outdoors, TV or videos have been shown to help dogs while away the hours. There are even videos especially made for dogs. Do they work? You have to make this determination on your own, by watching your dog's response. We know that dogs can see things on TV; we don't know what particular dogs find interesting. According to NASA research, monkeys prefer to watch movies of other monkeys and of jungle scenes, so videos of this ilk are prescribed for their entertainment. Extrapolating from this, dogs might prefer videos of other animals, especially other dogs, and outdoor scenes. This is the basis behind what is marketed for them — video of agility trials, dogs herding sheep, and scenes of dogs playing. If you don't want to spring the cash for a dog video, you can always rent the movie *Babe*. It's full of dogs and other wildlife. There is a catch, though. Some dogs' engagement in what's on TV may take on unacceptable forms (recall Billy the beagle). Some dogs become territorially aroused when they see other dogs in their living room. Even when (or especially when) their owners are there, they may charge at the screen, barking frenziedly, or run around to the back of the TV, seeking to rout out trespassers. For these dogs, TV may be more of a frustration than an interest. Some behaviorists recommend music for dogs who must be left alone. If dogs are like cows, they might prefer country music to heavy metal. Cows apparently produce more milk when country music is played in the milking parlor. Dog-Cat Radio is a gimmicky new radio station that plays sounds for pets and supposedly takes their tastes into account. I don't know whether dogs appreciate such efforts, but any soothing sounds might be better than the unsettling sound of silence. One behavioral researcher claims that the taped sounds of "dog laughter" — a kind of huffing noise dogs make when they play — has a calming effect on kenneled dogs. I'm not sure about the validity of this study, but if its conclusions are correct, behaviorists might one day recommend such tapes as a way of buoying the spirits of dogs who must be left alone.

Dogs should always have something safe to chew on, especially when left alone. Note that real bones and toys small enough to pose a choking hazard are unhealthful and even dangerous. Booda bones, Nyla bones, and Kongs are fine, but may not be attractive to some dogs. The appeal of these chewies can be greatly enhanced by adding food, food flavors, or certain scents. Booda bones and Nyla bones can be made more attractive by adding your dog's favorite taste or smell to them. Vanilla, anise, and hunting lure scents can really focus a dog's attention on a chewy. Nyla bones can be drilled out and soft food packed into the drill holes. Kongs can be stuffed with peanut butter or spray cheese and then frozen to ensure hours of interest and gastronomic pleasure. One of the more sophisticated food puzzles is the Talk To Me Laser Treat Ball. It appeals to all five senses — not just taste and smell. When the dog nudges this ball, it rolls around the floor, delivers a recorded message in the owner's voice, emits motion-activated lights (good for visually orientated dogs), and spills out enclosed treats.

Ambient odors have been employed to make dogs feel more at ease in their environment. Lavender and chamomile are supposed to have the same relaxing effect on dogs as they have on people. A study showed that dogs who became distraught during car rides were significantly less upset when lavender scent was aromatized in the air. Some veterinarians are now recommending the use of so-called dog-appeasing pheromones (DAP) to calm troubled dogs. I do not use this product, as none of my clients who have tried this form of aromatherapy have reported any beneficial effects. To me it seems a bit like "The Emperor's New Clothes."

Outside of the house, physical provisions are a different matter. The larger the accessible area, the more enjoyable the experience is for the dog. Just imagine a home with a dog door providing access to a neighboring forest brimming with interesting creatures, sights, sounds, and smells. A dog in this situation would probably think he had died and gone to heaven. But this degree of freedom poses serious risks. Bad things can happen in the great outdoors: dogs can get lost; have a run-in with a coyote, porcupine, or rabid raccoon; or stumble onto a busy highway. A large, fenced-in backyard is a much safer, but still relatively entertaining, outdoor environment. The fenced-in component means that the dog can roam freely around the yard investigating anything that moves or smells interesting. A dog door providing 12–7 access to the yard gives a dog more choice over his environment, more autonomy and self-sufficiency. More choice leads to a better quality of life and less stress. A caveat applies for very small dogs who may be plucked from the backyard by a hawk. Luckily, dogs that small may find enough entertainment within the relatively cavernous interior of the home. For dogs in general, access to a small fenced-in yard or outside run is better than no access at all. Outside, a dog can see and smell what's going on and can relive himself at will without risk of rebuke. He can also run around and generate all those feel-good brain chemicals we discussed in chapter 1.

Mental Needs

In discussing appropriate channeling of dogs' predatory instincts, I listed a few outdoor activities, such as flyball and lure coursing, which are invaluable in this respect. Such activities are also beneficial in other ways as they provide much-needed exercise and mental stimulation. For a dog, chasing things is not only occupational therapy, it's also fun. Dogs, like us, need gainful employment. In short, they need a job. Without a purpose in life, dogs can become depressed or act out in ways that we find unacceptable. All-too-common — and sometimes very annoying — attention-seeking behaviors are the product of otherwise unoccupied canine minds. "Idle minds do mischief make," as my grandmother used to say. Some dogs even develop compulsive disorders (as described in chapter 8). A veterinary drug company put out a pamphlet with the striking caption, "Underemployment — the number one problem of dogs today." Dogs need to be provided with opportunities to become engaged in a variety of mentally stimulating and fulfilling activities. Some of the more useful such activities necessarily involve some time commitment on the part of the owner — but not all. Sometimes the desired goal can be achieved by enlisting the assistance of other people, like dog walkers and daycare providers.

For mental stimulation and exercise, dogs can be enrolled in activities like agility training (training them to navigate tricky obstacle courses), Schutzhund training (with its three components of tracking, obedience, and protection), freestyle dancing, and field trials. All of these activities are mentally stimulating for dogs, and all strengthen the human-animal bond by uniting owners and their dogs in an organized activity. For something a little less structured, hiking with his owners provides a dog with a great deal of mental stimulation and healthy outdoor fun. Even if a dog is not athletic or is older, there are still fun and educational things owners can do to provide him with an interest and a focus. Some people, even elderly people with elderly dogs, find that enrolling their dog as a service dog is doubly rewarding. As long as a dog has the right personality, he can be trained to visit people in the hospital or nursing home to cheer them up. Such an exercise — even just the getting-out-of-the-house aspect — provides new experiences and opens new vistas for the dog and owner alike.

Ongoing training to an advanced level is another way to ensure quality interactions between owners and their dogs. All owners should make time for their pet's continuing education. Even twice-daily training sessions of five or ten minutes will be appreciated by a dog as entertaining, quality, one-on-one time spent with his owner (as long as the training methods are positive — see chapter 3). Don't forget to play with your dog, too — fetch, hide-and-seek, whatever. Dogs just like to have fun, and playtime does them a lot of good. As mentioned earlier, the presence of another dog takes some of the pressure off owners, as dogs will often play and romp together. It's much less demanding to look after two friendly dogs than one needy dog, and, psychologically, it's better for the dogs, too.

Routine

It is well known that dogs like routine. To know what's happening and when on a daily basis definitely makes life less stressful for dogs. With routine, dogs always know what's likely to happen next, and this causes them to feel more confidence in their environment. This is especially important for shy dogs, but even macho dogs are happier when they know the ropes. Let's face it: we all like to know what's coming up next. Sensitive dogs may be particularly shaken up by departures from routine. Some dogs with separation anxiety have a meltdown on Mondays when their owners go back to work after a weekend at home again (that's why separation anxiety is sometimes called "Monday Morning Disease"). Just imagine how shaken up these dogs are when their schoolteacher owner goes back to school in the fall or when teenage children leave home for college. Routine means that dogs have events they can look forward to during the day and that they have nothing to dread because they always know what's happening next. One patient of mine sat by the refrigerator each morning at eleven o'clock waiting for his favorite Frosty Paws treat. It was the highlight of his day. Another brought his food bowl to the feeding station at six o'clock each evening, presumably to remind his owners it was time. Yet another showed signs of separation anxiety only if his owner came home later than the usual time of 5:00 P.M. Who says dogs can't tell time and who says they can't anticipate events to come?

Let's face it, dogs need more to keep them occupied than most owners realize. Some people think that to have the dog padding around the house all day and curling up to sleep for fourteen hours each night is a normal lifestyle for a dog. It isn't. Eating a lot and sleeping a lot can be signs of depression, as they are in humans. Owners should appreciate their pets' biological and psychological needs and try hard to provide appropriate outlets and diversions for them. For dogs to be able to spend quality time with their owner each day is a great start, but there's so much more that can be and should be done. Positive training incorporated into the daily routine is a big plus. Aerobic exercise and outside excursions as regular features of a dog's daily life provide physical and mental outlets and inspiration. Enrichment of a dog's environment when you have to be away is a must. You can

Pet Havens?

One high-end pet-products company has taken the environmental-enrichment idea several steps further. The company, Elite Pet-Havens, sells total indoor environments for dogs. If you have $50,000 to $200,000 to spend and want to make life really sweet for your dog, you can enlist their custom services. A typical such environment takes up about a quarter of a fairly large room. Movies (plain or IMAX) of wildlife scenes are projected onto the walls with appropriate auditory accompaniment (birds singing, water flowing, trees whiffling in the breeze). A treadmill and lap pool are available for aerobic exercise, as is a training area where the various skills necessary to use the equipment are taught. There is, of course, a drying-off area, complete with hair drying, for dogs who have taken the plunge, and a digging area when they can exercise their digging and burying penchants. Of course, no indoor environment for a dog would be complete without a tree and, yes, they have that, too. And did I mention the massage area? Here's how it all works together. In one scenario, the scene projected on the wall depicts a duck dropping from the sky. The owner encourages his dog to fetch the duck by swimming toward it in the lap pool. Swimming briskly "upstream," the dog eventually reaches the location — where the duck has "fallen," and there finds a dummy duck to retrieve. The dog is then called back to his owner, to swim against the now reversed current, and is rewarded for successfully accomplishing his mission. Maybe this is taking things a bit too far — but some would say you can't get too much of a good thing (if you can afford it).

spend thousands of dollars on the very latest devices to address this problem (see opposite), or you can accomplish similar ends relatively inexpensively. To make the right decisions about what is best, all you have to do is consider things from your dog's perspective and then design his lifestyle and environment accordingly. If you live in a town or city, the chances are that all this advice is very much needed even though you may have leash laws and a shortage of open space hampering your efforts. If you live in the country, you may not have to be quite as inventive, as your dog will be able to share and enjoy the lifestyle that comes with living in a rural environment. Nevertheless, having a dog requires that you sometimes think about things from his viewpoint to ensure that his life is both absorbing and purposeful.

Part 2

Maladjustment and Medical Matters

In the first section of this book I discussed the seven factors supporting the well-adjusted dog. In this section I outline the problems arising from maladjustment. I also discuss underlying medical issues that can make dogs feel strange and act differently — perhaps expressing themselves as behavior problems. For completeness, I cover various herbal and pharmacologic remedies for these and other behavior problems that, alone or concurrent with behavioral and environmental management, can get wayward dogs back on the road to recovery.

8

A Rock and a Hard Place

Compulsive Behaviors in Dogs

> We call them dumb animals, and so they are, for they
> cannot tell us how they feel, but they do not suffer less
> because they have no words.
> — Anna Sewell, *Black Beauty* (1877)

Some dogs live pretty idyllic lives even within the constraints of modern society and despite their total dependence on
human care providers. An owner's circumstances and capacity to
provide for his dog both play key roles in determining a dog's
quality of life. Of course, dogs are happiest and most fulfilled
when they are doing what they were originally bred to do. I
remember spending many long hours as a teenager hiking around
a private estate with a gamekeeper and his loyal companion, a
Parson Russell terrier called Scamp. As the gamekeeper and I
trudged around massive wheat fields, along fence lines, over hill
and dale, Scamp would busy himself with his own agenda, sometimes running a hundred yards ahead or to the side as he
explored burrows and flushed birds and small varmints from the
hedgerows. At the end of the day, this otherwise highly energetic
dog was tired and happy, his instinctive drives exhausted, as he
settled in for his evening meal and nap, no doubt reflecting on the
marvelous events of the day. Scamp led a life close to the one for
which his breed was created.

At the other end of the spectrum are dogs that are incarcerated or chained, sometimes all day, with little to occupy their minds and virtually nothing to do. An advertisement sponsored by the Massachusetts Society for the Prevention of Cruelty to Animals sums the situation up perfectly with a photograph of a pathetic-looking dog chained near some trash cans in a filthy-looking backyard; the caption reads, "It's a crime the way some people treat their dogs." Dogs sometimes wind up in these pitiful situations because their owners are neglectful or just plain abusive. Other times, dogs' freedom is denied for logistical reasons; for example, when owners are too busy to properly care for their dogs or when stray dogs must be impounded until an adopter comes along. Some working dogs, like a drug-sniffing Belgian Malinois I once treated for acral lick dermatitis, had to be kenneled for long hours each day for statutory and performance-enhancing reasons. Junkyard dogs are often tied by long chains and have little to do all day except bark at visitors — hardly a fulfilling lifestyle. When I visited Hokkaido, the northern island of Japan, I saw a group of Hokkaido inu bear-hunting dogs who were forced to spend their days chained within a very small radius. These dogs were treated as belongings, not as the sentient living creatures that they were. All of these situations, and many others like them, cause dogs great hardship. Such restriction leads to psychological problems that manifest as refractory behavioral problems and sometimes self-injury.

Things are not always as black and white as the circumstances described above. There are many shades of gray between the utopian situation in which Scamp found himself and the extreme deprivation suffered by the Hokkaido inu. Sometimes all is not well for dogs living within the confines of an apparently happy home. They may not have enough of what they need to make them whole. Dogs have a biological agenda that must be taken into account when providing for them. If dogs are short-changed in this respect, both they and their owners may suffer the consequences. But all things are relative, so how the lack of opportunity to engage in breed- and species-specific behaviors affects an individual dog depends on his genetic makeup, personality, and level of deprivation. A field-strain dog with a type A personality who is compelled to endure a relatively uninteresting, uneventful lifestyle may well suffer a negative psychological reaction. A couch potato pet dog with a type B personality in the same situation might manage to cope. All the same, it's best to optimize lifestyle factors for all dogs for humanitarian as well as behavioral reasons.

The Consequences of Deprivation

In situations where an energetic dog's biological objectives are thwarted by environmental shortcomings and restrictions, dogs, like other species, develop various coping strategies. These strategies often manifest as repetitive disorders, formerly called stereotypies but now more commonly referred to as compulsive behaviors. These behaviors have been misconstrued by owners and veterinarians alike as meaningless anomalies. A stereotypy, by definition, is a pointless, mindless, repetitive behavior that serves no obvious function. Scientists have argued for years about whether stereotypies indicate underlying stress and thus impaired welfare. The weight of scientific evidence now is that stereotypies *do* signify that all is not (or was not) well for the animal. But it is not so much the performance of the stereotypy that is a concern, rather, the circumstances that led to its development or allow for its propagation. Performance of the stereotypy may, in fact, have stress-alleviating effects. If a parrot is confined in his cage all day every day, there is a good chance he will become a feather picker, stripping feathers from any region of his body that he can reach with his beak. If a big cat is confined in a zoo exhibit, he will pace mindlessly for hours on end, sometimes to and fro, sometimes around in circles. Environmentally deprived seals swim in geometric patterns or ingest coins from the bottom of pools in which they are kept; captive monkeys engage in skin picking and compulsive masturbation. Dogs, when psychologically or physically deprived, evidence their own spectrum of stereotypic behaviors. Though many stereotypies are harmless to the dog, some are not and may cause self-injury. For the ones that cause injury, treatment, not merely restraint from performing the behavior, is what is needed.

One of the first canine stereotypies I became deeply interested in (in the mid-1980s) was acral lick dermatitis (ALD), a condition in which dogs repetitively lick the lower extremities of their limbs. At that time, I did not fully appreciate the welfare implications of what a colleague and I were studying. Our experiments demonstrated that nature's own morphine-like substances — the endorphins — were involved in ALD, because affected dogs' self-licking behavior decreased dramatically when the dogs were treated with endorphin antagonists. Since endorphins are released in stressful situations, our results appeared to confirm that stress was involved in the propagation of this curious self-directed behavior.

It was around this time that a child psychiatrist at the National Institutes of Health, Dr. Judith Rapoport, wrote her best-selling book, *The Boy Who Couldn't Stop Washing*, which was about childhood obsessive-compulsive disorder (OCD). Following her book tour, she returned to Washington, D.C., to find a slew of telephone messages from dog owners saying that their dogs had the same problem. I doubt that she had ever heard of ALD at the time, but when owners described their dogs as constantly "washing" (licking) their paws, Rapoport wondered whether this might be a canine version of OCD. If dogs also suffered from OCD, this would provide novel opportunities for study of the condition. Good scientist that she is, she set about conducting a study in which dogs were treated with the human antiobsessional drug clomipramine and then monitored for several weeks. The canine condition responded to this treatment in the same way human OCD sufferers might. Rapoport then conducted a more detailed study confirming her earlier work and showing that a variety of human antiobsessional drugs were effective treatments for what she referred to by its synonym, acral lick. Everything Rapoport found pointed to the fact that acral lick was an OCD analogue, and over the next few years she published a number of scientific papers in which she described the condition as a promising model for the study of OCD.

Veterinarians jumped on this bandwagon, and before too long, canine compulsive disorder, not stereotypy, was the accepted terminology for acral lick, as well as other repetitive behaviors. Purists preferred to drop the word "obsessive" from the label as obsessions are constantly recurring thoughts that cannot be confirmed in dogs. One of the questions Dr. Rapoport's conclusions raised was whether genetics play a role in canine susceptibility to ALD. She noted that certain large breeds of dog were commonly affected and thus may be genetically inclined to the condition. This was a logical conclusion, since other canine compulsions are more prevalent in certain breeds. Some scientists have debated whether acral lick and other canine compulsive disorders arise from a dog's nature (genetics) or nurture (environment). The correct answer is both.

Nature and Nurture

Recently, it has been shown that if an animal has a genetic predisposition toward a particular behavioral problem but circumstances are opposed to its development, the behavioral problem will often not materialize. Conversely, if circumstances are ideal for the development of a particular behavioral problem but the animal does not have a genetic predisposition toward it, the problem will not occur. So, viewed from this perspective, it can be argued that nature or nurture can make a 100 percent contribution to whether a certain behavior problem occurs. Consider a German shepherd from nervous, sensitive stock. Raise that dog under optimal circumstances and the result would most likely be a fine dog with few, if any, behavior problems. But take a high-strung shepherd and subject him to many long hours alone and unoccupied in a kennel, and a canine compulsive disorder of some sort may well develop. Most American German shepherds I see are a tad on the sensitive side, and many have suffered adverse environmental experiences at some time during their lives. This set of circumstances typically leads to the development of compulsive behavior as a coping mechanism. German shepherds caged for long periods of time tend to exhibit compulsive behaviors in the form of pacing to and fro, circling, or chasing their own tails. These manifestations stem from the so-called appetitive (hunting) phase of predatory behavior gone awry.

A former resident of mine, Dr. Petra Mertens, studied the development of compulsive disorders, then called stereotypies, for her Dr.Med.Vet thesis at veterinary school in Munich. Her conclusions were that singly housed shelter dogs had a significantly higher prevalence of pacing stereotypies than those housed in pairs — and now you know why. Being physically confined and socially deprived is more stressful than being confined with a companion.

Acute stress, not just chronic ongoing stress and boredom, can also precipitate compulsive disorders. Many of them develop for the first time in young dogs around the time of sexual maturity (six to eight months). One German shepherd I heard of found himself in an acute conflict situation when his police handler gave the attack command ("Fass") when confronting a robber in a furniture store who was brandishing a chair above his head. Unfortunately for the handler and the dog, "hands above the head" was the no-go signal for this dog, who was so confused he immediately started to run around in circles. This dog never recovered — I'm not sure what happened to the policeman. Some dogs develop compulsive disorders immediately after neuter surgery or following some other highly stressful event. Sometimes the precipitating event is known to us and sometimes it is not.

Compulsive Behavior and the Canine Brain

The longer a compulsive behavior has been in existence, the harder it is to treat, as the neural pathways become seemingly more well trodden and facilitated. At this stage, even when the precipitating conflict is resolved, dogs will continue to engage in the behavior. Trivial environmental perturbations, like the dog's owner leaving the house, will trigger the behavior, or it may be expressed spontaneously with no apparent triggers.

Should owners worry about repetitive behaviors that continue following the elimination of stress? That depends on whether the compulsive disorder causes the dog any physical problems and whether the behavior is so disruptive as to interfere with the normal relationship between the dog and his owner. A mild repetitive disorder might be tolerable in a dog whose lifestyle and environment has been optimally adjusted. However, a more serious case under similar circumstances might need to be addressed.

The underlying cause of canine compulsive disorders is anxiety. Dogs with anxious temperaments are the ones most likely to exhibit compulsive behavior when the going gets tough. Anxiety opens a veritable Pandora's box of possible compulsive-behavior manifestations in dogs. Behaviors that are vital for survival — like eating, grooming, and predatory behaviors — are encoded deep within the canine brain. Normally, these encoded behaviors are accessed in the appropriate context; that is, as and when necessary. If a dog sees a rabbit, his cerebral cortex sends messages to the region of his brain that activates predatory behavior, including searching, chasing, killing, and eating. When rabbits are not on the dog's radar, the above mechanism is not needed and shuts down. In compulsive disorders, isolated aspects of predatory behavior can be expressed out of context. For example, a dog may continuously search when there is nothing there to find or may chase dust particles or beams of light.

Common Manifestations of Compulsive Behavior

In seeking to circumvent or address compulsive behavior in dogs, it is helpful to know about breed tendencies and temperament. Specific manifestations of compulsive disorder can derive from behaviors especially well hard-wired for particular breeds of dog. Accordingly, it is possible for an informed owner to make the necessary environmental adjustments to ward off the development of canine compulsive disorders or take measures to address them at their humblest beginnings (see chapter 7). Humanitarian issues aside, prevention of a problem of this nature is far better than allowing it to develop and then having to call in the cavalry. Listed here are some common compulsive behaviors exhibited in dogs.

Self-Licking

Large breeds, such as Great Danes, golden and Labrador retrievers, Doberman pinschers, and German shepherds, are most prone to compulsive self-grooming leading to acral lick dermatitis (ALD). Almost always, excessive licking is directed toward the wrist area (carpus) of the foreleg or the hock region (tarsus or "back elbow") of the rear leg. The reason for this distribution may be that dogs tend to lie either (a) on their chest, with their heads resting on their forearms, making the wrist a convenient target, or (b) curled to one side, so that their one or other hock is positioned right next to their mouth. In ALD, continuous licking strips hair off the region, causing local baldness, and finally affects the skin, where ulcers form. The ulcers start to heal from the base up, forming strawberry-like granulation tissue. It's a dynamic process of repair and damage, with damage prevailing. Secondary infection of the area is common and can penetrate to deeper tissues, sometimes involving the underlying bone. One dog that was treated here at Tufts had to have his leg amputated because the bone was affected by a deep-seated infection.

Like other behavior problems, excessive licking is best nipped in the bud. Overgrooming of this nature often indicates that a dog is anxious, and once possible medical causes have been ruled out by your vet, attempts should be made to alleviate the source(s) of the dog's anxiety.

The natural function of grooming is to facilitate personal hygiene and survival. A well-kept coat is a healthy coat, and a clean coat will not give a dog's presence away to prey downwind. Grooming also serves a self-comfort function.

Dog carpus (wrist) displaying deep and wide "granulating" ulcer as a result of excessive self-grooming (acral lick dermatitis)

Grooming, as a behavior, is hard-wired in dogs. After a meal, lip licking may progress to nose licking, thereafter to licking of the forelimbs, forefeet, flank, rump, hind limbs, hind feet, and tail. Self-licking can also occur as a self-comfort behavior, not unlike human babies' thumb sucking, in moments of angst and uncertainty. As with other compulsive behaviors in dogs, overgrooming leading to ALD occurs only when stress is severe.

Curiously, ALD tends to develop in mature dogs. In one study we conducted, we found the average age of onset to be five years (the range was two to seven years). Affected dogs tend to be more highly strung than their unaffected counterparts and remain anxious and highly strung as they age. Boredom, injury, or acute environmental stresses first trigger compulsive licking, but once the pendulum has started to swing, it's hard to stop it without taking dramatic measures. Even so, dogs that have exhibited the tendency to lick compulsively are prone to develop the problem again even after its successful resolution — so it's a case of "till the next time."

As far as the treatment of ALD is concerned, the best remedy is to alleviate ongoing stresses, though this measure alone is rarely sufficient to arrest the problem. In one case, a couple's German shepherd started to lick compulsively when the husband left his wife. This dog stopped licking immediately when the husband changed his mind and returned home. That was pure luck for the dog. Most times the solution is not that easy or as dramatically effective — though there are often some obvious remedial actions to be taken. Environmental enrichment, as described in chapter 7, is often a much-needed first step. When all else fails, a medical solution must be sought and implemented (see more in chapter 10).

Surface Licking

Some dogs, for reasons unknown, develop licking compulsions that are not self-directed but rather are focused on external objects such as varnished surfaces, floors, carpets, and even metal stoves. The breeds of dogs that engage in this strange compulsion are not the same as those prone to self-licking and thus ALD. I have seen surface licking mostly in beagles and spaniels, but it also occurs in other breeds, including boxers and Lhasa apsos. It isn't hard to see why floor licking would be considered an OCD; after all, compulsive surface washing is a well-documented form of human OCD. Anthropomorphically speaking, you can almost imagine the repetitive thought that precedes every compulsive licking bout. One dog I once treated licked carpets so persistently that he wore deep groves in them. Another stripped varnish off wooden table legs, chair legs, and banister rails. But this condition may also be a manifestation of a form of seizure activity, which I discuss in chapter 9. In support of the seizure theory, surface licking often does not respond well to common antiobsessional medication, like Prozac, but may respond to treatment with an anti-convulsant. Like so many other areas of behavioral medicine, the final verdict on this suject is not yet in. Meanwhile, it is a good plan to optimize the affected dog's lifestyle to minimize stress and provide optimal outlets for species-specific behaviors. And as far as medical treatment is concerned, it's whatever works best!

Tail Chasing

Compulsive tail chasing is most common in breeds with high prey drive. Terriers, especially bull terriers, and herding breeds, like German shepherds, are most commonly affected. A dog with high prey drive that has no outlet for his predatory tendencies will invent one. I believe affected dogs see their tail out of the corner of their eyes and go for it. As they turn to grab it, the tail moves away from them, mimicking prey. Then the hunt is on. Some dogs engage in this behavior at such a low intensity that owners may not even consider it a problem. But things can get

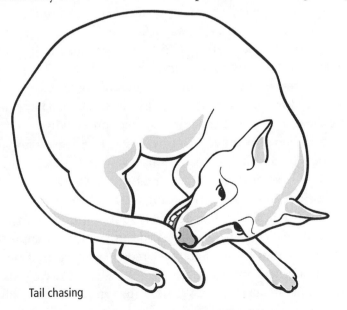

Tail chasing

much worse, depending on the circumstances, which is why it's so important to understand what the behavior signifies: boredom, frustration, and a dog with a conflicted agenda. High-intensity tail chasing, in which dogs spin for hours like a whirling dervish, is obviously a major problem that can affect the quality of life for both the dog and owner. I have encountered dogs that spin almost nonstop, pausing only to grab a mouthful of food or sleep from pure exhaustion. These dogs have no quality interactions with their owners and if physically prevented from engaging in the behavior will put up quite a struggle in attempts to continue. If dogs have obsessive thoughts — and I believe they do — this behavior provides an excellent example of the unrelenting voice within. Physical problems that occur as a result of extreme tail chasing include weight loss, abrasions to the foot pads, and damage to the tail. I heard of a German shepherd who lost his life as a result of tail chasing. Late one evening, this dog bit the tip off his tail and it bled profusely. The veterinarian hospitalized the dog overnight and applied a pressure bandage as an interim measure to stem the bleeding; the dog was scheduled for surgery the next day and hospitalized overnight. But the dog managed to tear the bandage off during the night and was found dead in a pool of blood the next morning. By the way, amputating the tail does not cure tail chasing in dogs that compulsively tail chase. They simply chase the stump or some imaginary "phantom" tail instead.

Clearly, no owner wants tail chasing to progress to such extremes. To this end, the solution lies in early detection and treatment. In some dogs, tail chasing is initially mild. This is the best time to address issues regarding the dog's environment and lifestyle. Specifically, it is a good idea to minimize the time the dog spends in confinement and provide him with more appropriate opportunities to dissipate his predatory energies. There is probably a genetic influence aside from high prey drive causing susceptibility to tail chasing. Whether the gene or genes involved promote an anxious type-A personality is not known, but clinical impressions point that way. Tail chasing, like other compulsive behavior in dogs, seems to result from interplay between genetic susceptibility and a suboptimal environment. The behavior has never been observed in wild dogs, probably because they are not inbred and do not have to deal with the same environmental tedium that confronts many of their domestic counterparts.

Sometimes the full-blown relentless tail chasing and tight circling develops immediately after neuter surgery or following a geographical move. Other times the triggers for the behavior are much more subtle or may not even be evident. Most dogs are first affected when they are pubescent (five to nine months of age), but a few develop the condition when they are fully mature. One bull terrier I treated first exhibited the behavior when she was six years old following a move from New Hampshire to Long Island, New York. The condition reversed when she was returned to her original home and family. Another geographical solution to the problem involved a bull terrier living with a feuding couple in a small apartment in New York City. This dog was rehomed to a farm in upstate New York following the couple's separation, and subsequently his tail chasing ceased altogether.

German shepherds are a law unto themselves when it comes to tail chasing. First of all, they don't always spin in tight circles. Some wander aimlessly in a larger radius and some run in figure-eight patterns. It can be argued that German shepherd tail chasing and circling is analogous to the bull terrier condition, but it does not always respond the same way to treatment. Some affected German shepherds respond well to therapy only when anticonvulsants are included, along with more conventional antidepressant treatment, as part of the therapeutic regimen. This observation points to the possible involvement of partial seizures in the behavior (discussed further in chapter 9). I have found abnormal brain wave patterns in tail-chasing bull terriers but have not yet conducted controlled studies of this nature in German shepherds. A neurological, seizure-based impetus for tail chasing seems quite plausible in German shepherds, as this breed is prone to epilepsy. The boundary between compulsive disorders and seizures is not always clear, even in human medicine. Some 43 percent of people with bulimia have abnormal electroencephalograms (EEGs). But that begs the question, why don't all bulimics have abnormal EEGs? We don't know the answer to that yet.

Light Chasing and Shadow Chasing

Shadow and light chasing, like tail chasing, can also be attributed to the repetitive misfirings of the predatory brain. Seriously affected dogs relentlessly chase any light or shadow that crosses their path and continue to seek will-o'-the-wisp shadows or lights long after real ones have disappeared from view. While light chasing may seem like fun to an onlooker, it's not. These dogs are driven to distraction, compelled to give chase for hours each day at the expense of other aspects of their emotional and behavioral agendas. Owners' attention, positive or negative, may exacerbate the problem because of the attentional reward it supplies, but that is usually not the cause. Many dogs begin and continue this pattern of behavior when their owners are not around. One owner was alarmed to wake up and find her dog careening around her living room, chasing "imaginary rabbits down imaginary rabbit holes." The deluded dog kept pouncing on the floor, barking in frenzied excitement as if he had run a varmint to earth. Curiously, this dog, a Dalmatian, was deaf — as are many light and shadow chasers — so maybe not hearing makes seeing a more intense experience. The first three shadow-chasing dogs I saw were all deaf Old English sheepdogs. Deafness, however, is not a prerequisite for compulsive light or shadow chasing. My fourth case was a field-strain springer spaniel who could hear perfectly well.

The ingredients necessary to spark light chasing appear to be (a) high prey drive (terriers and field-strain dogs are overrepresented), (b) an anxious temperament, and (c) a less-than-challenging — let's face it, boring — environment. It's another case of a dog with an anxious personality who, metaphorically speaking, is all dressed up with nowhere to go — and that's where we come in.

Light chasing can be triggered in susceptible pups by unsuspecting owners who play with their anxious, prey-hungry youngster using a flashlight. This is the behavioral equivalent of giving a teenager with an anxious, addictive personality a pack of cigarettes as a gift. A normal dog might just enjoy a quick game of light chasing and then call it quits. The potential addict cannot stop. There are many parallels between addiction to a behavior and addiction to drugs. Both involve a constantly recurring thought — the obsession — driving the mechanical process that is the compulsion. Potential or early-stage light chasers should not be exposed to triggers for the behavior, especially at a formative time in their lives (say, less than one year of age). If the behavior begins to surface, flashlights should be put away for good, curtains should be drawn shut at key times (sunrise/sunset), and affected dogs should be denied access to environments that spark the compulsive chasing behavior. If this fails to check the behavior, it may be necessary to "dog proof" the house to minimize damage to property as the dog charges around. Increased exercise, environmental enrichment (including providing the dog a job), and pharmacological treatment (see chapter 10) can provide relief. Even so, the behavior may not necessarily be completely eliminated, merely reduced in intensity and duration. Sometimes, as with human OCD, a useful level of improvement may be the best that can be achieved.

One dog, Tucker, a Cavalier King Charles spaniel, exhibited a variation on this theme. Instead of chasing light beams, Tucker stared into dark places, stared at furniture, stared at clothing, and stared at sunlight streaming through windows. He seemed especially obsessed with dust particles dancing in the sunbeams and any areas of contrast between light and dark. Tucker would sometimes bump into furniture, seemingly on purpose, in order to get dust particles to fly — and then he would chase them. Sunny days completely consumed him, but windy days were worse because he would focus on and pursue anything that moved. Interestingly, Tucker's odd "autistic" behavior was completely absent when he was on his owners' boat. That was an environmental solution to his problem, but his owners could not remain at sea indefinitely. On land, his distraught owners tried to light- and draft-proof their Florida home, but in the end it took medication to get Tucker back to normal. Who knows why Tucker got this way? My theory would be through a combination of high prey drive, anxiety, and boredom.

Snapping at Imaginary Flies

Compulsive fly-snapping behavior, bizarre as it is, is also common in dogs with high prey drive. Terriers and herding breeds are most commonly affected. There is nothing wrong with a dog snapping at real flies; it's when the snapping occurs in the absence of flies that there's a problem. My sister's German shepherd used to leap in the air and bite yellow jackets in half with a single snap. I could never understand why the dog didn't get stung, and I marveled at the accuracy of his bite, which severed the critters midthorax. I regard this behavior as normal — and useful. But one Norfolk terrier patient of mine leapt and twisted in the air, snapping at nothing, apparently seeing things that weren't there. Now that's just plain weird. Fly snapping has been described as a canine compulsive disorder, which it may well be. But this behavior has also been reported in association with seizures, so, like tail chasing, it may stem from abnormal brain wave activity. Treatment is the same as for other compulsive behaviors — environmental and lifestyle enrichment — but may extend to the use of antiobsessional medications and/or anticonvulsants in some cases.

Flank Sucking and Blanket Sucking

Flank and blanket sucking derive from nursing behavior and are the canine equivalent of thumb sucking. Often the dog's coat be-

Flank sucking

comes wet with saliva where the dog has "nursed," but usually there's not much else to note other than the behavior itself. Occasionally, the coat becomes denuded of hair and, even more occasionally, the skin becomes ulcerated. In Doberman pinschers, who are most commonly affected, genetics clearly plays a major role in the expression of the condition. In most other breeds, environmental factors, notably early maternal deprivation, are instrumental.

If a Doberman sucks his flank only occasionally, you can argue it's no big deal. But if the behavior is frequent and intense, or causes local damage, it's time to act. As with other compulsive behaviors, the chief message an owner needs to get is that the dog's environment and lifestyle may both need adjustment. The stress of boredom and lack of opportunity to perform species-typical behaviors may underlie the performance of flank sucking, especially if it is severe. Biologically speaking, flank sucking derives from the suckling behavior of young pups as they latch on to mom's teats, but there's also self-comfort that derives from suckling. Whenever things in the outside world get big and scary for a young pup, he crawls back to mom's milk bar — even when her milk supply is drying up — for a quick comfort suckle; touching base, so to speak. When mom's not around, worried pups may have to resort to a mother substitute, hence the development of flank sucking in (relatively speaking) maternally deprived pups.

Dobermans may be especially prone to displaced nursing because they naturally nurse longer than most other breeds and are deprived of real nursing opportunities when weaned at the traditional seven or eight weeks of age. If this concept is correct, a Doberman pup with constant access to his mom for the first three to six months of life might not develop flank sucking in the first place. The jury is still out on this one. A fact that seems to fly in the face of the early weaning theory of flank sucking is the age of onset in some dogs. Some Dobermans do not exhibit the behavior in the first year of their lives, so what is holding them back? An explanation for the apparent anomaly is that compulsive behaviors can be primed at an early age and may be expressed later only when conditions are "right." There is some scientific evidence to support this view.

Other breeds that may develop flank-sucking behavior are Weimaraners and dachshunds — interestingly, also both German breeds — but the incidence is lower in these breeds. Other breeds, particularly retriever-type dogs, occasionally nurse on soft, furry toys to excess. However, if I see a retriever or any other breed that sucks on his flank, my first question is, When was he weaned? The last time I posed this question to a Labrador retriever owner the answer came back: "When he was five days . . . his mom died."

Blanket sucking, whose form is self-evident from its description, is another way that misdirected sucking behavior can be expressed. It's probably driven by the same internal forces, but affected dogs have access to a blanket on which to vent their sucking penchant. And yes, blanket sucking also primarily affects Dobermans, too. A recent study compared and contrasted flank sucking and blanket sucking in Dobermans to see if there was any distinction between the two compulsive behaviors other than in their form. Except that blanket sucking occurred a little earlier, both behaviors were remarkably similar, indicating similar if not identical underpinnings.

Treatment for flank sucking or blanket sucking is to adjust the affected dog's environment and lifestyle to provide appropriate outlets and distractions. Extreme versions of the behavior may lead to problems requiring medical intervention (see "Compulsive Eating Behaviors"). When it comes to medical treatment, optimizing thyroid hormone levels, if they are somewhat borderline, may be helpful. Dobermans are no strangers to thyroid issues (hypothyroidism). Other medical interventions are rarely necessary. I did treat one flank-sucking Doberman using a pharmacological approach — an endorphin blocker— and it worked well. This dog, Taylor, was a show dog who had developed unsightly lesions on one flank as a result of the behavior. Not only did his flank sucking stop after he was treated with medication, but an acral lick lesion he had developed also healed.

Compulsive Eating Behaviors

Some dogs like to chew and swallow things that are inedible or are, at least, not appropriate food items. The diagnosis of a compulsive-eating problem hinges on ruling out underlying medical causes and the extent to which the behavior is performed. Basically, eating behaviors deemed excessive or unhealthful can be considered compulsive behaviors.

Blanket eating

Some compulsive blanket suckers actually ingest (swallow) the material they "suckle" on, posing a health hazard. In a study of forty-four blanket-sucking dogs, ten were reported by their owners to have medical complications resulting from their habit. The problems ranged from worn teeth and lower-lip callus to digestive upsets, including vomiting and intestinal obstruction. Flank suckers also may have an indiscriminate eating penchant (pica) that can lead to intestinal obstruction.

Coprophagy

Stool eating is a normal behavior in young pups, who may be simply emulating their mom's normal nest cleanup behavior, but it can become excessive and persist into adulthood. Stool eating can be regarded as a compulsive behavior when it assumes habit proportions and becomes a preoccupation for the dog. Some dogs eat only the feces of horses and farm animals when such material is available. This behavior is relatively normal and is typically not expressed compulsively. Other dogs eat their own stool. This can also be normal, depending on the age of the dog and the frequency of the behavior. Some dogs eat only other dogs' stool, and some eat poop only in the winter when it is frozen ("poopsicles"). Yet others are totally indiscriminate about their stool-eating behavior and will even eat stool as it is being extruded from themselves or another dog. The age of the dog and extent of the problem determine whether the behavior has transcended some arbitrary limit of normality and assumed compulsive proportions. A truly compulsive coprophagic may well have anxiety and displacement at the root of his behavior and may eat other inedible items, too. Bark mulch and tree bark are high on the list of alternative substrates. A healthy lifestyle and environmental enrichment may help, but specific measures such as dietary manipulation (high-fiber diet) and antiobsessional medication may be called for. Failing this, careful management — eliminating a dog's access to feces — may be the only solution. One thing's for sure, dietary additives, such as meat tenderizer and peppermint breath mints fed to the dog, do not work. Coprophagy, as disgusting as it is to us, is not harmful for the dog. The worst it does for a dog is to cause bad breath, but for us the thought of receiving a doggy kiss after a dog has indulged himself in this way is repugnant.

Stone/rock chewing

Rock chewing is another mystifying (to humans) behavior. Affected dogs pick rocks up in their mouths and chew on them like gum — finally either spitting them out or swallowing them. This behavior derives from the eating ("consummatory") phase of predatory behavior. In all probability it arises as a displacement behavior. A dog finds himself outside (no rocks inside!) with nothing to do and rocks in front of him. He might lick or gnaw on a rock first and then, finally, take it into his mouth. The clicking of the rock on his teeth might provide a new and entertaining sensation, and the masticatory movements might satisfy some short-changed consummatory requirement. Either way, the behavior starts. In some cases it may peter out or be performed only occasionally in odd moments of boredom. In other cases the behavior escalates, becomes ingrained, automatic, and ranks as a true compulsive disorder. So what's the big deal? you might ask. Baseball players chew tobacco and spit throughout many a long game. That's true, and this type of chewing may also warrant an OCD label in some players! One method of deciding whether a repetitive behavior is compulsive or not is whether it causes harm. Rock chewing does. Teeth can be worn down to the gum line, and swallowed rocks can cause serious intestinal problems, even blockage. Surgery is indicated in the latter situation. The best way to deal with rock chewing is early detection followed by logistical and other measures designed to make sure that it does not continue. In other words, owners should nip the problem in the bud. In extreme cases where a dog's health is at risk or where medical intervention has been required in the past, environmental modification, lifestyle enrichment, and medication may all be required.

Grass eating/dirt swallowing

People always ask me whether grass eating (plus or minus dirt) is a normal behavior for dogs. The answer I give them is yes. A lot of dogs munch an occasional blade of grass, perhaps because they like the taste. Dogs are, in fact, omnivores, which means they eat both meat and vegetable matter. Wild dogs get both meat and vegetable in one meal if they consume an herbivorous prey animal, intestines and all. Or they might eat a plant or two for dessert from time to time. Domestic dogs are often fed carnivore rations only. Perhaps this accounts for their urge to eat something else. But, as with other "normal" behaviors, grass eating could theoretically be expressed compulsively under the right (or wrong, depending on your viewpoint) circumstances. It is also well known that dogs that don't feel well eat grass, perhaps because they feel nauseous and want something in their stomach or because eating wads of grass makes them vomit and thus purges their upper intestine. Finally, dogs subject to certain types of seizure may eat grass frenetically during or following seizure bouts. The solution to grass eating is either (a) don't worry about it (for mild occasional grass scarfing), (b) roll out the anti-compulsive-behavior lifestyle and environmental-enrichment strategy (if your dog seems obsessed by grass eating), or (c) consult a specialist veterinary neurologist or behaviorist if the behavior occurs in bouts and appears frantic.

Pica

An abnormal craving or appetite for nonfood substances, pica involves the eating of all manner of inedible objects, such as plastic, candy wrappers, toilet paper, and socks, often with dire consequences. You should always have your veterinarian rule out medical causes of pica before labeling it a purely behavioral problem. Pica can be caused by a number of medical conditions, ranging from brain tumors to hormonal problems, but anemia (too few red cells in the blood) ranks right up there as a possible cause. Once a medical cause is ruled out, behavioral issues can be addressed.

Pica can be an attention-seeking behavior; some dogs will steal almost any item from eyeglasses to wineglasses if their kleptomania gets a rise out of their owner. Any attention, even if it's the negative kind, is better than no attention. The answer to this problem is to ignore the thievery as far as possible and deny the dog any attention at all until the object is relinquished (see chapter 5). Compulsive eating of inedible objects can be a real — and potentially fatal — problem, and, for some reason, it is extremely difficult to treat. I have come out with all environmental and pharmacological guns blazing and still not been able to resolve this problem. One owner of a compulsive wirehaired fox terrier with pica, who had conscientiously dog-proofed her home and employed other corrective measures for years, finally decided to euthanize her dog (for financial as well as logistical reasons) following his second intestinal obstruction. The treatments I know for this problem are environmental enrichment and the use of antiobsessional medications, and neither seems particularly effective. Finally, seizure activity can also provoke pica; this is discussed in the next chapter.

Compulsive overeating of food

Being environmentally stressed and deprived of usual species-typical outlets for natural behaviors can drive a dog to, almost literally, eat his heart out. Constant eating of as much food as possible combined with an inactive lifestyle leads to obesity, one of the greatest scourges of the canine nation today and one that affects some 40 percent of the nation's 70 million dogs. Not all obese dogs are compulsive overeaters, but, in my opinion, many are. These are the chowhounds who live and die for the love of food. Excessive calorie intake shortens a dog's life span, not to mention affecting his health span. The effect of obesity is to increase the likelihood of many different diseases, most notably cancer. To address this very serious problem, ensure that a dog gets adequate exercise and has outlets for natural (species- and breed-specific) behaviors as well as a user-friendly environment. And start the dog on a veterinary weight-loss diet.

An Ounce of Prevention

Canine compulsive behaviors are just another reminder that dogs have emotions similar to our own and suffer from an analogous gamut of behavior problems. These disorders affect anxious, more sensitive dogs who do not endure the confines of a tedious environment. When stressed, these dogs engage in one or more ritualistic "coping" behaviors as a psychological escape. The behaviors take the form of natural behaviors gone awry and, when they have assumed compulsive proportions, bear no obvious relevance to the situation in which they are expressed. Rock-and-a-hard-place dilemmas activate conflicting psychological drives in sensitive dogs, leading to these behaviors.

Long hours in crates or kennels are typical situations that favor the development of displacement behaviors in dogs, and these behaviors can morph into hard-wired compulsive behaviors either suddenly or over time. The proper care and management of dogs is essential in preempting these behaviors. Dog owners who are knowledgeable about situations that can lead to the development of canine compulsive disorders can avoid them. While most domestic environments are far from ideal for dogs, knowledgeable dog owners can strive toward providing more user-friendly environments and species-typical activities for their dogs. Such action on the part of owners can offset the development of compulsive behaviors in dogs. Remember, for a dog, a home can be like the Eagles' "Hotel California": "You can check out any time you want, but you can never leave." The quality of a dog's life is in his owner's hands. Owners who give high priority to optimizing their dogs' lifestyles go a long way toward circumventing the situations that give rise to compulsive behavior in dogs. Know what to anticipate, what to look for, and what to do about it if problems arise.

9

Physical Health Concerns

The Influence of Underlying Medical Problems on Dogs' Behavior

Where there is health, there is hope, and where there is hope, there is everything.
— Arabian proverb

As I have said, my approach to resolving behavior problems in dogs is to some extent holistic. "Holistic" literally means treating the dog as a whole, as an entity, not just the presenting problem that's obviously in need of attention. In many cases the presenting problem, especially in the case of behavior problems, is the tip of an iceberg of maladjustment. Having read this far, you will have some appreciation for the various factors influencing dogs' health and well-being: the importance of exercise, an appropriate diet, good communication, strong leadership, an engaging environment. Now I want to deal with another component of the whole-dog management program: the potential impact that underlying medical problems can have on your dog's welfare and how to address these issues. I believe that owners should have at least a modicum of understanding as to how physical ailments can affect their dog's quality of life and behavior; forewarned is forearmed in this respect. Veterinarians appreciate vigilant, well-informed clients because, after all, an owner is a key partner in a dog's medical-management team. With the right knowledge, owners can approach their veterinarian for advice about appropriate screening tests when the likelihood of a medical problem is high (based on the dog's breed and predisposition). Also, the informed owner is in a better position to recognize subtle signs of disease early on and to summon veterinary help immediately.

Holistic medicine is often thought of as a trendy, New Age type of approach to health management, but "holism" is actually centuries old. The term implies treatment of the mind and body as a unit and emphasizes the critical relationship between these two entities that is necessary for optimal functioning. Most of us appreciate that psychological pressure in the form of stress can have a profound impact on our medical status. Well, the same is true in dogs. One dachshund I saw recently lost 25 percent of his body weight as a result of extreme separation anxiety that started when his formerly housebound single male owner took a job away from home. Bereavement is another situation in which anguish can lead to very real health problems. Exactly the opposite can happen too, when boredom or stress leads to overeating and weight gain.

Emotional problems clearly can and do affect a dog's physical well-being. The mind-body connection is a two-way street, with the mind affecting the body and a dog's physical condition affecting his psyche. Geriatric-onset nocturnal separation anxiety provides a prime example of the latter (see later in this chapter) as does the influence of skin allergy on a dog's propensity for irritability and aggression (as we saw in chapter 2). The connection between mind and body is not an ethereal concept; it is nuts-and-bolts reality with very real therapeutic implications. When a dog is suffering from almost any physical ailment, altered behavior often provides the first clue to the owner that all is not well. The bottom line is that medical problems can and do contribute to many behavior problems including aggression, anxiety, phobias, compulsive behavior, house soiling, and age-related issues. This doesn't mean that every time a dog barks excessively, or cowers during a thunderstorm, an underlying medical problem is to blame. What it does mean is that some thought should be given to possible medical involvement in virtually all cases of altered behavior.

Being a veterinarian, it is second nature for me to consider and, if necessary, investigate potential medical problems prior to embarking on what might otherwise be futile behavioral modification. Medical involvement is often signaled by one or more of the following:

1. Sudden change in behavior. If a dog that formerly ate well becomes inappetent, a dog that formerly slept well becomes an insomniac, or a dog that formerly had copious energy becomes subdued, something must have happened to promote these altered patterns of behavior. Granted, changing circumstances can trigger sudden behavioral change, but if there have been no social or geographical changes in your dog's life and no environmental or management changes, the possibility of a medical problem is high.

2. Physical signs preceding or accompanying the behavioral change. Pale gums, prematurely gray muzzle, drooping eyelids, a dry coat, allergies, or gastrointestinal disturbances — to name but a few — are all signs that something may be wrong medically. One dog that was brought to see me for pica was found by one of my students to have almost white gums. A blood sample showed the dog to be severely anemic, and that accounted for the problem. No need for diet change, retraining, or Prozac here. Steroids addressed this dog's autoimmune problem.

3. Extreme dysfunctional behavior, such as untoward aggression or manifestations of intense anxiety or fear. Extreme behaviors are quite unlike their functional, ethological equivalents and serve no useful role in the pet's life. A bull terrier that frequently woke up in the night and attacked his sleeping owner provides an example of extreme, mindless,

functionless behavior that would (did) raise my eyebrows (as well as the owner's). This dog had seizure-related aggression ("rage") and responded to anticonvulsant therapy.

4. Runts of the litter may have developmental shortcomings that can affect their behavior. A runty, one-and-a-half-year-old Scottie I learned of recently started having strange panic attacks at night. This dog was found to have a congenital liver shunt (in which blood bypasses the liver instead of being "purified" by transit through it). The treatment in this case was not behavior modification but surgery to address the underlying vascular plumbing problem. The panic attacks subsequently subsided.

5. Marked behavior problems existing from puppyhood tend to indicate genetic or medical problems. Two bulldogs I saw exhibited extreme, unreasonable aggression from an early age. One also exhibited head bobbing and the other bizarre chewing motions — both since puppyhood. Because of these manifestations I suspected a congenital "wiring problem" in the brain and treated them accordingly. Both dogs improved immensely.

6. When a dog's behavior changes later in life, say, when the dog is around eight to ten years of age, medical problems are often to blame. One Afghan hound started to act anxiously for the first time in his life when he was about eleven years old. Our internists were unable to make a diagnosis despite sophisticated tests, but at least I was able to make the dog more comfortable and less anxious with a course of anxiety-reducing medication and analgesics. Some time later, the dog suffered a "spontaneous fracture" of a limb and that led to a diagnosis of bone tumor. Pain from this widespread tumor was the cause of the anxious behavior. Unfortunately the tumor was untreatable, so the dog eventually had to be put to sleep. At least he didn't suffer anymore after he was brought to Tufts.

Behaviors with a Possible Medical Cause

House Soiling

The most common causes of what is euphemistically referred to as "inappropriate elimination" are (a) lack of proper housetraining and (b) urine marking. That said, no veterinarian worth his or her salt would dream of proceeding with a behavior-modification regimen without first ruling out possible medical causes of the problem, particularly if it arises for the first time in a formerly housetrained dog. Even if a dog was never properly housetrained, a vet will still want to rule out any possible medical causes of the problem before proceeding with behavior modification. I once made the mistake of not checking for a medical problem first when treating a Yorkshire terrier who had been urinating around his owner's home for quite some time. Circumstantially, the problem appeared to be one of simple house soiling. The dog was of a breed likely to exhibit this type of problem, lived with a pack of fellow Yorkies, and had previously been "paper-trained" (bad news). Because I felt so sure of my ground, I forwent the requisite medical testing and proceeded with a conventional retraining program. Two weeks later, when not one iota of progress had been made, I elected to take a urine sample and found it seething with bacteria. The cause of this dog's problem was bacterial cystitis. A few days on the right antibiotic resolved the problem — and I had learned a valuable lesson.

It is not only the age of the dog and the history of inappropriate elimination that provides clues as to what's going on; the form of the behavior also can alert an owner or vet to the nature of the problem. A young dog that walks around the house dribbling urine from time to time and appears incontinent may have a congenital problem. Two such problems are ectopic ureter and pelvic bladder. In the first condition, the tubes that carry urine from the kidneys to the bladder do not connect properly into the bladder. Consequently, there is no reservoir for accumulating urine, which therefore dribbles out as it is formed. In the pelvic bladder condition, the bladder is physically restricted in terms of its expansion because it is incarcerated within the dog's pelvis. The frequent low-volume urination that results predisposes affected dogs to house-soiling problems. Both conditions can be corrected surgically once they have been properly diagnosed, but the diagnosis can be tricky, often necessitating the use of sophisticated techniques. A dead-giveaway medical cause of house soiling is urinary incontinence following spaying. Again, the history provides the key to diagnosis. Another diagnostic giveaway regarding post-spay incontinence is the form that the behavior takes: affected dogs dribble urine and leave puddles of urine when asleep or lying down.

Some cases are not so clear-cut. Take the situation of an adult dog who, in midlife, suddenly starts having accidents in the house — typically in one or two locations, on rugs or in the corner of rooms. Such a dog may well have a purely behavioral reason for his sudden change in elimination habits. For example, he may have been left alone for too long and been forced to use the living room rug as a bathroom. Or, if he urinates when his owner is away, he might be having a flare-up of formerly latent separation anxiety. However, medical factors may also be involved. Bladder infection (aka cystitis) is certainly on the diagnostic agenda. A simple urine test is all that is required to rule out or confirm this troublesome condition. However, it is also possible to find things other than bacteria that should not be present in normal urine, like sugar, protein, or blood cells. Sugar indicates sugar diabetes. Sugar diabetes causes an increased thirst and increased urination — hence an increased tendency for house soiling. Increased protein in the urine can indicate a kidney problem. Kidney failure usually leads to the production of large volumes of dilute urine — and hence increased risk of house soiling. Large amounts of blood in the urine can indicate bladder stones or bladder cancer. All of these various conditions — and more — must be ruled

The Importance of History in House Soiling

- A dog who has urinated inside the home since puppyhood was most likely never properly housetrained.
- A dog who suddenly starts to have "accidents" in the home after years of eliminating outside might have a medical problem, might have suffered a breakdown in housetraining, or might be exhibiting anxiety-related urine-marking behavior.
- A dog who eliminates in the home only when his owners are away most probably has separation anxiety.
- A dog who eliminates in his crate either has separation anxiety (owners away) or has been forced to break a canine cleanliness code as a result of lengthy confinement (owners home or away).
- An adult dog adopted from a shelter who eliminates in his new home from day one almost certainly has a housetraining problem.

out if a middle-aged dog inexplicably starts to soil in the house.

Marty, a boxer, drank water like a fish and consequently had accidents on the floor. His frustrated owner had tried withholding his water (bad idea), training him to urinate outside (didn't work), and finally consulted with her vet. After extensive tests, including all manner of blood and urine tests, the vet could not explain Marty's problem and sent him to me, suspecting a compulsive-behavior problem. I tried treating Marty with antiobsessional drugs — but they did not work. Eventually I revisited possible medical causes of the problem. Despite the vet's workup and "rule outs," it turned out that Marty had a form of diabetes — diabetes insipidus. He responded dramatically to treatment with a hormone (vasopressin) and the house soiling ceased. In diabetes insipidus, a hormone deficiency results in the production of large volumes of dilute urine. You can see how this deficiency would lead to house soiling.

How to Retrain a House-Soiling Dog When Medical Matters Are *Not* Involved

1. Take him out on a leash at regular intervals, always to the same location — morning, noon, evening, and night PLUS anytime he transitions from one activity to another (e.g., sleeping to waking).

2. Walk him back and forth for fifteen minutes, verbally encouraging him to remain focused on the job at hand. Do not allow him to become distracted by surrounding events.

3. Praise and reward him immediately for a successful mission outside. Treats given at this time should be high value, like freeze-dried liver or thin slices of hot dog, so that they are well worth waiting to go outside for.

4. If no success, bring him back inside and confine him for fifteen minutes (either on short leash or in an enclosure) to prevent any accidents. Another method is to tie the dog to your belt on a short-ish lead while you busy yourself for fifteen minutes. This is sometimes called "umbilical cord training."

5. Take him back outside fifteen minutes later and try again.

6. Repeat this cycle until you meet with success — leave nothing to chance!

7. When your mission outside meets with success, praise him, reward him, and allow him some degree of freedom when he returns inside the house (e.g., perhaps restrict him to a downstairs area where you can loosely observe him).

8. If you catch him urinating in the house, DO NOT PUNISH HIM. Instead, create a loud noise as a distraction and then quickly escort him outside on leash to finish the work.

9. PROPER CLEAN-UP of the previously soiled area is imperative. Trying to mask odors is hopeless. You must eliminate odors completely.

10. Stick with it. All dogs can be properly housetrained — even older ones who were never properly housetrained in the first place.

Some drugs that veterinarians prescribe can cause house soiling. Two classic examples are cortisone and the anticonvulsants phenobarbital and potassium bromide. If house soiling begins immediately after a veterinarian has instituted a medical therapy, a drug-induced cause should be considered.

If an older dog, say, over ten years old, suddenly loses control of his bladder or bowels without any apparent medical cause, canine Alzheimer's disease (aka canine cognitive dysfunction) must be considered — but more on that later.

It is always inappropriate and counterproductive to punish dogs for urinating in the house, but it should be *a crime* to punish a dog with a medical problem, because he can't help himself. That's another reason why it's so important to check for medical problems before proceeding with retraining.

Overactivity, Reactivity, or ADHD?

Many dogs are overactive due to inappropriate management or they are simply reactive by nature. *Overactive* dogs may be the product of insufficient exercise, an inappropriate diet, lack of clear communication, lack of proper control, and lack of opportunity to engage in species-typical behaviors. *Reactive* dogs are hair-trigger when it comes to any perturbation in their immediate environment, such as the sound of an approaching stranger or an icicle falling from the roof, but otherwise conduct themselves peacefully. (Reactivity is a familial trait.) *Hyperactive* dogs — dogs with attention-deficit/hyperactivity disorder, or ADHD — barely settle and are in almost perpetual motion. Hyperactivity or ADHD is relatively uncommon in dogs — so uncommon, in fact, that some veterinary behaviorists are not even sure if it occurs. If it does exist, and I believe it does, the classic presentation is that of a dog on the go, one that is exuberant beyond all reasonable limits and who, quite frankly, is a bit of a pain to be around. Such dogs can be thought of as being "mentally noisy," the exact opposite of cool, calm, and collected. A proper diagnosis of ADHD can be applied, however, only if a dog is tested for it by a veterinarian. The test involves administering a stimulant, any stimulant, but notably Ritalin or amphetamine, and observing the effect. The stimulant is administered in progressively increasing doses until an effect is seen. At an effective dose, normal dogs become stimulated and may run around like they have just consumed sixteen cups of coffee. In dogs with ADHD, on the other hand, a paradoxical calming effect is observed; these dogs become more mellow — or, in the words of one owner, *normal.* That is not what you typically see following the administration of a stimulant! Treatment of ADHD, which can be thought of as a chemical imbalance in the brain, is by ongoing administration of a stimulant drug. The results of treatment can be quite dramatic in terms of the relief it seems to provide for the dog . . . and the owner.

Emma, a beagle, was brought to the Tufts Behavior Clinic because she had separation anxiety, but her owner also considered her to be hyperactive and somewhat compulsive in terms of her insatiable appetite for food. I treated her for separation anxiety using a behavior-modification program (see chapter 6) and mood-stabilizing medication. When Emma's owner brought her back for a recheck appointment one year later, she reported only a 30 percent improvement in Emma's separation anxiety with no change in the other behavior problems. While Emma's owner was satisfied with her improvement, I was disappointed with the result and asked her questions to shed further light on Emma's problem. The word "hyperactive" cropped up again, so I decided to try a Ritalin challenge to see if Emma was genuinely hyperactive. The test was positive: Emma became calm and attentive following the Ritalin. I treated Emma with a course of Ritalin to see how she would fare. As it turned out, all three of Emma's behavior problems improved to the point that her owner considered her to be behaving "like a normal dog." Emma's appetite also returned to normal.

Geriatric-Onset Nocturnal Separation Anxiety

When I see an aged dog with nocturnal separation anxiety but without dementia, my mind turns to medical causes underlying the dog's nighttime anxiety attacks. Affected dogs are usually over ten years of age and usually have shown mild signs of separation anxiety earlier in their lives. When an already sensitive dog develops a painful medical problem, it becomes even needier, especially when alone at night. During the day, the owners are usually around and there are other distractions that take the dog's mind off his plight. But at night, when all is quiet and the dog's owners are asleep, there is nothing for him to do but dwell on his predicament, so pain and discomfort are magnified.

Dogs with this problem whine or pace, paw at the sheets or the owner, or become destructive. One dog I saw broke into closets at night and chewed up his owner's shoes. It is possible for vets to diagnose this problem on the first visit by listening carefully to the story, examining the dog, and running a few laboratory tests. Other times, confirmation of the nature of the underlying problem is not that easy. Medical problems that I have found underlying nocturnal/geriatric separation anxiety include brain tumors, arthritis, abdominal tumors, and eye tumors. A medically oriented client of mine told me that nighttime anxiety also occurs in human cancer patients and with such frequency that all cancer patients are given a handout on how to deal with it if it occurs. In dogs, treatment is to address the underlying cause — when that is possible. If the condition is treatable, the improvement is often dramatic. If the problem is incurable, palliative treatment is the only option.

Tucker, a forty-pound neutered beagle, was no spring chicken. Almost fourteen years old, he had enjoyed a good life but for the last few months had shown extreme anxiety at night, pacing, panting, and barking. If he fell asleep, he would wake up in a panic, leap to his feet, and start pushing doors or other objects with his nose.

Tucker was showing none of the usual signs of cognitive dysfunction. I assessed that he had some underlying medical problem — but what? Clinically, there wasn't much to see. I decided to take him for a blood sample, and as I went to leave the consulting room, his owner made a comment that caught my attention. She mentioned something about him having difficulty defecating. I thought about this as I led Tucker down the corridor. So, as well as taking blood, I also engaged in the relatively unusual practice — for me — of giving Tucker a rectal examination. When I touched his prostate gland, he screamed. I stopped and he was silent. I touched it again, he screamed. I had found something painful, something unusual, something that might account for his distress. At his age, prostate tumor was high on the list of possibilities. Further tests confirmed this suspicion. The good news was that I had found something that could account for his problem; the bad news was that it isn't easily treatable. The definitive treatment was with a nonsteroidal anti-inflammatory drug called piroxicam, which has some cancer-suppressing effects. In addition, I treated Tucker with antianxiety medication and sleep aids. The results were initially good. Tucker's nighttime anxiety subsided and he regained much of his youthful vigor. Sadly, though, all I was able to do for him was buy him a little extra quality time, as the improvement faded over time. Eventually his owners had to have him put to sleep, but at least his last few weeks of life were less stressful and less painful than they would otherwise have been.

Pica

As discussed in the previous chapter, dogs with pica have an appetite for inedible things, which they chew and eventually swallow. If the behavior becomes excessive, it can be extremely hazardous to a dog's health. The results of depraved eating are gastrointestinal disturbance (vomiting and diarrhea) or intestinal obstruction that may require surgery. It is said that medical problems frequently underlie such wanton eating behavior, and that is probably true, but there are purely behavioral causes of the problem, too. A variety of digestive disorders, some endocrine disorders, and anemia may all lead to pica.

Diagnoses with Behavioral Implications

Subclinical Hypothyroidism

Subclinical hypothyroidism is currently a hot topic in the dog-behavior world and in the world of veterinary science as well. It refers to suboptimal functioning of the thyroid gland and, controversially, may be linked to certain behavior problems. While hypothyroidism in dogs can be easily diagnosed by vets because of its unmistakable clinical signs of weight gain, lethargy, and skin conditions — coupled with well-defined acceptable limits of normal for all thyroid parameters in the dog's blood — the diagnosis of subclinical hypothyroidism is much more subtle. Unlike the full-blown condition, subclinical hypothyroidism is a bit of an enigma. Some dogs with borderline-low thyroid status show no obvious physical signs of the classic condition (see box next page). What subclinical hypothyroidism may cause, though, is increased anxiety and wariness, both of which can exacerbate various behavior problems. Increased aggression has been most commonly associated with borderline hypothyroidism, though other manifestations of anxiety are also possible. In humans, anxiety and depressive symptoms are more marked in patients with hypothyroidism, so it is not unreasonable to presume that dogs may follow suit. Many dog owners are convinced of the validity of testing for and treating subclinical hypothyroidism in their dogs. They read opinions about it on the Web and swap success stories. Some veterinarians are onboard with this diagnosis, but others remain skeptical despite numerous favorable case reports on the subject in the veterinary literature. Nonbelievers stick to their scientific guns, stating that no conclusive study has yet been per-

Signs of Hypothyroidism

Excessive shedding, patchy hair loss, or "rat tail"

Dry skin or dull, dry coat

Recurrent infections (especially ear, skin, and foot infections)

Tendency to gain weight

Heat-seeking behavior

Increased sleep time

Hyperactivity

Slow learning

Seizures

Worried look, tragic facial expression, or looking "old"

Reduced hearing, sight, and scenting ability

Chronic gastrointestinal symptoms

Loss of muscle or bladder tone

Head tilt

Change in character of bark

Exercise intolerance

Infertility, false pregnancy, or weak, dying, or stillborn puppies

Recurring eye infections

formed. They are right to be cautious but will not have to wait long to get the proof they need, as formal studies — with very promising preliminary results — are now under way.

Meantime, let's assume, as anecdotal reports imply, that subclinical hypothyroidism *does* contribute to mood disturbances in some dogs. In that case, how is the condition defined? Oversimplifying a bit, what we have come up with as an empirical definition here at Tufts is that if the most stable component of the thyroid hormone complex, total thyroxine (TT_4), and its free or unbound form (FT_4), are within the lowest twentieth percentile of the normal range (say, 1.2 units when the normal range is 1.0–4.0), then a borderline, suboptimal situation may well exist. (Of course, there are other blood results and clinical manifestations that we consider when making a diagnosis.) The response of most vets to finding a T_4 level of 1.2 is: "His thyroid level is within the normal range." It's true that it is within the normal range but, in our opinion, may be too low for comfort. By way of analogy, if a car's gas tank is registering in the red zone, it has gas — but you won't get far on it. In fact, you may run out at any time. That's how it is when thyroid levels are in the low-normal range. Affected dogs may show subtle signs of hypothyroidism, helping to confirm the diagnosis, but not all dogs evidence such confirmatory clues.

Let's suppose a dog that exhibits owner-directed aggression has a borderline T4 level, sheds all year round, and has dry, flaky skin. This dog might well benefit from a four- to six-week trial of thyroid hormone replacement therapy (THRT). Following the trial treatment period, the dog should be reevaluated to assess any change in its behavior and physical condition. A blood test will show the boosted T4 level. The goal of THRT is to elevate T4 to the top twenty-fifth percentile or even slightly above the normal range. If the dog's coat and demeanor improve, the treatment is considered a success and should be continued indefinitely. Sluggish thyroid glands — if that's the problem — do not suddenly get a new lease on life and begin to function normally. If the dog's condition fails to improve, THRT should be tapered off and discontinued. There's no point in continuing to treat a dog that is not benefiting from the treatment. Other anxious dogs with low

Breed Susceptibility to Hypothyroidism (the top twelve breeds)

- Golden retriever
- Shetland sheepdog
- American cocker spaniel
- English setter
- Boxer
- Doberman pinscher
- Labrador retriever
- German shepherd
- Akita
- Irish setter
- Old English sheepdog
- Collie

Note: All greyhounds have low levels of thyroid hormone as a "normal" feature of the breed. Toy breeds are least likely to be affected by hypothyroidism.

T4 that might benefit from the same therapeutic approach include those with noise phobia, global fear, separation anxiety, and compulsive behaviors.

Recently I saw a magnificent red Doberman cavorting on the veterinary school grounds. His owner, who I didn't immediately recognize, greeted me, and then I remembered: the woman worked at Tufts and had been to see one of my colleagues because her dog was a flank sucker and had been somewhat anxious and depressed to boot. "He's great now, isn't he?" she said. "No more flank sucking, no more depression, he's terrific — and it's all thanks to that thyroid treatment. That's all that we did." This dog, who had been a participant in a genetic study we are conducting, was found to have borderline-to-low thyroid hormone levels. According to his owner — and what I could see for myself — he had done extremely well with THRT. That's one case for the records.

Partial Seizures

Back in the 1960s it was quite common for vets to diagnose dogs exhibiting bizarre repetitive behaviors as having partial seizures. That was in the days before the diagnosis of canine compulsive behavior came into being (see chapter 8). Since then, attributing bizarre behavior to partial seizures has become unfashionable. In fact, some behaviorists today are extremely skeptical about the diagnosis. But Dr. Steven Schachter, a neurologist and epilepsy expert at the Beth Israel Deaconess Medical Center in Boston, shared with me that partial seizures are more common in people than grand mal epilepsy. If the "one medicine" concept that has stood me in good stead as a veterinary behaviorist continues to hold true, the same should be true in animals. One reason partial seizures are so well documented in people — but not dogs — is that people are able to verbalize the strange feelings they have. People experiencing a partial seizure may feel and act very strangely — having heightened sensations, with sounds seeming very loud, lights appearing almost painfully bright, and touch too heavy.

Some sufferers may even have auditory, visual, or olfactory hallucinations. Consciousness is altered but not necessarily lost during a bout. Memory of the events is usually impaired, though the person may continue to perambulate around like a character out of *Night of the Living Dead.*

Now consider what would be the canine equivalent. Imagine that a dog is going about his business when he suddenly feels lightheaded, tingly, and warm all over, possibly also experiencing some foul taste or weird smell. The dog may simultaneously get abdominal cramps or become confused. Anger, fear, or impatience may result, if the human experience is anything to go by. But a dog can't tell you how he's feeling, so we can only tell by his actions — but what might these actions be? My belief is that the behavior that results depends on where in the brain the electrical storm is occurring, because different regions control different functions and perceptions. If the seizure activity occurs in an area of the brain called the hypothalamus, predatory (chasing) manifestations, depraved eating, or aggression may occur. If the disturbance is centered in an area of the brain called the amygdala, extreme inexplicable fear might arise, with the dog literally cowering, shaking, and trying to hide. If a brain region that controls movement is affected, there may be some twitching, lip smacking, chewing, or head bobbing. Partial seizures in people (and I presume in dogs) also cause "autonomic" (involuntary) effects, such as widening of the pupils, drooping of the eyelids, drooling, or sweating (foot pads only in dogs).

The question becomes, How do we know if these different behaviors are attributable to partial seizures or something else? Chasing things or fear, for example, can be absolutely appropriate responses to certain environmental cues. What differentiates a seizure-related problem is not a single item but rather a whole gestalt of events. In many cases the behavior tends to be episodic, occurring with an interval of hours, days, or even weeks between incidents. Most dogs exhibiting partial seizures seem out of sorts before the event and may fall asleep afterward. The aberrant behavior that constitutes the seizure bout is often sudden in onset and serves no obvious purpose. If muscle twitching, jaw movements, or autonomic signs accompany the "attack," that again is evidence in favor of a partial seizure underlying the problem.

A friend of mine e-mailed me from Las Vegas asking for help regarding her daughter's dog. Her daughter had recently had a new baby and the dog had started to behave very strangely. Here's what she wrote. Read it and then see from what I have just described if you think this dog's behavior might have arisen from partial seizure activity:

> Please help if you can, Nick, our daughter and son-in-law are getting very worried. You see, they have two other "babies" besides our new grandson: Jake is a seven-year-old neutered lab/rot mix and Ginger is a five-year-old spayed pit/ridgeback mix. Jake was a stray and Ginger came from the pound and they have owned both dogs since they were less than a year old. These dogs are VERY well cared for both physically and mentally. They have their own doggie door to go in and out at will day and night, but are also walked every single day to the park for a run; they have a multitude of toys; and sleep with the rest of the family "pack" (Rebecca, Scott, and baby Jonathan) in the same room. Nothing has changed in their play/walk routine since the baby was brought home three weeks ago (except that they have had more company).
>
> Last night Ginger woke Rebecca and Scott up because she was pacing, panting, and sniffing, with tail wagging but with a nervous demeanor — she was kind of "crouched" as she sniffed all the bedroom, hall, nursery area, and when they got up, she followed them through the rest of the house but doing the exact same thing (like sniffing and searching for something). The other dog was snoozing away oblivious to whatever was causing Ginger's behavior. With a new-

born, Rebecca and Scott were exhausted and called Ginger back to the bedroom and tried to get her to lie down but was nervous and aggravated and got up and did it all again. Finally, she went to her bed and lay down and they fell asleep mystified.

Just now, Ginger went through this whole scenario again but during the day and we could all see what was happening. Rebecca called out to me to watch Ginger because she spotted her in the backyard in her sniffing, nervous pacing, crouched posture, and "searching" for something. I tried to coax her into the house by pushing on the doggie door flap (to show her the way) rather than opening the doorwall because her dogs prefer to come in through the doggie door and do not use the doorwall even if it is open. However, she acted like she did not even know the doggie door was there! I had to try to get her attention and show her how to come in the house through the doorwall! She continued her sniffing and searching through the family room/kitchen and when Rebecca tried to call her to come to her, which would have normally resulted in a bound around the sectional couch into her lap, Ginger stood behind the couch as if she didn't know how to get to Rebecca. Like the door, she didn't know how to get to her and I had to show her. Although she appeared to know Rebecca, it appeared to us that this whole sniffing time, she didn't really know where she was. I wanted to see if she remembered where her treats were kept and asked her if she wanted one. She seemed to recognize that I was at the pantry door and she wanted to come to me but again didn't know how to get to me (simply get off the sectional couch and go around the short end) and stayed on the couch pacing back and forth looking over the back of it. I showed her how to come around and she went to her dish to await her treat (normal behavior). After she ate her treat, it was like the "bout" was over and she was her normal self again. She found the couch, jumped up, and went to sleep, very relaxed. What on earth is going on. Please get back to us asap. Thanks, Jo Anne

I replied to Jo Anne that Ginger was most likely having some sort of seizure and that they should bring her to the local veterinarian for a neurological examination and some blood work. In my mind I had pretty much dismissed other possibilities like canine Alzheimer's (too young, not a classic presentation) and predatory behavior toward the new baby (dog got on fine with the baby and was not so much excited during the bouts as scared and confused). Things in favor of the partial seizure diagnosis were sudden onset, bout-like behavior not precipitated by any obvious external event, dysfunctional manifestation involving searching for something that was not there, and fatigue/sleep occurring immediately afterwards. Add to this the fact that the dog was part pit bull, part Rhodesian ridgeback — neither breed a stranger to seizure disorders — and the fact that the dog had several more bouts of the same behavior the very next day spaced at approximately two-hour intervals. The local veterinarian agreed with my hypothesis and treated the dog with the anticonvulsant phenobarbital, following which Ginger returned back to her old self with no further incidents of the abnormal behavior. But what caused the seizures in the first place? We will never know — but it could have had something to do with all the comings and goings in the house related to the new baby's arrival. Ginger could have been overwhelmed and thus stressed, and stress is a major factor promoting seizures. There's that mind-body connection again.

Diagnosis of the disorder does not have to be as circumstantial and subjective as it was in Ginger's case. Partial seizures can often be confirmed by electroencephalography (EEG) — looking at the dog's brain waves. We look for spiky wave patterns on the EEG trace, particularly in the temporal lobe of the brain where the hypothalamus, limbic system, and other emotional centers are housed. A second, less convincing way to diagnose partial seizures is by observing a positive response to treatment with anticonvulsant drugs (as occurred in Ginger's case).

Let's consider a few possible expressions of partial seizures to illustrate the problem further.

Seizure-related behaviors

Rage: A man sat at his kitchen counter reading his daily newspaper. As he turned the page, his two-year-old spayed female pit bull attacked him savagely and just kept on coming. Fortunately, the man managed to escape with minor injuries. The dog finally regained her composure and returned to her happy-go-lucky old self. This attack was unprovoked, extreme, out of character for the dog, and there was no obvious explanation for it. Other similar attacks followed. I saw this dog many years ago and wondered about the possibility of seizure activity underlying her sudden mood change. Another odd thing, a clue as it turns out, was that the dog compulsively groomed her left flank to the point of hair loss. A short course of treatment with an anticonvulsant abolished the aggression and flank licking, seemingly confirming the involvement of seizure activity in both of these problems.

Rare though it is, rage in dogs is important to recognize and understand because it poses a human health hazard. In 1977, Cornell professor Alexander DeLahunta, in his famous clinical neurology textbook, *Veterinary Neuroanatomy and Clinical Neurology,* described behavioral seizures originating in the temporal lobe of the brain as a cause of rage in springer spaniels. However, like other partial seizure diagnoses, the seizure theory of rage came to be doubted. In a veterinary behavior textbook, Dr. Benjamin Hart of the University of California at Davis referred to the violent, dysfunctional aggression shown by some dogs as "idiopathic" — meaning without known cause. Dr. Ilana Reisner, a veterinary behaviorist whose PhD dissertation dealt with aggression in springer spaniels, said that she did not believe in springer rage when she started her studies. But following many years of detailed study, she conceded that something bizarre was going on in some of the aggressive springers she studied. I gathered that she was wavering in her acceptance of springer rage as an entity. Here at Tufts, we have been a little more cavalier in our claims and have published reports of dogs with explosive aggression who, according to EEG evidence and response to treatment, appear to have suffered from seizure-related aggression (we called it "episodic dyscontrol" — a term borrowed from human psychiatric medicine). Some dogs express rage only out of the depths of sleep. They wake up abruptly attacking whatever is in front of them; sometimes a person, sometimes another dog, sometimes a piece of furniture. Sleep, as it turns out, is a well-known trigger for seizures, so rage surfacing from the depths of sleep makes perfect sense. Some people have seizures almost exclusively at night when they are sleeping. I have seen several bull terriers with this nocturnal version of the problem — and one golden retriever.

All in all, I have seen rage in springer spaniels, cocker spaniels, bull terriers, a pit bull terrier, a Chesapeake Bay retriever, a beagle, a couple of bulldogs, and the aforementioned golden retriever. I believe rage is a real entity and is a consequence of partial seizure activity in the brain. It's rare, that's for sure, but it does seem to occur — particularly in seizure-prone breeds (which again makes sense). Some of the dogs I have diagnosed with this problem have subsequently manifested classic seizure activity, such as stiffening, falling over, shaking, twitching, jerking, jaw chomping, drooling, and so on. That's fairly conclusive.

The big problem when it comes to treating seizure-related aggression is that while it can be successfully controlled with medication, treatment must be virtually 100 percent effective to ensure the safety of people living with the dog. This goal can be difficult to achieve. Nevertheless, some owners choose to have their dogs treated and learn to avoid their dogs when they see (certain) premonitory signs heralding an attack. For treatment, I usually employ the old standby, phenobarbital. If the result is unsatisfactory after three weeks, I supplement the treatment with another seizure-controlling medication, potassium bromide. Things can get tricky if phenobarbital and bromide don't produce the desired effects, but fortunately there are new anticonvulsants around these days that can be tried instead. The most important thing for owners to remember is to exercise caution around the dog when he appears in a strange mood and never, under any circumstances, try to handle or physically control the dog at these times.

Fear: As mentioned above, one of the more common feelings that epileptic people experience before or after having a seizure is fear. It seems that brain regions mediating fear response are spuriously activated as a result of the precursory or "aftershock" ripples of the electrical conflagration. The same appears to happen in the case of partial seizures, though, with respect to the latter, the conflagration is perhaps more locally confined. I have seen only a handful of dogs who I thought were suffering from this disorder and confirmed the diagnosis by EEG in only one of them. The other suspected cases responded to anticonvulsant therapy, providing some vindication for the presumed diagnosis. The first time I saw this problem it was in a bull terrier. The dog was globally phobic — that is, exceptionally frightened of everything and everyone all the time and for no good reason. I accidentally dropped a manila file on my desk during the appointment and the dog jumped about a foot in the air with his feet splayed out sideways like a cartoon cat. This dog also "moonwalked," raising his feet higher than normal off the ground with each step and moving as if in slow motion. One of Dr. Schachter's epileptic patients reported that, during a seizure bout, he would feel as if he was "walking on air" and had to pick his feet up "real high" in order to walk. That sounds like what I was seeing in this dog. Though EEG results indicated that a diagnosis of (partial) seizures was correct, the proof of the pudding was in the treating. Days after starting phenobarbital, the dog was angst-free and acting like a puppy again. It was as if a great weight had been lifted from her shoulders.

A German shepherd mix I saw was frightened of the sun. When the sun came out from behind a cloud, the dog would shake, drool, and try to hide. When the sun went behind the cloud, the dog was hypervigilant—constantly looking skyward, still afraid. Again, quoting from one of Dr. Schachter's patients: "I have noticed that certain environmental factors have become more difficult to manage, *including bright sunlight . . .*" I felt sure this German shepherd mix had partial seizure activity underlying her unusual fear. As vindication of my reasoning, the problem was well controlled using phenobarbital and Valium (also an anticonvulsant).

Recently, I have seen a couple of Bernese mountain dogs with the same type of inexplicable, extreme fear. One of these always ran from the house when visitors came and spent days cowering at the bottom of the yard following each unwelcome visit. It was an extreme and unusual reaction. Because there was no early environmental dysfunction to account for this dog's fearfulness, I reasoned that it was genetic in origin. The fact that Bernese mountain dogs are prone to seizures led to the conjecture that it could be some sort of seizure disturbance. I treated him accordingly and his confidence improved considerably. Though he was still obviously unhappy about visitors, at least he did not run away and hide at the bottom of the yard for days after they came over.

Snapping at "Imaginary" Flies: Although snapping at imaginary flies can be a compulsive disorder, as discussed in the last chapter, the behavior has also been attributed to partial seizures. Not only does fly snapping affect predominantly seizure-prone breeds, such as bull terriers, Norfolk terriers, Greater Swiss mountain dogs, and German shepherds, but it also often responds to anti-convulsant therapy. My behaviorist colleague, Dr. Alice Moon-Fanelli, had a coydog as a pet. (A coydog is a cross between a coyote and a domestic dog, in this case a beagle.) One day she unwittingly put a flea collar containing a potentially seizure-promoting ingredient on her dog. Shortly afterward, he began to snap at imaginary flies. When she took the collar off, the problem ceased and never recurred. It seems that her dog was seizure-prone and that the chemical in the collar pushed him over the brink. The fact that the dog was part beagle was probably relevant, too, as beagles are seizure-prone.

Tail Chasing: Tail chasing is a problem that primarily affects bull terriers, German shepherds, and dogs derived from either of these breeds. There are also a few small terrier-type dogs that chase their tails; curiously, many of them are white. Tail chasing, like fly snapping, is often described as a canine compulsive disorder (see chapter 8), but that may not be the whole story. We conducted a study of six tail-chasing bull terriers at Tufts Cummings School and found that all of the dogs had epileptiform EEGs. Five of them also had moderate to severe hydrocephalus ("water on the brain"). These findings suggest that the problem may have a medical explanation, too — as opposed to being purely behavioral. The positive response of tail-chasing German shepherds to antiepileptic medication makes a strong case for the involvement of seizures in tail chasing in this breed. As mentioned earlier, tail-chasing German shepherds do not respond that well to antiobsessional medication alone, but many get much better when also treated with an anticonvulsant like phenobarbital. I am not completely sold on the notion that partial seizures always underlie tail chasing, so usually begin treatment with an antiobsessional drug, but the possible role of seizure activity and the possible value of anticonvulsants in treatment are important to bear in mind. The same may be true for bull terriers, though antiobsessional drugs alone are often effective treatment for tail chasing in this breed. The bottom line is that dogs with extreme forms of tail chasing, from whatever cause, usually need medication of some sort to settle them down. And the medication may have to be in place long term, if not for life. The only other solution I have found, occasionally, is that of a geographical cure. What I mean by this is moving the dog from one environment — one geographical location — to another in which the dog's lifestyle is very much enhanced. The "cure" in these cases might result from anxiety reduction — which would have a positive impact whether the problem was compulsive in nature or arose from partial seizure activity in the brain.

Shadow and Light Chasing: Some bored dogs, usually ones with high prey drive and often ones that are deaf, chase shadows and lights to the point of distraction, theirs and yours. It has been suggested that this condition may result from partial seizure activity in the visual cortex of the brain, but I do not think that this is the case. My reasoning is that the condition does not occur primarily in seizure-prone breeds, does not respond well to anticonvulsants, and, in the only case in which I performed an EEG, the brain waves were normal. The dog in question was a wirehaired fox terrier called Bumbly. Bumbly became absolutely frantic at the first sign of lights or shadows. In fact, when his owners had to leave him alone at home, they had to "Bumbly-proof" their home before they went out by drawing curtains, moving breakables on high, hanging the shower curtains over the rail, and so on. Bumbly's EEG was performed live on camera as part of the television show *20/20* and was eventually aired in front of a large national audience. The trace, even from the part of the brain responsible for visual interpretation, was entirely normal, so I did not pursue the seizure theory or the anticonvulsant route of treatment with him. Shadow chasing, however, does respond reasonably well to antiobsessional drugs like Prozac, and Bumbly did respond to this line of treatment. So much for the seizure-basis theory of shadow chasing. It seems to me shadow/light chasing fits in more closely with the compulsive disorders described in chapter 8.

Glugging: I once saw a man who told me his springer spaniel was "glugging." By glugging he meant making swallowing motions accompanied by gulping sounds. I immediately thought the dog must have swallowed something that got stuck in his throat. But when I looked, his throat was clear of any debris. I watched a video of the dog that the man had brought with him. "Here he goes," the man said on the soundtrack. At that, the dog switched from relaxed to agitated, looking startled, worried, and had large black pools for eyes (dilated pupils). Then the dog started to graze on the linoleum floor. I could tell from the copious strips of duct tape that he had chewed up the floor on previous occasions. Next he cruised the perimeter of the kitchen floor like a hungry shark, hoovering up dust bunnies and other detritus as he went, seemingly unstoppable in his mission. Then he stopped and walked over to the door. "Let me out," his expression said. The man obliged and followed him with the video camera. In the backyard, the dog proceeded to eat great globs of grass and dirt in a frenzied fashion. Eventually the dog's mood passed and he returned to normal. This behavior, as it turns out, was a form of partial seizure. One of the giveaways was the boutlike nature of the behavior. It was as if a switch had been thrown. Another clue was his breed — springer. The focus of the seizure activity was most likely in an area of the brain responsible for controlling eating behavior. The dog's response to anticonvulsant therapy was spectacular and complete. It wasn't long after I saw this dog, my first case of glugging, that an owner told me that his dog was a "snoofer." Yes, you guessed it, it was the same problem. Since then I have seen several such cases and have become *au fait* with respect to the diagnosis.

REM Sleep Disorder (aka REM Behavior Disorder)

Some dogs wake suddenly from a deep sleep to run around and perhaps, out of character, attack the nearest object or living thing. While this sounds similar to partial seizure attacks, it is sometimes a result of rapid eye movement (REM) sleep disorder. The mechanism of REM sleep disorder is like that of night terrors that occur in children. When we (or our dogs) fall into a deep sleep, the body is totally relaxed — paralyzed, in fact. The reason is that serotonin mechanisms responsible for executive control over muscular activity are — or should be — shut down. At this time the mind is racing with dreams that replace rational, organized thought. During this dreaming phase of sleep, small muscles outside the control of the serotonin system — eye muscles and digital muscles — may flick or twitch. Only large antigravity muscles are completely turned off. In REM sleep disorder and night terrors, the serotonin system fails to shut down and dreams can be physically acted out. The result is that a person or dog can perambulate and show emotions — eyes wide open — while unconscious and asleep. The perambulation and mood swings may not last long, and following an episode the person or dog simply goes back to sleep, unaware of what has transpired. Treatment for this rare behavioral disturbance is by means of a Valium-like drug called clonazepam. Treated dogs respond quite well.

Narcolepsy

Narcolepsy is a sleep disorder that primarily affects Doberman pinschers, dachshunds, and Labrador retrievers. When affected with this condition, dogs literally fall asleep on their feet and enter a REM-like state. A faulty gene responsible for the manufacture of a stay-awake neuropeptide (hypocretin) is responsible for the disorder. In dogs, food is usually the trigger for a narcoleptic attack; dogs may fall asleep over a treat or with their nose in the food bowl. Excitement can be a trigger, too. A dog eagerly heading outside with his owner may suddenly fall asleep in his tracks.

It's weird to see. Treatment is necessarily medical, using stimulant drugs such as Ritalin and amphetamine — though codeine and antidepressants may be helpful too.

Canine Cognitive Dysfunction (aka Canine Alzheimer's Disease)

If an older dog who was previously housetrained suddenly starts to have accidents around the house and there is no medical explanation for the behavior, canine cognitive dysfunction, an Alzheimer's-like deterioration in mental processing, should be considered. Of course, it's not up to you, the owner, to make the diagnosis — your vet will do that — but here are a few other signs to watch out for. First is disorientation. Affected dogs tend to become disoriented, getting stuck behind furniture, standing at the wrong side of the door to go out, or walking someplace and then seeming to forget why they went there. Another sign is altered social interactions with people. For example, dogs that would have greeted owners become indifferent to their homecoming. Dogs that formerly shadowed their owners throughout the day become detached and fail to respond to their names. Some owners think their dog has become deaf because he is so unresponsive to sound cues. But it's not that the dog doesn't hear, he's just not able to process the signal properly. Another change occurs in sleeping pattern. Affected dogs usually sleep more during a twenty-four-hour period but sleep fitfully at night. Some even appear to suffer from a sundowner syndrome in which nightfall makes them restless and anxious. Finally, as already mentioned, loss of bladder or bowel control, causing house soiling in a formerly housetrained dog, is a cardinal sign of the condition. Canine cognitive dysfunction is a bona fide medical problem that affects some dogs as they age. It is not usually seen in dogs less than ten years of age, but its incidence in the canine population increases year by year after that.

Dogs with canine cognitive dysfunction have physical changes in their brain architecture that parallel measured changes in their behavior. While the pathology is not identical to that of Alz-heimer's disease in humans, it is similar. One key change in the brain is the buildup of a protein called beta-amyloid. Amyloid for-mation represents an attempt by the brain to repair ongoing damage and is not the cause of the brain dysfunction per se. Fortu-nately, treatment for canine cognitive dysfunction is available and is effective in many cases. Anipryl, marketed by Pfizer, is extremely effective at reversing signs of canine cognitive dysfunction in about one-third of cases. In another one-third of cases, the effects are positive but not quite so remarkable. The effects of Anipryl do not last forever because the underlying disease is progressive. So, six to twelve months after beginning treatment, you may find the drug losing efficacy as the disease process overwhelms its beneficial effect. However, buying the dog additional quality time, especially when you consider that one year in a dog's life is equivalent to seven or more in ours, is a worthwhile endeavor.

Recently, some reports of other treatments for "canine Alz-heimer's" have appeared. Documenting what we were beginning to explore ourselves at Tufts, the reports indicate that other novel treatments — sometimes using combinations of components — are effective in reducing the clinical signs of the condition. One approach is to try to stabilize cell membranes and another is to prevent oxidative damage to brain cells. Both seem to work. Hill's Pet Nutrition now markets a prescription antioxidant-rich diet called Hill's b/d (brain diet) to postpone aging in dogs. The efficacy of this diet in delaying the onset and progression of behavioral changes attributable to old age has been documented. The company reports that some dogs with established cognitive function improve, too.

Where Your Vet Comes In . . .

The list of problems affecting dogs' behavior discussed in this chapter is not comprehensive. Neurological problems like brain tumors and rabies can and do affect behavior, as can metabolic problems, like liver failure. Any condition that makes a dog feel uncomfortable will affect his behavior. Arthritis can make dogs cranky and cause them to growl or worse if someone touches them where it hurts. Lyme disease causes arthritis and neurological problems, and various behavior problems, including pain-induced aggression, have been associated with this condition. Deafness and blindness can lead to dogs being easily startled because they can't see or hear peoples' approach. This can lead to their reacting out of surprise — sometimes aggressively. Suffice it to say that if your dog is behaving oddly in any way — showing a sudden aggression or acting anxiously — it may not be a trainer that you need but a veterinarian. When in doubt, a visit to the vet's office is always a good first choice. Your vet is your best ally when it comes to recognizing and dealing with the medical aspects of behavior problem management.

10

Healing Potions

Behavior-Modifying Agents: Natural and Pharmacologic Remedies

> Healing is a matter of time, but it is sometimes
> also a matter of opportunity.
> — Hippocrates

Even when an owner is doing everything right for a dog, behavior problems can and do sometimes arise. When genetic factors are stacked against a dog, or when his early upbringing has been dysfunctional, even the most favorable lifestyle will not ensure a problem-free pet. We are beginning to realize that some of the most obstinate canine behavior problems, like phobias and compulsive disorders, involve chemical imbalances in the brain similar to those that can occur in humans. Behavior modification can favorably alter brain chemistry and affect behavior issues when effective, but, paraphrasing Hippocrates, recovery sometimes necessitates having an opportunity to heal. Some behavior problems are so severe that it is difficult to break the vicious cycle of "exposure-response-reinforcement" long enough for a new veneer of positive learning to be applied. In such situations, behavior-modifying drugs can be a lifeline.

Medical interventions, when necessary, can improve the quality of dogs' lives when nothing else seems to work. When dogs feel better, the behavior problem that had made life difficult for the owner is often substantially improved or, in some cases, disappears completely. Psychopharmacology involves treating the dog from the inside out, instead of from the outside in. Although behavior-modifying medications can and do work without concurrent behavior-modification therapy, the combination of medication and retraining strategies produces the fastest and best results. The goal is to taper off the medication at the first opportunity, and ongoing behavioral therapy is usually necessary to ensure that any improvement is maintained. In situations where the withdrawal of medication leads to a relapse, most behavior-modifying medication can be continued indefinitely with appropriate veterinary supervision.

For those opposed to treating dogs with behavior-modifying medication (on the grounds that dogs don't have a choice in whether to be medicated), remember that as dog "parents," owners always have to make decisions for their dogs, because dogs, like children, are not in a position to decide for themselves. We are the ones who decide to have them vaccinated, administered antibiotics when they have an infection, and surgically treated when the need arises. Giving them drugs to help them get around one of life's really sharp corners is no different. If a dog were able to weigh in, I am sure he would consent to medical treatment that would alleviate an intractable behavioral problem that could otherwise lead to his relinquishment. *Let me see*, the dog might ponder, *a six-month course of Prozac or euthanasia in a shelter. It's a tough call, but I guess I'll take the Prozac.* Many dogs who are presently alive and well would not be either if it were not for behavior-modifying drugs; their owners would have simply given up on them. I know this for a fact. These days, drugs are frequently prescribed by veterinarians to reduce aggression and anxiety, quell phobias, and check severe compulsions.

When a Pharmacologic Treatment Can Save a Dog's Life

Barney the bulldog suddenly started to behave like a raging bull when he hit young adulthood. Though his owners loved him, even they were finding it difficult to live with a dog who would suddenly charge at them and pin them against the wall, growling, for the most trivial of reasons. Barney had taken up resource guarding and territorial guarding with such gusto that it was impossible to be in the same room with him when food was around, and his owners were finding it difficult to get back in their own house when they came home. When they returned from an excursion, Barney's owners would find his nibs guarding the door, and they'd be afraid to enter. And there were no flies on Barney. If they crept around the house to another entrance, they would find him running from window to window growling and keeping tabs on them. Their solution of throwing food to distract him was working to some extent, but they were having a few near misses and wondered how long they were going to be able to deal with Barney's unacceptable behavior. By the time they came to me, they were ready to put Barney to sleep if they couldn't get his behavior problem under control in short order. Bulldogs are an unusual breed. Their flattened faces make them susceptible to airway trouble and some neurological problems. I suspected the latter were involved in Barney's case because he also occasionally exhibited head bobbing. Treatment for Barney involved implementing a leadership program and medication: Prozac to control his aggression and an anticonvulsant to quell presumed nervous irritability. The result was spectacular and Barney's life was spared. When we later tried to reduce the dose of medication, Barney's raging bull behavior reappeared, so for him treatment was (literally) for life.

Like Barney before his treatment, Lief, a rescued German shepherd, could not help himself. In almost all situations he became overexcited and was constantly running around yelping, snapping, spinning, and biting his tail. In Lief's case, he loved and respected his owner, so aggression toward his owner was not an issue. Lief's antics made life very difficult for his owner, who had to tolerate the dog's noisy, hyperkinetic behavior in his small downtown Boston apartment. The neighbors were none too pleased either. Lief's owner was more concerned for his dog's welfare than his own predicament. Behavior modification had not worked for Lief, yet it was impossible to imagine him continuing in this constant state of red-alert hyperreactivity. Something had to be done. After medical tests and some trial-and-error therapeutics, I finally found the right combination of medications to help Lief. Like Barney, he responded to mood-stabilizing medication and an anticonvulsant. In Lief's case, I also had to adjust his thyroid hormone levels. With these treatments, Lief's behavior normalized. Even years later during his annual checkups, Lief would sit calmly next to his owner, his hysteria gone. An older dog now, Lief is beginning to have a few age-related medical problems. He is lucky to have made it this far. Had his owner not toughed out the issues, Lief's quality of life would have been severely limited, and the situation may have simply become untenable for his owner.

Not all dogs with behavior problems need to be — or should be — medicated. Pharmacological treatment options should be considered in situations in which behavior modification alone is unlikely to produce the desired result or has failed to produce results. Another good reason to consider medication is if a behavior problem is life-threatening for the dog or poses a serious risk to other dogs or people (e.g., aggression). The sooner such dogs can be brought under control the better, and psychopharmacology, if nothing else, accelerates the response time. Finally, behavior-modifying drugs may be called for when a dog's owner has lost patience with behavior-modification therapy or when owners are constrained in their ability to implement a retraining program because of their advanced age or infirmity.

Natural Remedies

For owners in need of extra help in managing their dogs' behavior but who are unwilling or reluctant, for whatever reason, to embark on a pharmacologic regimen, a variety of herbal and nutraceutical remedies are available that may be usefully employed to treat behavior problems in dogs. This is to be expected, as plant remedies predate drug remedies and quite a few medicinal drugs are derived from plants. The cardiac drug digitalis, for example, is an extract of plants in the foxglove family (e.g., the common foxglove, *Digitalis purpurea*). Salicin, originally extracted from the bark of the willow tree (*Salix alba*), was modified to form aspirin. Morphine and codeine are extracts of the opium poppy (*Papaver somniferum*). Though heart patients could scarf down great wads of foxglove and people in pain could chew on willow bark or sun-dried poppy latex for relief, they would probably prefer chemically pure, accurately dosed, medicinal forms of these drugs. However, the active ingredients of many plant medications — like valerian — have yet to be isolated and purified, leaving no other option than to consume the plant directly if you want its special effect. Conversely, many modern medicines have been fabricated and have no botanical equivalents, leaving proprietary forms of the drugs the only ones available.

Some but not all herbal remedies work. I have confidence that valerian root has a sedative property in dogs but little faith in the calming effects of Bach flower essences. To find success with botanicals, you must use the right herb or plant for the purpose at hand, employ the correct dosage, and make sure the medicinal herb or plant is in the correct form. This is not something you can or should try to fathom on your own. You will need input from a veterinarian, preferably one who specializes in animal behavior or alternative medicine. One of the drawbacks of herbal remedies is that none has yet been clinically proven to work in dogs, so their efficacy must be taken on faith. Another problem is that — assuming they contain a pharmacologically active compo-nent — the amount of whatever-it-is will vary considerably from batch to batch. A good batch may be stiff with the stuff, while an improperly stored or weedy batch may contain little or none. Since studies of the pharmacological profile of the active ingre-dient in the body will not have been performed, the frequency of dosing is determined by trial and error. In some cases, it is not known which plant chemical is producing the effect, so detailed study is impossible.

Some people think that because a remedy is herbal it must be safe. Not so. Many plants are poisonous and herbal remedies sometimes produce serious, even fatal, side effects. Check out bel-ladonna (aka deadly nightshade), for example: so named because would-be beautiful Italian women (*bella donnas*) used it cosmet-ically to enlarge the pupils of their eyes. Belladonna, containing the alkaloid atropine, can kill you if you eat it. Some herbal-therapy aficionados believe that the hotchpotch of compounds found in medicinal plants is advantageous when it comes to ther-apy. They think the ancillary components present somehow for-tify the action of herbs because of some "natural" balance effect. I disagree. Plants did not arrange their components for optimum therapeutic efficacy in humans. The fact that willow bark con-tains lignin, suberin, and cellulose is neither here nor there; it's the salicin that has the effect. Give me the chemically pure, easily absorbed, relatively stomach-friendly derivative acetylsalicylic acid (aspirin) any day. On the other hand, chamomile helps a col-icky pup get over his stomach problem through some unknown, unpurified component — so there's no other choice but to use it if you want its unique effects. Ditto when it comes to kava kava and some other botanical products.

There are so many herbal products available, it's hard to keep track. My clients tell me what they have tried, and, from what I gather, the following seem to be most popular: Bach flower essences (Rescue Remedy) to treat anxiety; valerian root for sedation/calming; Saint John's wort for depression and restlessness; chamomile for gastrointestinal problems and insomnia; and kava kava as a mood stabilizer. These remedies are given either alone or in various combinations. Since it is beyond the scope of this book to discuss every herbal therapy in detail, I have elected to say a few words about each of these popular herbal remedies to give the reader some idea of what is known about them and how they are employed. Anxiety reduction and sedation/sleep promotion — sometimes panacea efficacy — are common themes.

Rescue Remedy

Originally intended for use in humans, Rescue Remedy has found its way into the therapeutic armamentarium of pet owners, shelter workers, and trainers. Many people swear by its efficacy. It is used in dogs for the treatment of a variety of emotional and behavioral ailments and has been deemed effective in just about all situations in which it has been tried. Bach flowers are the flowers of some thirty-eight plants and trees, the essence of which is extracted in 40 percent brandy as "mother tinctures" that when ingested either neat or in diluted form are thought to provide relief from various unpleasant feelings. Each flower extract was tested and cataloged by Dr. Edward Bach for use in a variety of human ailments. Rescue Remedy, a popular combination of five such flower essences, namely, cherry plum, clematis, impatiens, rockrose, and star-of-Bethlehem, was designed to reduce a variety of fearful states. While this remedy has never been properly tested for safety or efficacy, it has been around for years and no ill effects have been reported. Even if it does not work, at least in using it you do no harm.

Uses of Rescue Remedy

- Rescue Remedy has been used in dogs to treat fear-based behaviors, such as thunderstorm phobia, separation anxiety, and anxiety caused during car travel or veterinary office visits.

- Rescue Remedy has also been employed as a treatment for anxiety-based urine marking in cats and dogs.

Precautions and Side Effects

- There are no known precautions and no side effects have been reported to date.

No client of mine has ever reported any useful effect from giving Bach flower essences Rescue Remedy to their pet. That's why they come to see me. You could argue that when it does work, they do not need to come and see me, so I would never learn about its benefits. Nevertheless, at this time I remain skeptical that it produces any useful effect.

Valerian Root

Valerian officinalis is the botanical name of the plant from which valerian root extract is prepared. The plant's root contains yellowish/brownish/green oil rich in isovalerianic acid that is apparently the cause of valerian's unpleasant smell. The root also contains alkaloids. Two main ones are chatarine and valerianine. Valerian has been used as a sedative for about two thousand years and continues to be used as such today. There is little doubt that valerian has sedative/calming properties in humans and animals. Its nervous system effects are thought to result from an action on the same inhibitory neurotransmitter system that Valium works on. Valerian is also said to have antispasmodic properties (reducing spasm in muscles). Valerian — as valerian, valerian root extract, or tincture of valerian — is an over-the-counter drug in the United States. Quite a lot of anecdotal information has been published about the use and effects of valerian in dogs.

Uses of Valerian

- Valerian is used as a sedative or anxiety-reducing drug and sleep promoter.

- It has also been used as an antispasmodic and anticonvulsant and has been recommended for the treatment of hyperactivity.

Precautions and Side Effects

- Since valerian has not been properly tested in dogs, it should be used only with caution — though it is probably reasonably safe.
- Valerian should not be used in animals with known hypersensitivity or allergy to it.
- Valerian may interact with other medications (e.g., antidepressants, barbiturates, and other "behavior-modifying drugs").

Quite a few owners have reported to me that valerian root causes their dogs to become sedated, so I have some faith that valerian works — at least as a sedative. However, the great strength of modern pharmacological treatments is that they do not produce generalized depression or sedation — as this seems to be what most owners dislike, even fear, the most about the concept of any medicinal treatment. This is not to say that sedation is never useful, only that it is not what behaviorists want — or are trying to achieve — when using behavior-modifying drugs.

Saint John's Wort

Saint John's wort is an herbal remedy with a long and somewhat controversial history as a treatment for anxiety and mild to moderate depression in humans. It has also been used to treat stomach upset and insomnia, and as a topical painkiller and antibiotic. The beneficial effect of Saint John's wort in humans remains controversial. The benefits in dogs and other animals are even less clear. Saint John's wort is available over the counter but should not be administered without the supervision and guidance of a veterinarian. Note that Saint John's wort is marketed for use in humans, but there are a number of preparations sold for use in animals that contain Saint John's wort.

Uses of Saint John's Wort

- Saint John's wort is sometimes used to treat mild depression. In dogs, conditions that might respond to therapy include grieving, long-term separation, or day-to-day separation anxiety.
- Saint John's wort has also been used to treat various other anxious states.

Precautions and Side Effects

- Although essentially safe, Saint John's wort may cause side effects in some animals. One of its notable side effects is photosensitivity. Dogs treated with Saint John's wort should probably not be overly exposed to bright sunlight.
- Saint John's wort may interact with other medications (e.g., antidepressants).
- In addition, as with other herbal remedies, it should not be used in animals who have previously exhibited hypersensitivity to it.

A Harvard-based review of the scientific literature concerning the use of Saint John's wort in people indicated that it is effective for the treatment of mild depression and that its use was not associated with any notable side effects.

Chamomile

There are several different varieties of herb known rather loosely as chamomile (or camomile), but only two of the daisy-like species have had significant use as medicinal herbs. These are the perennial "noble" chamomile *Anthemis nobilis* or *Chamaemelum nobile,* also known as English or Roman chamomile, and the annual *Matricaria recutita,* also known as German or wild chamomile.

Uses of Chamomile

- As medicinal plants, chamomiles traditionally have been used as antispasmodics (to alleviate intestinal cramping).
- Chamomiles have also been used as carminatives (to reduce bloat/intestinal gas) and as aids to digestion.

Precautions and Side Effects

- Chamomile may cause toxic reactions in individuals sensitive to ragweed or other allergens.

The supposed sleep-inducing properties of chamomile may be due to the purported settling effect it has on the gastrointestinal tract. I was informed by a reliable source, a highly credentialed human anesthesiologist, that chamomile tea helped his young child to sleep through the night while he was a resident in training. This gave him a chance to catch some much-needed rest. I believe that the reason it worked so well in this case was that it settled the child's gripes (stomachache) and allowed the child — and thus the anesthesiologist — to get some sleep. It is possible, though, that chamomile has a more direct sleep-inducing effect.

Kava Kava

Kava kava is a tropical herb that supposedly has an effect similar to that of aspirin. Kava kava is also a mild tranquilizer and has been used to treat anxiety. Pacific Islanders brew up a kava kava concoction that is used the same way as alcohol to produce a relaxed intoxicated state. There is no data to support the therapeutic use of kava kava in dogs, and its safety has not been evaluated in them. Kava kava is classified by the FDA as a nutritional supplement. Many different preparations of kava kava are available from a variety of manufacturers and distributors.

Uses of Kava Kava

- Kava kava has been used in veterinary medicine as a mild sedative to relieve anxiety-based behaviors, such as separation anxiety in dogs.
- It has also has been employed as a painkiller, a muscle relaxant, anticonvulsant, mood stabilizer, and sleep inducer.

Precautions and Side Effects

- Yellowing of skin, nails, and hair
- Eye irritation
- Insomnia
- Difficulty maintaining balance

There is no doubt in my mind that kava kava has a biological, mood-altering effect, but I need to learn more about its use in a veterinary clinical setting before I would feel confident about its efficacy in a particular situation with respect to dogs.

Other Natural Remedies

Other remedies classed as "natural" include nutraceuticals, like tryptophan, hormones like melatonin, and various homeopathic medications. Amino acids, like tryptophan, building blocks of protein, do have some biological action, and I recommend them from time to time for treatment of dogs whose owners are reluctant to give their dogs pharmacologic drugs. Tryptophan used to be available as L-tryptophan before the eosinophilia-myalgia (EM) scare some years ago. This debilitating condition is associated with muscle pain (myalgia) and a high count of particular white cells (eosinophils) in the blood. The cause was contamination of a batch of L-tryptophan shipped from Japan. Because of this incident, the FDA had L-tryptophan withdrawn from the market; it is no longer for sale over the counter. L-tryptophan is an essential amino acid for dogs and is present in dog food. What is available over the counter is a derivative of L-tryptophan, 5-HTP.

5-HTP (5-hydroxytryptophan) is actually a tad better than L-tryptophan, being better absorbed and more rapidly transported to its site of action — the brain. Here it is metabolized directly to the mood-stabilizing neurotransmitter serotonin. In Europe, 5-HTP is more often prescribed for mood stabilization in people than Prozac. 5-HTP is relatively safe in dogs and somewhat effective for treating a variety of mood disorders that might otherwise lead to aggression, phobias, or compulsive behaviors. It has as broad a spectrum of activity as Prozac (see later) and produces its effects similarly by augmenting serotonin concentrations at synapses (nerve connections) in the brain. It appeals to naturalists because it's not a "drug," though its effects are almost the same.

The sleep hormone melatonin is another treatment popular with the natural movement for treatment of sleep disturbances and anxiety. Melatonin can be helpful in some situations, but in my experience it is only minimally effective. On the positive side, melatonin is incredibly safe. Laboratory rodents could not be given enough of it for scientists to calculate a lethal dose. Melatonin, which is secreted by the pituitary gland, influences the sleep-wake cycle and reproductive cycles of some domestic species. Its levels fluctuate during the day and over the course of the year. Melatonin's precursor, serotonin, whose concentration is highest on waking, is converted to melatonin over the course of the day. Higher levels of melatonin at the end of the day help trigger sleep. Low levels of serotonin at the end of the day increase the likelihood of irritability and aggression at this time, especially in already aggressive dogs. The use of melatonin is unwise in depressed patients because it can decrease serotonin formation by negative feedback, thus worsening depression.

Proponents of melatonin claim ever more numerous behavioral benefits for it that go well beyond sleep induction. Anxiety reduction is one far-reaching claim, because anxiety can promote aggression, phobias, and separation anxiety — as well as seizures. And melatonin has been touted as being effective in any and all of these conditions in dogs. I must admit, I have had some seemingly positive experiences myself when prescribing melatonin. One dog — a golden retriever with severe fear of fireworks — coped remarkably well one Fourth of July when, at our suggestion, his owner gave him a robust dose of melatonin. Another dog with fear of red-winged blackbirds overcame this fear when treated with melatonin. A Great Dane with a nasty ALD lesion (caused by licking his wrist raw during his owner's absence) was completely cured when given melatonin before his owner left home each day. I presume he slept instead of worrying, but you could argue that he may have been awake, yet not anxious. Finally, a bull terrier exhibiting nighttime "rage" attacks — presumably caused by behavioral seizures — was controlled with melatonin. Despite these few apparent successes, I must admit that the majority of cases I have treated with melatonin have not fared so impressively. The usual effect, in my experience, is no effect — but it never hurts to try. By the way, it is better to use chemically pure (synthetic) melatonin than the "natural" product that is extracted from bovine brain tissue. Eating anything derived from cows' nervous tissue is probably not so wise in this age of prion infections and mad cow disease. Although there is no known canine equivalent (mad dog disease?), you don't want to be the first owner to find that one exists.

Homeopathy — wherefore art thou, homeopathy? Though it's popular in Europe, I have serious concerns about this branch of alternative medicine. The theory, of course, is that a little dose of what ails you does you good. I can see how that concept applies to vaccination and desensitization to allergens, because inoculates stimulate an immune response — but I can't see how it applies in other situations. Various homeopathic behavioral remedies containing microscopic concentrations of herbal products are now on the market. One such remedy — antianxiety drops — was originally developed by an Irish veterinary practitioner who whipped up a dilute concoction of herbs to treat mastitis (inflammation of the udder) in cows. Being a large-animal vet, cows and mastitis were dear to his heart. In a moment of brilliance, he decided to bottle the cattle remedy for use in dogs to treat what else but . . . anxiety. And thus antianxiety drops were created. Whether the product actually works is doubtful, but bottles of the stuff are practically flying off the shelves. Naturopaths are positively swarming for it. Testing of this product presumably went something like this:

- Take a worried-looking, barking dog and film him.
- Put the anxiety drops on his tongue.
- Wait until he has calmed down.
- Film him again.
- He's calm.
- It's a miracle!

The point they seemed to miss is that the only mental state that can follow a disturbed one is calm. It's just a matter of time. I sent a sample of these antianxiety drops to the Department of Biochemistry and Experimental Therapeutics at Tufts medical school to see whether I was missing something about the ingredients. The reply came back, "Nick, there's virtually nothing here. It's water." I guess that's the point.

Pharmacologic Remedies

Some dogs, like some humans, need a little extra help to get through difficult phases in their lives. Specific conditions for which medications might be helpful include the following:

- High level of owner-directed aggression
- Mistrust of strangers, leading to fear aggression
- High level of aggression toward unfamiliar dogs
- Severe storm phobia
- Severe separation anxiety

- Global fear
- Refractory compulsive behavior
- Motion sickness
- Severe fear of the vet's office

Having read this far, you are aware of how to optimize lifestyle factors for your dog to make him the best he can be. But these measures alone do not always completely resolve behavior problems, particularly ones that are severe and ingrained. In these situations, and sometimes for medical or logistical reasons, I advise some clients that behavior-modifying medications might help improve their dog's welfare, the effectiveness of his rehabilitation, and thus their situation. Some owners are quite open to the idea. Others are leery, and some are positively resistant, usually because they fear what they do not understand. With these owners, I often find myself addressing a variety of common misconceptions about behavior-modifying drugs to make sure that their decision is an informed one.

Common Misconceptions about Behavior-Modifying Drugs

Behavior-modifying drugs are needed only for dogs whose owners are too lazy to follow a behavior-modification regimen.

Not true. Some people are physically or psychologically incapable of successfully implementing a particular behavior-modification program for their dogs. Some people have difficulty enforcing a "tough love" (leadership) program, because it requires a change of mindset that they find difficult to adopt. High-strung individuals may not be able to radiate the calmness necessary to guide an underconfident dog through a desensitization program. And some owners do not have the time or opportunity to engage the ideal treatment recommendations. Owner personality and circumstances aside, medication may be the only hope for some dogs, even if their owners are keen and capable and able to make the time commitment.

Behavioral medications will not work without concurrent behavior-modifying therapy.

While it is true that combined behavior modification and drug therapy is often the most effective approach for clients seeking rapid and dramatic behavioral change, drugs will work on their own — and may have to in some cases. Antidepressants stabilize a dog's mood and can reduce aggression without the owner having to engage in any behavior-modification therapy. Compulsive disorders, like ALD, may not respond at all to behavior modification but can often be controlled with antiobsessional drugs.

Behavior-modifying drugs are too new to have been adequately safety-tested.

Again, this is simply not true. Veterinarians have been prescribing medications to modify dogs' mood and behavior since early in the last century. First came the barbiturates and then the antipsychotics. The wonder drug of its time, Valium, was introduced into veterinary medicine in the 1970s. Hormone therapy for aggressive dogs using synthetic progesterone was also commonplace at this time. The only difference between then and now is that now we have a better array of safer, more side-effect-free medications. What's not to like about this newness?

Behavior-modifying drugs cause sedation.

Older drugs used to cause sedation — that's what got behavioral pharmacology a bad name. Newer drugs, on the other hand, exert their action without producing sedation and usually have few, if any, other side effects (when used correctly). So when my clients say, "I don't want him to be sedated," my response is, "He won't be." Many of these clients' friends are probably taking some sort of human mood-modifying medication — based on what are multibillion-dollar sales — but no one would know simply by looking at them. Individuals on this type of drug therapy aren't sleepy and don't have their tongue lolling out of the side of their mouth. In fact, you could never tell that they were receiving medication. Well, it's the same for dogs who are medicated in this way. Today's psychoactive drugs are often referred to as "smart drugs." They fix the problem without causing collateral damage (affecting the patient in other ways). While it is occasionally possible for some dogs to become groggy, especially when medicine is first introduced, this side effect is temporary and can be addressed by reducing the dose.

Drugs are habit-forming and, once started, cannot be stopped.

Valium and related drugs are dependence-producing if given at robust doses for a long period of time. I do not use them in this way for this very reason. But even if a dog did develop dependence, it would simply be a matter of weaning him off the medication at the end of the course, as opposed to discontinuing the medicine suddenly. One thing is for sure, you will never find your dog breaking into the pill bottle to get his "fix." It's not that kind of dependence — and anyway, dogs don't have opposable thumbs. The antiseizure medication phenobarbital is another drug that can lead to dependence. But if a dog needs this medication to treat a seizure problem, he really needs it and it should probably never be discontinued. After all, the potential for seizures doesn't just go away.

The majority of mood-altering drugs used today are antidepressants — like Prozac. These drugs are not habit-forming. Though it isn't a great idea to stop them suddenly — for behavioral reasons — they are definitely not addictive. It's true they tend to be long-term drugs, but they can be tapered off whenever a veterinarian decides or whenever an owner wants. We often try discontinuing antidepressants at the owner's request. Sometimes the unwanted behavior does not return because learning has taken place or because beneficial structural changes have occurred in the dog's brain. If a dog's behavior deteriorates when the antidepressant is discontinued, the owner usually asks to resume treatment with the medication. Yearly, we ask owners of dogs receiving this type of treatment to reconsider whether they want their dogs to remain on medication. If they do, and if the dog's health and blood work are normal (which, in our experience, they almost invariably are), we continue with the medication for another year — until the next follow-up visit. An Eli Lilly representative client of mine told me that if an owner asks how long a dog should be on Prozac, my answer should be "forever," as long as the dog is doing well on the treatment. I said forever seemed like a very long time and that many of my clients do not want to hear this opinion. He then replied that "one year" was the next best option because it can take that long for brain changes to consolidate after beginning treatment with Prozac.

Drugs affect a dog's memory and ability to learn.

The good thing about most modern behavior-modifying medications is that they do not affect learning or memory — except in a positive way. Dogs on such treatment usually remain bright and alert and their new confidence facilitates learning. Dogs don't learn well when they're anxious or scared, and this can result in a Catch-22 situation when attempting to retrain them. The only drugs we use that do impair memory are those in the Valium class, but then we don't use these drugs much, and when we do, it is for a minimum time and at a minimum dose. Valium-type drugs can produce so-called retrograde amnesia, which means you can't remember things for some time before you took the medication. This can be a useful side effect in some instances — for example, when these drugs are used preoperatively — but more often not.

Types of Behavior-Modifying Drugs

Antidepressants

Older tricyclic antidepressants have been around for scores of years and they work well for the treatment of some conditions. I have employed these drugs for their original use — to treat depression in dogs — and also to treat behavior problems ranging from aggression to phobias. Tricyclics are even helpful in some cases of house soiling when some physical problem prevents a dog from being able to "hold it all night" or when a spayed bitch shows post-spay urinary incontinence. This class of drug is employed to treat refractory bed wetting in children, so there are parallels with human usage. Tricyclics can be used to attenuate a dog's leg lifting in the home, though the success I have had using them in this situation is limited. The prototypical tricyclic antidepressants are Elavil and Tofranil, but there are others, most notably Clomicalm (the veterinary trade name for clomipramine). Clomicalm is a cut above the rest because it preferentially increases serotonin while having much less of an effect on other brain chemicals.

The big breakthrough came with the discovery of Prozac — a selective serotonin reuptake inhibitor (SSRI) — now available for the treatment of separation anxiety in dogs under the trade name Reconcile. To understand how Prozac works, you need to know that certain nerve cells in the brain "talk" to one another using serotonin as the chemical messenger. Serotonin is released into the gap between these nerve cells, facilitating transmission of the conversation between the nerves. Following its release, serotonin is vacuumed up at a so-called reuptake site for later recycling. Prozac blocks this site so that serotonin stays around longer in the junctions between nerves. It's a bit like putting the plug in the bath to stop the water from draining away. The resulting increase in serotonin in the gap between nerves has a mood-stabilizing effect. Low levels of serotonin are associated with depression, impulsivity, and aggression. Prozac can dramatically alleviate these conditions. The suicide rate in the United States has fallen significantly since the introduction of Prozac and other SSRIs. Low serotonin is also associated with a lack of confidence, so humans and dogs with "social phobias" and other anxiety disorders often respond positively to SSRIs. Other SSRIs are Zoloft, Paxil, Celexa, Lexapro, and Luvox. They all work in the same way, though most are chemically dissimilar. Prozac and the other SSRIs are the nearest thing to a silver bullet for treating behavior problems. They can be used with advantage to treat almost any behavior problem. The course of treatment is necessarily long because these drugs take some time to work. The maximum effect is not achieved in some cases for three months or more. The reason for the delay has been the subject of much discussion, but the answer now seems clear. It is not just that these drugs take a long time to build up in the system, as so many people think. It is that they facilitate the development and migration of new nerve cells in the brain. Under the influence of Prozac, precursor nerve cells in an area of the brain responsible for memory, the hippocampus, mature into fully fledged nerve cells, which then migrate to where they are needed. This is a totally new concept because previously it was believed that animals are born with a set number of nerve cells, a number that only decreases over time. But it turns out that Prozac causes new growth of nerve cells and has an effect like adding extra memory to a computer. Perhaps the new nerve cells, by providing an additional substrate for memory, allow treated dogs to learn new tricks and add a veneer of new learning over old themes.

Of course, everything comes at a price, but the price exacted by Prozac and other SSRIs is not too high. Side effects of Prozac include reduced appetite, lethargy, intestinal disturbances, twitching when asleep, lack of playfulness, and aloofness. Most of these side effects are temporary, often lasting only a couple of weeks. If side effects become troublesome, the dose of Prozac can be — should be — reduced. The dose can be increased again sometime later, often without the same side effects recurring. Most dogs receiving Prozac over the long term show no side effects at all. Increased aggression, a common reason for veterinarians not to prescribe Prozac, is not a feature of Prozac's use.

In one study we did here at Tufts, dogs' aggression toward their owners was reduced almost linearly over four weeks as a result of Prozac treatment alone. One of the dogs in the study was biting his owners some forty times a week. A few days after beginning a Prozac regimen, his aggression disappeared completely and remained absent for six months, at which time his male owner forced an aggressive encounter and then had the dog put to sleep. We have also shown that Prozac works to treat separation anxiety, and its efficacy in treating compulsive disorders is not in question. Because of its wide applicability in treating behavioral cases, the late Frank Loew, former dean of our veterinary school, referred to Prozac as the behavioral equivalent of the broad-spectrum dewormer ivermectin. Before ivermectin, vets had to carefully choose which dewormer to use to treat intestinal and other worm infestations in dogs, cats, and farm animals. After ivermectin, vets could reach for this one medication to deal with practically all of these problems. All I can say is thank heavens for Prozac and the other SSRIs. They make behavior problem resolution much more feasible in difficult-to-treat cases and have to date saved thousands of dogs' lives.

Anxiety-Reducing Drugs

Antianxiety drugs, often referred to as anxiolytic (or anxioselective), are of two basic types. First on the scene were Librium and Valium. Revolutionary at the time, Valium was thought to address anxiety with little or no serious downside. But as a drug that reduces inhibitions in a manner similar to alcohol, it was soon found out that Valium could disinhibit (i.e., increase) aggression. The term "paradoxical aggression" has been on veterinarians' minds ever since and has rightfully discouraged them from prescribing it to potentially aggressive dogs. In some cases, Valium causes obvious agitation — another paradoxical effect. Also, Valium does not seem to work as well or reliably in dogs and other animals as it does in humans, but there are occasions when it is

---

The Cost of Treatment

Most of the drugs discussed in this chapter are now available in generic form at prices far below brand-name versions. When it first came on the scene in the late 1980s, Prozac retailed at $3 per capsule. At one or two capsules per day for a mid-size or large dog, respectively, that would cost $90–$180 per month — out of most dog owners' reach. Buspar was also in the $1–$2 per tablet range and is a twice-daily drug. Today, generic Prozac (fluoxetine) is available at 25¢ or less per capsule and generic Buspar (buspirone) is also inexpensive. Older drugs like phenobarbital and Inderal (propranolol) are dirt-cheap. Prices of individual drugs vary considerably from retailer to retailer. So shop around, and bring your prescription to the outlet offering the best deal.

---

helpful (e.g., for the acute treatment of purely fearful conditions, like separation anxiety and storm phobia). One problem with Valium is that it doesn't last long, so other drugs of the same family may be a better choice. Valium and all other Valium-type drugs are addictive and should be used only for the least time possible and at the lowest dose that is effective. Valium increases appetite (a side effect sometimes employed by vets to advantage), can cause weight gain, and can overly sedate dogs, especially at higher dosages, affecting motor skills (watch out for your dog falling down stairs). All in all, it's best to avoid using Valium, but as the old saying goes, there is a time and place for everything.

Another less problematic antianxiety medication is Buspar. I first tried Buspar in storm-phobic dogs in the late 1980s and found it to be partially effective. Treated dogs became much calmer at the sound of distant thunder but still became distressed if a storm passed right overhead. Other fear-related conditions I have treated with Buspar, including fear aggression and social anxiety, do respond positively, though the beneficial effects are rarely spectacular. Buspar can also be used to treat urine marking in dogs, and it is quite effective for this purpose. It can also be helpful in separation anxiety when other medications have failed. I prescribe Buspar less frequently these days now that many modern antidepressants, including Prozac, are finally off patent and thus more affordable. That said, there are still occasions when Buspar is just what this doctor ordered, either alone or in combination with a Prozac-like drug. As well as being a mild anxiety-reducing drug, Buspar is also effective against motion sickness and helps prevent vomiting, thus it is indicated for carsickness in dogs (though another drug, Cerenia, has recently been FDA-approved for this purpose). Though its efficacy in dogs varies, Buspar is extremely safe, has almost no toxicity, has few side effects, and is not addictive.

Other Drugs

A number of other medications may be used to get a dog around a tight behavioral corner. The classical veterinary prescription is for acepromazine, a sedative that is very helpful to tranquilize dogs before anesthesia, for chemical restraint, and for short-term management of behavior problems. But acepromazine ("ace") is not really suitable for long-term treatment of behavior problems. Acepromazine realizes dog owners' worst fears — their dog is, and appears to be, sedated — so the behavioral advantage is obtained only at the expense of the dog's personality. While it is better to have a dog with thunderstorm phobia sedated than panicking, it is also desirable to use drugs with less depressant activity to resolve the problem. Acepromazine makes dogs staggery, sluggish, bleary-eyed, and generally out of it: not what we desire in modern behavioral therapy. Also, its effect lasts for several hours, if not all day.

Phenobarbital is also still used sometimes to treat behavior problems, but, to my mind, this drug should be reserved for when it is specifically indicated, for example, when partial seizures underlie the behavioral problem. Phenobarbital is a depressant, like alcohol, and has many potential side effects, including paradoxical hyperactivity, increased appetite, and thirst. It is also toxic to the liver if used in high doses for a prolonged period. Monitoring of blood levels and liver function are mandatory with phenobarbital.

If fear is the issue, drugs that block the fight-or-flight response, called beta-blockers, can be very helpful as stand-alone or adjunctive therapies. The part of the nervous system that oversees fight or flight is called the "sympathetic" nervous system. There are alpha and beta components of this system, with the beta component being most relevant when it comes to the perception of fear and in modulating behavior. Beta-blockers prevent the heart from pounding inside the chest during a fearful situation; they lower blood pressure, eliminate the "butterflies in the stomach" feeling, suppress trembling and sweating, and relax muscles. Much of their effect is peripheral (in the body, as opposed to the brain), but there are central (brain) effects, too. Beta-blockers like Inderal, though principally "heart drugs," are also used in human medicine to treat fear of public speaking, stage fright, and performance anxiety in musicians. They can be used similarly to quell fearful responses in dogs. Because Inderal is so short-lived, I prefer the long-acting version, Inderal LA. There are few, if any, observable side effects of Inderal, but it is prudent to monitor a treated dog's heart rate in case it gets too low. Fewer than fifty beats per minute is too low for a medium- to large-sized dog.

Finally, a treatment for canine cognitive dysfunction (CCD) is available thanks to Pfizer's Animal Health Division. Anipryl is an antidepressant of the monoamine oxidase inhibitor (MAO) variety but is now employed for its action of increasing an epinephrine-like substance, dopamine, in the brain. About 60 percent of dogs with CCD who are treated with Anipryl do amazingly well, as mentioned earlier. Anipryl is definitely worth trying in any dog seemingly suffering from dementia. If Anipryl does not work or begins to lose its efficacy, various antioxidants like melatonin, vitamin C, and vitamin E can be tried. Alternatively, or in addition, a number of compounds that improve brain function or slow deterioration can be used. Acetyl L-carnitine and coenzyme Q10 and Huperazine A are three such compounds.

Future of Drug Therapy in Dogs

Many new treatments for use in dogs are on the horizon. Drugs get more specific and safer by the year. Different forms of older drugs, like once-a-week Prozac and Paxil CR (controlled release), have appeared and may offer some advantages. Many new neuroleptics (acepromazine-type) drugs have also been developed. There are even new uses for existing medicines that have recently come to light. We have found that drugs that block an excitatory substance in the brain, glutamate, are effective in treating some compulsive disorders and perhaps fear-based problems. The glutamate blocker we are currently using to treat dogs at Tufts is on the market for the treatment of Alzheimer's disease in people. This drug, Namenda, has shown efficacy in the treatment of compulsive disorder in humans and dogs. With benign drugs now available to control aggression, alleviate anxiety, and treat compulsive behaviors in dogs, and new remedies being developed all the time, dog owners have more options than ever before in caring for their dogs' emotional and physical well-being.

Part 3

A Second Chance

Although this book has dealt primarily with the factors promoting dogs' health and well-being and optimizing the relationship between dogs and their owners, I felt it was important to include a third short section on adoption. Too many dogs are brought to the nation's shelters and pounds each year as unwanted commodities, and many will meet an untimely end if they are not rescued and given a second chance. Many shelter dogs are adoptable and will do well if placed in the right home with a knowledgeable owner. The purpose of the following chapter is to point out how adoptable shelter dogs are, to help you choose the right one for your family, and to assist in successful integration of adopted dogs of various personality types into their new homes.

11

Adopting a Dog

Assessing a Rescue Dog and Integrating Him into the Home

> No one can sincerely try to help another without helping himself.
> — Charles Dudley Warner

Thus far this book has dealt with how best to treat, train, and understand your dog, as well as how to troubleshoot and prevent behavior problems. The supposition has been that you already own the dog and want to optimize the experience. However, if you have not yet taken on the responsibility of dog ownership, but think you might like to, or if you are thinking about getting a second dog, consider adopting a shelter dog — please. To adopt a rescue dog is to save a life and at the same time, with any luck, to find the canine companion of a lifetime. Only about 1 million out of 4 million dogs passing through United States shelters each year (25 percent) are adopted, while 2.4 million (60 percent) are destroyed. Clearly there is room for improvement here. Not many shelter dogs are puppies and not many are strays. Most are adult dogs dropped off because their owners failed to develop a proper bond with them and/or became fed up with them as a result of behavior issues; typically, owners either don't know or don't care what will happen to these dogs upon surrender. These dogs deserve a second chance, so please consider adopting one to reverse the odious trend of surrender and euthanasia. We may live in a disposable society, but this should not extend to our companion animals, who depend on us and can contribute so much to our lives.

Shelter dogs typically get a bad rap. People generally conclude that they come with a certain amount of psychological baggage. And some do — I call them project dogs. Some have an aggressive history, and few of these dogs — though some could easily be rehabilitated — are wittingly adopted out. Remember, many owners will not tolerate a growl from their dog — let alone a snap or bite— though they may be far from temperamentally perfect themselves. How reasonable is it to hold a dog to standards higher than our own? No aggression, no complaints — ever — is not a reasonable standard of expectation for anyone or any dog. Child grabs dog's tail and pulls it — dog turns and snaps (doesn't even bite) — dog is ejected from household. It should be the owners who are ejected for not protecting their dog from the child's unwelcome advances. Some dogs in shelters are there because they are destructive — but this problem can often be addressed. Some are noisy or not housetrained — again, resolvable problems. However, some dogs in shelters are perfect angels and find themselves incarcerated for no fault of their own. Perhaps their owner has left the country, is ill, or has died. Take a close look at what your local shelter has to offer and carefully consider your options. A shelter dog can sometimes be the perfect fit for a potential owner.

Choosing a Shelter Dog

Finding the right dog is a bit of a dating game. No one dog personality fits all. Some people like energetic dogs — the kind that bound right up to you and lick you all over. Others prefer shier, more retiring ones, while yet others go for middle-of-the-road personalities. The dog you choose might fit right in with your family from the get-go with little need for special arrangements or retraining. Other dogs require work and an investment of time. Some people prefer the easier route; others are up for a challenge. Whichever type of dog you decide on, choose carefully and with forethought. This should not be an impulse decision (and most shelters have guidelines in place to ensure that it's not). Returned adoptees are the bane of shelter life. Just when the shelter staff thinks they have found a dog a good home, he appears back on their doorstep. That is a big disappointment to all concerned. Consider the dog's breed, temperament, energy level, age, size, the expense of upkeep, grooming requirements, and compatibility with your lifestyle and family members. The shelter staff can be extremely helpful here because they get to know the dogs and can address potential incompatibilities.

Here are some key questions to ask as you pursue your quest:

Question 1: Why is the dog in the shelter? Sometimes the answer to this question is known — but not always. Some dogs are found wandering in the street or are left tied to the shelter gate. Even if a reason for the dog's surrender is given by a previous owner, the information can be inaccurate or frankly misleading. People make up all kinds of excuses when dropping dogs off at shelters as they try to appease their consciences or justify their actions to the shelter staff. Typical reasons people give for surrendering dogs to shelters include: He's grown too big for us (*you couldn't see that coming?*); I can't train him (*why not?*); there's a baby on the way (*so?*); we're moving (*why not take him with you?*); I'm getting divorced (*so why have the dog suffer, too?*); I can't afford to keep him (*duh*); I don't have enough time (*you should have thought about that before*); he doesn't get along with other pets (*so work with him — get help*).

If the previous owners have admitted to a behavior problem, find out if shelter staff can corroborate it. If so, can you and your family accept and address this particular problem?

Question 2: What sort of temperament does the dog have? Is he easy to be around, rambunctious, aggressive, retiring, noisy? The shelter staff will help you make this assessment. Dog people know dogs. Don't settle for one opinion. Ask around until you have a consensus and feel comfortable with the assessment, and use that information in your decision-making process.

Question 3: How does the dog act around you and others? To answer this most important question, you have to spend time with the dog and use your powers of observation. First, ask to take him out of the kennel or shelter context. Dogs do not behave the way they might usually behave when they are in a kennel environment, with all the associated clamor and distractions. Find a quiet place nearby and, with the dog on lead and a member of the shelter staff on hand in case you need assistance, interact with him. See if he will follow you or if he's a more independent type. See if he startles when you make a loud noise. Find out if he tolerates petting and handling (of his feet or ears, for example). Assess his energy level. Does he jump up? How does he respond to being held? Does he resist restraint? Does he pull on lead? Can you roll him over and pet his tummy, or does he wriggle to right himself? Is he good around children, or does he cringe or bark and lunge at them? How does he behave around unfamiliar adults? Obviously, to answer these latter questions you must expose the dog to various individuals. Arrange to introduce him to a variety of people (e.g., children, tall people, bearded men, and people wearing uniforms) and gauge his response. Also, see how he responds to other dogs. These are just a few of the interactions and observations upon which you can — with the help of the shelter staff — base your assessment. Spend at least fifteen minutes with the dog conducting your evaluation. Ask yourself the following questions:

1. Is he a willful dog? Might he need a leadership program at home to learn his proper place in the family? And are you

prepared to invest the time and energy it takes to teach him this important lesson?

2. Is he anxious or fearful? If so, can you — are you willing to — accept and work to address any fear-related problems?

3. Is he in a world of his own, indifferent to your presence, and preoccupied with his own agenda? In this instance, do you think you may be able to win him over and make him a sociable pet?

Different dog personalities suit different people. A dog with a strong personality might fare well in a home with a person of similar character. A dog that is fearful of children might do best in a home without them. A dog with separation anxiety might be a perfect fit for a person who spends lots of time at home — perhaps an elderly person. A dog with "too much energy" might do well with a physically active individual who loves to take long walks.

Bringing the Dog Home

Let's assume, for a moment, that you have found your perfect match, and you're ready to bring your new charge home. Now what?

How you introduce your new pet to family members should depend on the dog's personality. For a confident, outgoing dog, no special precautions may be necessary. Such a dog will likely view the whole experience as a big adventure. Hold on to the lead when bringing a dog like this home as he may dart away from you and go places you would not want him to go — like onto a busy road or into the neighbor's flower garden. Ditto when it comes to introducing a bossy, in-charge dog to new people. Unless family members or friends are dressed down and don't care, they may find themselves getting jumped upon, muddied, maybe even scratched or knocked over. With this kind of dog it is best to start out by maintaining control and setting limits. A dog's bounding enthusiasm is not always appreciated by family or friends, so it is a good idea to make introductions low-key and keep the dog on

244 A Second Chance

Adoption into a Home Where There Are Other Pets

Sometimes a would-be adopter already has other pets in the home. The question then arises, for the adopters and adoptees, how well the new dog will get on with the other pets, and vice versa. While some discrete questions by the shelter personnel may help to pin down the likelihood of mutual *bon accord* between a dog and other dogs or between a dog and cats, there is nothing like actual controlled exposure — a trial marriage, if you will, to see how things are/will be between the various factions. Questions shelter people should ask — or adoptive owners can quiz themselves on — are:

- Does the dog to be adopted have any issues with other dogs or cats?
- Does the incumbent dog or cat have any adverse reaction to other dogs?
- Was the incumbent dog or cat raised in the company of dogs?

If the dog to be adopted is aggressive toward or fearful of other dogs, the adoption may not work, or at least should be handled very carefully. Ditto if the existing pets are known to have issues with unfamiliar dogs. The likelihood that pets will get on is in part determined by whether they

continued on next page

lead for a while after returning home. Start training him to greet people by sitting or with four feet on the floor — "Off" is a good command to address jumping up (not "Down," which will confuse him). A walk around the perimeter of the property shortly after arriving home is in order, and possibly up and down the local streets — though you could reserve that pleasure for the next day. A dog toilet area should be identified and shown to the dog as soon as possible to prevent any unfortunate accidents in the house. A dog's got to go when a dog's got to go, and all the excitement of the new place and new people only increases the possibility of a mishap.

Adoption, *continued*

were raised with others of the same kind. Dogs learn dog etiquette when raised with other dogs and communicate in ways that avoid fights. Cats learn to tolerate and understand dogs when they are raised with them. But take a dog-friendly dog or dog-friendly cat and put him with a dysfunctional dog or cat and there's often trouble. Questionnaires can only go so far toward answering the question about how well pets will get on. The acid test is to introduce the two parties together at the new home — with both under strict control, perhaps with one in a crate at first. If things don't work out, you can sometimes try to forge a relationship — especially when fear is a factor and neither pet is actually attacking the other. But if there is overt aggression, it may be better to try again with another adoptive dog. Incumbents don't appreciate their home being invaded and adoptees might not appreciate being forced to live in a combative environment. Discretion is the better part of valor sometimes. Ellen DeGeneres found out too late that her newly adopted dog, Iggy, did not get on with her cats. If the shelter had asked the right questions and made the right suggestions, the brouhaha that followed when Ellen rehomed Iggy may never have happened. That should be a powerful lesson for shelters and would-be adopters alike.

You should, of course, have all the supplies you need on hand even before the dog comes home: dog bed, food and water bowls, chew toys, other toys, and a supply of familiar food. Sometime after arriving home, if the dog hasn't eaten for a few hours, you could try offering him some food — but don't worry if he's too excited to eat. Dogs do not have to eat three square meals a day to survive. If he doesn't want to eat, he doesn't have to. It is counterproductive to try and convince a dog to eat. It's his job to figure out that there's food in his bowl (that's right, just leave the bowl down — for the first night, anyway). Spend quality time with him and let him know you are there and that you care. Petting, games, and your responsiveness to his reasonable demands are all fair game at this early stage. But you don't have to be — and shouldn't be — a complete pushover. Good behavior should be rewarded; bad (unacceptable) behavior should be ignored. That should be your maxim going forward, too. At the end of the day, you should take your dog for one last walk to the designated area and stay with him until he is successful in his endeavor — success that you should enthusiastically reward. Then he should be introduced to his new dog bed, which ideally should be located in your bedroom. If he prefers to sleep elsewhere, that's fine, too. It's his choice as long as he behaves well and earns the privilege.

Get him in a routine from the start. Dogs thrive on routine — knowing what to expect and when. Introduce him to his crate, but do not shut him in until he is comfortable enough to go in it voluntarily. Never close him inside his crate for punishment or for extended periods of time. Show him all his new toys — but don't give him access to them all, all at once. Toys should be rotated for maximum benefit. Make sure he gets a suitable diet. If his former diet was less than ideal, gradually switch to an appropriate ration. Implement the change gradually over several days to avoid intestinal upset. Make sure your new dog gets a healthy dose of exercise each day, and make sure you communicate with him using words of one syllable right from the start. He may already know a few words, like "Sit" and "Down." But don't stop there. As I expressed earlier, learning should be a lifelong experience. Identify a nearby doggy daycare center in case you have to go away without him, and introduce him to new dog friends there. If possible, enroll him in some appropriate occupational therapy — such as agility or obedience training. In time, chances are that he will settle down and become a fine family friend.

Some adopted dogs have specific issues that need to be addressed as they emerge. If your new dog growls at you or other family members, immediately address this behavior by means of a leadership program. If he spooks at something, remain calm and assertive. Think positive and be positive. If necessary, implement a desensitization program. Some dogs may not get on well with other dogs. Some may engage in excessive barking. Others might be generally anxious. Each problem can be addressed utilizing behavior-modification techniques and other measures as described in this book.

Many shelter dogs have fear-based problems, and introducing an anxious or fearful dog into a household can be a delicate matter. These shrinking violets must be carefully managed for humanitarian as well as behavioral reasons. Make sure that dogs of this disposition have your support but not your sympathy (which can reinforce fear). Ensure a smooth transition from shelter to home by making provisions for the dog before he arrives. All positive moves on the part of the dog — coming forward, confident body postures and affect — should be rewarded with encouraging words, petting, and delicious food treats. All negative moves — cowering, hiding — should be ignored. No active attempt should be made to hasten a fearful dog's acceptance of people, or other animals or things. A fearful dog should not be forced to confront his fears but rather allowed to acclimate slowly at his own pace. Dogs that have specific fears should be protected from exposure to the feared person, thing, or situation, except as part of a desensitization program (see chapter 6). Nonaggressive dogs with general angst and uncertainty around people should be treated using a reverse-leadership program — one in which "everything in life is free." Food should be provided liberally. Petting, if enjoyed by the dog, should be offered gratis and often. Toys should always be available. Tug of war and other "rough" games will help as long as the dog enjoys them (though there comes a time when they may need to be curtailed as the dog's confidence builds). Training should be exclusively positive with rewards for a job well done and no punishment — ever. In time, the shrinking violet will grow to like his new quarters and the kind people who surround him. Fearful pets often make the best friends a family could have — as long as fear-inducing people and situations are kept at bay.

Unfortunately, it is not possible for fearful dogs to live a sequestered life. They will be exposed to the comings and goings of people as well as of other animals. They will also have to be left alone from time to time. And lightning storms and other scary events will happen. That's why, after a fearful dog's introduction to and acceptance of the family, it is important to start work attenuating whatever fears trouble the dog for his own good as well as that of the family. Nobody wants their dog to shiver and quake his way through life, lunge at their visitors, or damage their property when they are away. Fearful dogs are worthwhile projects who require work of a different kind from their more confident counterparts. They require confidence to be instilled, whereas more pushy dogs need to have their egos reined in.

If the above provisions are met, adopted dogs can flourish and be a joy to live with. To me, the trick is finding the right dog for the right home — with realistic expectations and the will, desire, and knowledge to meet the dog's needs. Which brings me back to the seven steps at the core of this book. Never underestimate the importance of exercise, diet, and clear communication. Know how to physically restrain your dog when appropriate, and how to earn a dog's trust and respect by being a good leader. Be able to manage fearful situations, and ensure that your dog's environment is an engaging and fulfilling one. With all these things in place, you will be able to appreciate why dogs, including rescue dogs, can be your best friends.

Epilogue

A dog is, or should be, a friend for life. I know a woman whose eleven-year-old dog is so dear to her that when he dies, she is going to have him cremated and have his ashes returned to her; then, when she dies, his ashes will be buried alongside her in the coffin. (I don't suppose there will be room for her husband, too.) When such close two-way bonds develop between people and pets, you can be sure that a lot of things are going right. In order to optimize the chances of having one of these very special close relationships, all interactions should be based on mutual understanding and trust. Dogs don't get attached to people who physically punish them or compel them into submission to achieve their goals. The topics I have dealt with in this book are the underpinnings necessary for any dog to have a happy and healthy life and from that platform to develop and sustain good relationships with human "pack members." To help you visualize the relationship and interdependence of the measures I advise, I offer here a modification of Maslow's triangle — a human psychological concept depicting a hierarchy of human needs. Of course, my triangle refers to canine needs and realizations.

At the base of the canine hierarchy-of-needs triangle, as a foundation for all other needs, is the requirement of sound physical health and well-being. These aspects were addressed in the chapters herein on exercise and diet and necessary medical interventions. When these needs are met and a dog is fit and healthy, the next layer of needs can be addressed. For dogs, these are safety and environmental needs. I addressed these factors in the chapters on physical restraint, environmental enrichment, and fear management. When these needs are taken care of, the next layer,

**HIERARCHY OF
CANINE NEEDS**

**HELPING
OTHERS**
Dog willing
to share his joy,
works willingly,
optimal bonding

REALIZE POTENTIAL
Dog is happy, relaxed, fulfilled

KNOW & UNDERSTAND
Dog knows place in family and
realizes expectations

SELF-ESTEEM
Confidence without "dominance"

PACK & AFFECTION
Clear communication, leadership, and love

SAFETY & ENVIRONMENTAL
Alleviation of fear, proper control, environmental enrichment

PHYSICAL & HEALTH
Exercise, diet, medical well-being

concerning communication, leadership, and affection, can be addressed. Once these needs have been seen to, a dog is able to develop self-esteem, feeling confident in himself and having nothing to prove. This, in turn, leads to the dog's being able to relax and accept his position in the family, even understanding and enjoying the various comings and goings of friends and family. This is the well-adjusted dog of this book's title, epitomized by the classic all-American golden retriever with laughing face and eyes and long-suffering nature. Such a dog, at the peak of the triangle of basic needs, wants to share his joy and works willingly simply to please those around him. Call it canine karma. All of this may sound a little transcendental, but I can assure you that an integrated program of health, communication, leadership, environmental enrichment, and care as outlined in this book will lead to a happy, healthy, well-adjusted dog, one that will be a joy to live with and that you will remember forever.

Acknowledgments

I would like to acknowledge Jan Corning and MacInfy ("Mac") Emory for their kind and generous support of the behavior program here at the Cummings School of Veterinary Medicine at Tufts University. Jan and Mac made it possible for me to develop our behavior service and help thousands of dogs and cats with behavior problems survive and thrive when they might otherwise have prematurely gone the way of all flesh. The programs and advice that we offer — and that I have shared with you here in this book — are possible not least because of Jan and Mac's unwavering support, allowing so many pets that were in trouble to live happy, fulfilling lives and be a joy to their owners.

Index